D0092931

STRANGE *and*
DANGEROUS DREAMS

STRANGE *and* DANGEROUS DREAMS*

GEOFF POWTER

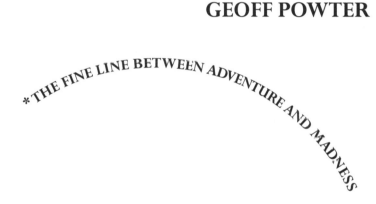

*THE FINE LINE BETWEEN ADVENTURE AND MADNESS

THE MOUNTAINEERS BOOKS

For Mr. T. and Ms. C.

THE MOUNTAINEERS BOOKS
*is the nonprofit publishing arm of The Mountaineers Club, an organization
founded in 1906 and dedicated to the exploration, preservation, and
enjoyment of outdoor and wilderness areas.*

1001 SW Klickitat Way, Suite 201, Seattle, WA 98134

First edition, 2006

Manufactured in the United States of America

Acquiring Editor: Cassandra Conyers
Developmental Editor: Don Graydon
Project Editor: Mary Metz
Copy Editor: Carol Poole
Cover Design: Ani Rucki
Book Design and Layout: Mayumi Thompson
Cartographer: Moore Creative Design and Hermien Schuttenbeld
Cover photograph: *Aleister Crowley, master of magick (Courtesy Ordo Templii Orientis).*

Library of Congress Cataloging-in-Publication Data
Powter, Geoff, 1957-
   Strange and dangerous dreams : the fine line between adventure and madness / [Geoff
Powter]. -- 1st ed.
      p. cm.
   Includes bibliographical references.
   ISBN 0-89886-987-0
   1. Explorers--Biography. 2. Mountaineers--Biography. I. Title.
   G200.P68 2006
   910.92'2--dc22

                           2006000676

contents

preface

IT HAS BEEN SAID THAT BOOKS find their writer just as often as writers find their subjects, and this was certainly the case with this book. From the time I first encountered adventure writing as a young boy, stories like the ones that follow have called to me. While I was absolutely in awe of the apparently invulnerable superstars of exploration and adventure, I have always been more intrigued by less perfect explorers who battled through difficult journeys. Too often, the grand heroes, with their steel will and unbounded endurance felt intangible, and even improbable, while the more unsettled characters in adventure literature, with their fragilities and troubled motivations, seemed far more real and sympathetic.

Long before I actually sat down to write this book, several trails in my life wound their way toward it. Along one, I turned the love of adventure tales into a life of my own adventuring, canoeing, and then climbing, giving me an even deeper interest in the thorny lives of the characters I had discovered. My own experiences with risk, and especially with the demands of expedition life, left me with a thousand questions about the motivations, and sanity, behind their patently aberrant stories.

I also developed a growing fascination with the difficult lives of several adventurers I met personally. I first thought it an odd contrast that such people lived lives of apparently glorious depth, accomplishment, and reputation, yet battled confusions, demons, and self-doubt to a degree that I rarely saw in the world outside adventure. I have since come to understand just how often such contradictions lie near the heart of many great adventures.

Along another path, I became a psychologist with a clinical practice in Canmore, a mountain resort town in the Canadian Rockies. That role drew not only clients trying to balance the complexities and contradictions of a risk-sport life, but also attracted, from time to time, calls from a media struggling to explain the troubles that often seemed a dominant part of adventure. Reporters asked me difficult questions about the sometimes terrible costs of expeditions— conflicts, bitter rivalries, even deaths—which appeared in their critical eyes to stem from little more than outsized egos and stunning selfishness. Again and again I was asked if there was simply something "wrong," or even "crazy," with the people who chose to pursue risk. Most often, I could argue that the reporters were seeing normal, emotionally healthy people pushed to their limits by the hardships of adventure, but there were times when something darker and more complicated seemed to be at play: truly troubled souls acting out their difficulties on the stage of adventure. I was convinced that there were right and wrong adventures, but I often found it a challenge to explain the difference to non-adventurers who often saw any voluntary risk as a sign of stupidity or lunacy.

If there was a single spark that finally lit this book, it came when I was asked to write a story for *Explore* magazine about Earl Denman, a Canadian who traveled to Everest alone in 1947, ludicrously unprepared but convinced he could be the first to climb the mountain. Telling Denman's tale helped me realize how much these stories show us about the nature and appeal of adventure, but it also reinforced just how controversial these characters are. The published story connected me with people—readers, adventurers, historians, and especially Denman's family—with very polarized perspectives on the man. Some considered him a quiet hero; others saw him as a naïve fool; others a romantic, if sad, innocent. In the view of some, he was little more than a suicidal misfit, barely worthy of a footnote in the history of the mountain.

Denman's story was hardly unique. Over the past two years I have come upon scores of stories, past and present, in every genre of adventure writing, about adventurers with dubious, dangerous ambitions, whose stories are full of doubts, turmoil, despair, and even madness. In the process of writing this book I've discovered that there are many people who simply dismiss these characters, but there are also many who believe these controversial personalities, warts and all, are the only "true" adventurers, and that they show us the deeper, dangerous truths of exploration.

I am personally aligned with both camps. I understand the deeply human desire for heroes of virgin promise. There is good reason that every culture, in every era, has adventure myths: The golden hero willing to walk through fire elevates us all beyond our fears and limits. But I also see the value in understanding the darker reasons for dangerous pursuits. In the end, understanding these more difficult but utterly human stories helps us both comprehend the deepest purpose and allure of adventure, and ultimately, I think, more honestly measure ourselves. The pull of adventure, the hope for redemption through heroic challenge, and the willingness to take chances against terrible odds—these all whirl at the core of human nature.

acknowledgments

MANY PEOPLE HAVE PLAYED SIGNIFICANT ROLES, directly and indirectly, in this book, but first thanks have to go to the writers who have previously mapped out the lives of many of the characters here. In several cases, some writers have been the sole source of material available, and I am deeply indebted to their groundwork and their conversations with me. Special, and admiring, thanks go to Ian and Caroline Mackersey for their deeply insightful and compassionate research into the life of Jean Batten, to Dennis Roberts for his unflagging faith in the importance of Maurice Wilson's story, and to Chip Brown for his remarkable understanding of the life of the Waterman family.

Another strong thanks needs to go out to the families that agreed to cooperate with the project. The stories they told were often difficult, but the families shed a great deal of light by telling them. I am especially indebted to Georges Juedel, Graham and Sandy Denman, Paul Denman Thompson, Vivian and John McLintock, Simon Crowhurst, Laura Waterman and Alice Morrison.

Conversations with several friends also helped immeasurably, by encouraging me to look at new subjects or see familiar ones in a new light. Special thanks go to David Roberts, Dr. Charlie Houston, Chris Bonington, Henry Barber, Maria Coffey, Pat and Baiba Morrow, Bob Sandford, Dwayne Congdon, Sharon Wood, Barry Blanchard, Karen McDiarmid, Judy Otton, Brian and Shawna Wyvill, Colin Wells, Doug Leonard, Jerry and Sasha Kobalenko, Tim and Sherry Auger, Will Gadd, and Gareth Wood. Over the years I have also been helped tremendously by the connections through and support from James Little and the staff at *Explore;* and by my friends at the Centre for Mountain Culture at the Banff Centre, with special thanks to Bernadette McDonald, Shannon O'Donoghue, Leslie Taylor, and Anne Ryall.

A number of others helped guide the research, including Margaret Pope at the archives of the Alpine Club in London, Amanda Pullin-Faber of the BBC, Thomas Noy, Audrey Salkeld, Nicky Watson, Dean Rau, and Kate Walkey at the History Channel in Britain.

I also am indebted to Gary and Shirley McLaren, and to Steve De-Keijzer and Marni Virtue, for their hospitality. I hope the spirits of their lake and mountain retreats can be felt in the book.

Helen Cherullo, Cassandra Conyers, and Don Graydon of The Mountaineers had faith in this project that far exceeded my own, and I'm grateful for their patience and encouragement in the face of my uncertainties. Don and Carol Poole worked editing wonders, keeping the stories and thoughts in line.

And finally, this book would not be in your hands without the considerable sacrifices and accommodations made by my wife, Christie McLaren. The shadow of a book can be a cold and dark place, but she added warmth and light throughout.

introduction

EVERYTHING ABOUT IT SEEMED WRONG.

At only thirty-two feet, *Le Soleil Noir* appeared dangerously inadequate for rounding the Cape. Even in experienced hands, the ketch would have struggled in the tortured seas that were forecast for the Cape Horn season, and the twenty-six-year-old Belgian at the helm was, even by her own admission, hardly experienced. Claudine Juedel had been sailing for barely more than six months when she set off on her solitary "pilgrimage" around the world in 1974.

Juedel, however, didn't see her lack of skills as a problem. In fact, as she explained in her journals, she believed being a novice was an essential part of the adventure, somehow guaranteeing what she called its "purity." Juedel wanted the voyage to be a "cleansing," a chance to shed the skin of the life she suffered through, and to "discover the truth" beneath. This ambition, she insisted, meant facing the sea completely "on its own terms" and "being taught about the ocean by the ocean." She told almost no one of her plans, took no sailing lessons, read only a few books on navigation and sailcraft, gave her systems only a cursory test through a couple of relatively benign nights off the French coast, and then cast off into the Atlantic, bound for Cape Horn and the worst seas in the world.

Though Claudine Juedel may have had little actual sailing experience, she was certainly immersed in the mythology of sailing as transformation. The cabin of *Soleil* was cluttered with dog-eared copies of the classics of ocean adventure—among them Joshua Slocum's *Sailing Alone Around the World*, Francis Chichester's *The Lonely Sea and the Sky*, and especially Bernard Moitessier's mystical *The Long Way*—all of them obsessively annotated in Juedel's meticulous script. In retrospect, her notes seem like self-help admonitions designed to get her past her doubts about the trip: "Every wave that washes over me will only make me stronger!!!" she insisted in the margins of one of Moitessier's many dramatic storm chapters. "Everything," she predicted, "will change."

For the first two months of the voyage, the sea did little to dissuade Juedel of the naïveté of her scheme; from the Normandy coast of France to the Canary Islands, *Soleil* saw barely a day of storm, and the crossing of the Atlantic proved even less eventful. Juedel's log from this first leg of the trip was filled with days of easy winds and gentle swells. A more typical mid-Atlantic autumn would have dramatically tested both the boat and the captain, but rather than seeing herself as somehow blessed by this luck, or capitalizing on the opportunity to hone her skills, by the time Juedel coasted into Puerto Deseado on the Patagonian shoulder of Argentina, she wrote that she was thoroughly "bored." Juedel tied up in the dry, wind-scoured town on the edge of the pampas and went in search of excitement.

By all accounts, Claudine Juedel was a troubled woman, born into a family worthy of a gothic romance. She was an exotic beauty, the daughter of a Vietnamese mother and a Belgian father, and was raised in Paris and other European capitals. She lost her mother as a young child and carried out a tempest of a relationship with her wealthy, perpetually absent father for years. She rolled through a series of brilliant beginnings of several careers in Brussels, but also made considerable money in a string of more marginal pursuits. She had brief brushes with the law, typically for disorderly conduct. Her love life mapped out much the same way: Juedel ran through a chain of flammable romances, culminating in a dramatic explosion of a relationship with a married man twenty years her senior in the year before her voyage. Four months before she set sail, Juedel was charged with assault against the man's wife. She cast off in *Le Soleil Noir* just before the court date.

News reports on the fate of Juedel's pilgrimage indicate that she cut a similar swath through Puerto Deseado during her short stay for refit of the boat. Her brother Georges recalled that a postcard she sent from Argentina—the only indication her family had that his sister had even considered such a trip—ended with the not-so cryptic comment "I've done it again." After only two weeks' stay, she left angry memories and unpaid bills in her wake when she sailed off to Tierra del Fuego. She paid no attention to the Argentine Navy's direct warnings of storms hooked on the Cape. They may not have been "storms of the century," but they were Cape Horn storms, and Juedel was advised on several occasions that it would be better for her to wait for the end of the storm season before continuing. Instead, she cast off in the middle of the night on November 23, 1974.

Just after the turn of the year, a Chilean fishing trawler stumbled upon the wreck of *Le Soleil Noir* drifting in placid seas nearly 350 miles northwest of Cape Horn. Her mast was broken clean, her rudder had been ripped from the stern, and none of her sails remained on board. There was no sign of Juedel, and the ship logs deteriorated from vague to blank just a few days out from Puerto Deseado. Juedel described rising seas, then stopped writing entirely. No one had called her in missing—her father said he did not even realize his daughter knew how to sail—and Juedel had refused to carry an emergency beacon despite demands by the Argentine maritime services. Claudine Juedel simply disappeared, as anonymously as she had come, into the slate-gray sea.

There are hundreds of stories like Claudine Juedel's in adventure legend and literature, and as the aftermath of her death illustrated, they are often haunted by controversy. In Juedel's case, critics came fast and rabid, insisting that she was nothing more than a naïve fool; that hers was a stupidly arrogant psychodrama that had nothing to do with "real" adventure; that she simply had no business sailing; and that she would have immorally endangered the lives of anyone sent to rescue her. The criticisms of Juedel were very public and very passionate, and one particularly caustic accusation wove through all of them: Juedel was mentally ill.

Every species of a diagnosis of madness surfaced in the controversy: that Juedel was completely blind to her limitations and was therefore a certifiable risk to herself, was so narcissistic that she believed she was immune to the sea, was possessed by bizarre thoughts, and worst, that she had always been a troubled soul with a self-destructive bent who fully intended to die when she began the trip. The journey, her life insurance company and several other people with less-vested interest argued, was therefore "nothing more than a suicide."

The condemnations cast in Claudine Juedel's wake have been leveled in various forms at all the characters whose stories follow. Everesters Earl Denman and Maurice Wilson were similarly derided as naïve and ill-prepared. The Italian climber Claudio Corti was judged naïve, and even immoral, for the blind risk of his plan to climb the deadly North Wall of the Eiger. The aviatrix Jean Batten, the polar balloonist Solomon Andrée, the Arctic explorer Sir John Franklin, and the mountaineer Aleister Crowley were all labeled pathologically, and even fatally, arrogant. The polar explorer Robert Falcon Scott has been called a "willing martyr" ready to die for the mystical deliverance of adventure. Wilson and the American mountaineer Johnny Waterman were both said to have embarked on climbs with suicidal intent. The explorer Meriwether Lewis was said to be suicidally lost in the world after his great western exploration ended. All of the characters in this book were weighted with emotional turmoils that made their adventures seem at least in part to be escapes from troubles and dissatisfactions rather than pursuits of pure dreams. The thread that connects all these stories is that, like Claudine Juedel, everyone in this book has been called "mad."

The term "madness" is used throughout the book in admittedly the bluntest layperson's sense of the word. The choice is intentional, for it is the layperson's verdict that is most often laid on these people. To non-adventurers, voluntary risk-taking is often seen as "crazy" regardless of preparation, expertise, or state of mind. To them (and, in fact, to many psychological theorists, who have variously diagnosed risk-taking as "neurotic" or "unevolved," or even as "masked self-destructive behavior") going off to sail the ocean or climb Mount Everest is inherently disturbed, because the choice in itself seems to ignore normal self-preservation.

Adventurers understandably ridicule the notion that all risk-taking is madness, but they too recognize the dangerous wrongness of *some* adventures. They join the layperson in judging some of the people in this book as mad, condemning many of the protagonists for taking questionable chances with their own lives, endangering the lives of others, or having motives that were dangerously compromised. They also recognize that several of the characters here had personalities or behaviors that invited anger, ridicule, or pity, and in a few instances began their adventure "mad" by even the strictest psychiatric standards.

In many cases though, including some in this book, the line between adventure and madness is less distinct. Even when terrible, questionable risks are taken, they can be forgiven if they are woven around a noble dream, or if they fit into a social context that celebrates adventure. In Claudine Juedel's case, for example, her aspiration to become the first woman to circumnavigate the globe, and her faith in a mystical rebirthing through adventure, both won her support in the debates after her death. Some sailors, for example, insisted that Juedel's ambitions were little different from those of a Columbus or a Lindbergh; others said the mystical healing power of the sea was exactly what motivated them to sail as well. And others still asked the very relevant question: Would we look at Juedel differently if she had succeeded?

Probably. Success is one factor that reliably keeps the line mobile: When the summit or the Pole is reached, when the ocean or desert is crossed, whatever dubious motivation came before seems to be forgiven. Lit by the favorable spotlight of conquest, ragefully obsessed sailors become "driven," suicidal climbers are reinvented as "committed," and the arguable immorality of extreme risk gets re-spun as heroic dedication. But when the climber falls, the sailor disappears, or the desert explorer perishes of dehydration, then the verdict is obvious: The person was mad for having the dream in the first place, or was foolish for having pursued it.

It is no surprise that the troubled are drawn to adventure. From Homer to Hemingway, literature paints its greatest adventure heroes not as invincible warriors, but as flawed souls redeemed by the hardship of their passage. The classics of the genre are very rarely the stories of the perfectly planned and executed expedition; they are more often the tales of climbers who stumble down from a ferocious mountain frostbitten and snowblind, or sailors who limp into port shattered by a great storm. The troubled among us can be powerfully drawn by the promise of heroics, redemption, and acclaim.

It was consequently not difficult to find examples of "madness" in adventure. But understanding the characters and seeing how they were related was the weightier challenge of the book. I chose to group the stories according to the driving issues and forces behind the characters—and their exploits. Those I've called *The Burdened* were all terribly haunted by the tremendous pressure to succeed, either from within or without. *The Bent* were likely drawn to adventure and acted the way they did because of a deeply seated malignancy in their psychological make-up. *The Lost* were people whose adventures ultimately had the same rudderless quality that the rest of their lives did, drifting sadly, frantically, or naïvely toward their unhappy conclusions.

I have tried to represent a range of eras, personalities, types of adventure, and probable psychiatric issue in the choice of characters in each of the themes. I have included some well-known stories and some obscure ones, as well as some stories in which the troubles of a well-known character might surprise the reader into seeing that the heroic versions told in adventure myths are rarely the whole truth.

There will be readers who like their heroes drawn larger and more handsome than life, and who will insist that stories like those of Claudine Juedel and the others in this book have no place in adventure literature. And yet, every one of these characters also embodied many of the same motives, passions, and even emotional hurdles that run through the greatest adventures. Each was drawn to the promise of the bliss that they believed lay in adventure, and each was willing to gamble just as heavily as the great adventurers for that promise.

The difference in these stories is that darkness of some kind—of ambition, of ego, of personal pain, of a need to please others—carried these characters in a much more perilous direction. Every adventure likely has moments of distraction and darkness, and every adventurer has troubles, but in these stories, the darkness clouded the exploit to a degree that it often became the story itself.

When Claudine Juedel pushed away from the Normandy coast in 1974, she sailed into one of the most complex currents in adventure: the line where ambition, passion, and dreams turn into something quite different.

part 1: the burdened

ome silver clouds have dark linings. For all their rich promise of grand experiences, challenge, and even fame, most adventures are freighted with enormous pressures and tensions. Serious expeditions entail months away from home, often in very remote, bitterly hostile places with ever-present threats of death or injury; and even the fittest, strongest adventurers have shown themselves vulnerable to the psychological weight of day-to-day expedition life. Adventure books are filled with stories of explosive tempers, despairs, and even complete breakdowns under the strain of expeditions.

But there are also other, less tangible forces, which can also shape the path of an adventure. These are the forces that sculpted the stories in this first section. Each of the characters here was swept along his journey by complex and ineffable undercurrents: the weight of obligation to others, the contemporary cultural myths about exploration, and the faiths of their time. All of these pressures, in one way or another, cost these men their reason and then their lives. Meriwether Lewis fell under the burden of devotion to a fatherly mentor, to his own ambitions, and then to the cumbersome saddle of fame. Robert Falcon Scott fell under a similar debt to a mentor and to his own ego, but more so succumbed to the chilling acceptance of martyrdom that haunted his era in polar exploration. Solomon Andrée was seduced, and then killed, by the unwavering faith in science that was such a sign of his time. Donald Crowhurst's is a more contemporary story, but with similar shadows of ego, obligations, deceits and finally, dissolution.

These four stories bridge nearly two centuries and reflect the evolving culture of adventure. The weights on Lewis at the beginning of the nineteenth century were the driving forces behind most of the history of exploration. Like most explorers before him, Lewis was sent out to find new lands for his people—an onerous responsibility for the serious, sad man. By the time of Scott a hundred years later, adventure had transformed into something quite different: no longer a search for Eden, but a siege of the barrens of the earth. Scott and many others of his time were pushed to incomprehensible limits conquering wastelands as proof of national virility, and were lionized by an increasingly bloodthirsty and sensationalizing press, even if they failed.

Andrée's and Crowhurst's stories, though separated by seventy-five years, were both encumbered with the unique twists of modern exploration. Both men pursued dreams that were completely, and fatally, reliant on technology; both were forced by finances to enter into devil's bargains with sponsors, media, and a public clamoring for drama and heroics; both staked their reputations on their schemes; and both arrived at a point from which they believed they could no longer return empty-handed.

But running more insistently beneath all four of these stories are the vulnerabilities that each man carried into their adventures. Their ultimately tragic tales were arguably not the necessary result of the burdens they shouldered; rather, they shouldered those burdens because they hoped they might cure far heavier despairs.

A lithographic version of Charles Willson Peale's 1807 portrait of Meriwether Lewis. (Licensed use, Jupiter Images)

CHAPTER 1

MERIWETHER LEWIS

Our Melancholy Hero

EARLY IN THE EVENING OF OCTOBER 10, 1809, a woman moved to the door of her rough Tennessee frontier cabin to follow the approach of a lone man riding in from the west. Smoke from the cabins' fires was just beginning to settle into the clear autumn air of the hillside clearing, but Mrs. Priscilla Grinder could make out the cut of the man. He was tall and broad-shouldered, with fair hair tied back in a ponytail, and he wore a loose white shirt striped with blue. The rider seemed strong in the saddle, though he was undoubtedly weary from the long journey to the isolated outpost and, like any sensible man riding the trail through Indian territory to Mrs. Grinder's inn, he was armed. He had "two handsome pistols and a dirk at his waist," a tomahawk ready for a quick draw, and a long-muzzled rifle sheathed in his saddle.

Mrs. Grinder likely knew well in advance that Meriwether Lewis would be coming her way that night, as there was always gossip following the heavy traffic back and forth along the Natchez Trace. Innkeepers usually knew whom to expect on the trail and the great explorer, now Governor of Upper Louisiana, was an unusually famous man to be riding the rough path. Governor

Lewis had been traveling the faintly blazed Trace through the Tennessee foothills for five days, making his way to distant Washington, and the Grinders' primitive stand of cabins was the only lodging within a day's ride. Lewis rode up and asked Mrs. Grinder for accommodation. She questioned whether he was traveling alone, and he indicated that he had two servants who should be along soon. Lewis unsaddled his horse, entered the mud-chinked log shack, and ordered a whiskey.

Like most Americans of her time, Mrs. Grinder was completely aware of the reputation of Meriwether Lewis. He was already a man of heroic proportions, having returned from his remarkable journey from the Mississippi to the Pacific with William Clark and the Corps of Discovery only three years before. He was, at thirty-five, a very young governor of an enormous—and enormously troubled—frontier territory, and he was the darling of the growing upper classes, invited to parties and grand balls. But although there were moments when Mrs. Grinder saw manners and bearing that lived up to Lewis's prestige, most of what she saw of the man that night at the inn simply terrified her.

When his servants arrived, Lewis had the two men carry his considerable baggage to one of the cabins. Then he asked one of them for his gunpowder. The servant didn't answer him, and Lewis began pacing frenetically in front of Mrs. Grinder, quickly coming toward her "as if to ask for something," then turning and hurrying away again. He talked loudly to himself, but then suddenly calmed down and appeared to be at peace. Mrs. Grinder fixed a meal, and Lewis had taken only a few mouthfuls when he was talking to himself again, this time violently and nonsensically. Mrs. Grinder said she "observed his face to flush as if it had come on him in a fit."

Then again, just as suddenly, Lewis's brittle mood passed. The Governor took a chair to the door of the cabin, sat quietly—"wistfully," Mrs. Grinder suggested—watching the western sky. He lit his pipe and said, "Madam, this is a very pleasant evening." He stood, paced the yard, came back to his chair, lit another pipe and remarked again what "a sweet evening" it was. Mrs. Grinder was puzzled by the mercurial change in Lewis, but less worried now. She even had moments of polite conversation with the man, and Lewis remained settled until nightfall. When Mrs. Grinder came to make a bed for him, he told her he would sleep instead on the floor, as he no longer enjoyed feather beds. His servants were called to lay out buffalo and bear skins, and then went off to their distant quarters.

Mrs. Grinder and her family went to their own beds, but were soon woken up by Lewis, who was again pacing in his room, talking loudly—"like a lawyer," she recalled. This went on, Mrs. Grinder explained, until the early hours of the morning, when she heard the explosion of a gun, followed by the loud crash of something falling to the floor. It was Lewis. "O Lord!" Mrs. Grinder heard him call out. In his pacings, by candlelight, Lewis had discovered his gunpowder, picked up his pistol, and shot himself in the head. According to one report, Lewis only grazed his temple; according to another, he knocked off a piece of his skull, exposing brain tissue. Either way, he somehow survived, only to reload the pistol, press it to his chest, and fire again.

A terrified Mrs. Grinder watched through the poorly caulked log wall as Lewis, still not fatally injured, dragged himself out of the cabin, calling as he went, "O Madam! Give me some water and heal my wounds!!" But Mrs. Grinder was paralyzed by fear and said nothing. The bloodied man fell back through his door onto his bedding.

It was hours before Mrs. Grinder pulled herself together enough to send her children out to fetch Lewis's servants. When the men came to Lewis, they found him with his razor in hand, "busily cutting himself from head to foot." He told the men, "I have done the business." Lewis then insisted that he had tried to kill himself to "deprive [his] enemies the pleasure and honor of doing it," but did not clarify who these enemies were. Finally, in his last words, Lewis begged his servants to finish the job, saying, "I am no coward; but I am so strong, [it is] so hard to die." As badly wounded as he was, it took another two hours, until the sun finally rose above the trees, for Lewis to die.

Immediately after news of his death reached the outside world, the arguments about Lewis's mental health that have lasted for nearly 200 years began. At the core, the debates revolve around the question of whether a "hero" such as Lewis could have taken his own life. That the dispute goes on says as much about our culture's glorification of adventure—and our continuing prejudice against depression and suicide—as it does about the facts of Lewis's end.

On one side, there were those who seemed quite able to suspend moral judgment and accept Mrs. Grinder's and the servants' accounts that Lewis had taken his life; on the other side was a smaller group of contemporaries and historians who were adamant that Lewis's death must have been far more complex, because, in their view, nothing in the man's heroic life predicted suicide.

The "suicide camp" insisted instead that there were signs pointing to self-destruction throughout his story. Several people close to Lewis—most importantly, his mentor and patron Thomas Jefferson, and his co-adventurer William Clark—felt that suicide was a tragic but completely understandable culmination of a moodiness and melancholy that had haunted Lewis for much of his life. They brought forward stories of Lewis's temper, revealed his history of drinking and narcotic use (following bouts with malaria and other illnesses from the trip), acknowledged his despair at not finding a wife, then added serious financial concerns and problems with his role as governor as dominoes that all fell toward a verdict of suicide.

The other side in the debate, arguably out of a desire to preserve a more heroic view of Lewis as the "conqueror" of the American wilderness, fervently insisted that Lewis would never have willingly taken his own life. "It seems to me," insisted Lewis historian Dr. E.G. Chuinard, "that Jefferson's ready acceptance of Lewis's death by suicide was a disgraceful way to treat a man." These doubters, including Chuinard, Vardis Fisher and David Chandler, have come up with alternative explanations for the tragedy at Grinder's Stand—for example, that Lewis was actually a victim of murder, either by some conspiracy of political enemies or at the hands of thieves who sometimes preyed on Natchez Trace travelers. Others, with far more tenuous evidence, conjectured that Lewis was robbed and killed by the Grinder family or by his own men. The historian Dee Brown suggests, for example, "Everybody knows what happened. Robert Grinder came home that night, found Meriwether Lewis in bed with his wife, and shot him. The rest of the story she just made up."

Following quite a different tack, other historians have insisted that if Lewis did commit suicide, his behavior was the forgivable result of physical illnesses such as malaria, or even syphilis—rather than some "disreputable mental weakness"—despite the fact that there is only fragile scientific justification for the claim that illness could have caused his suicide. Lewis biographer Flora Seymour summed up the anti-suicide camp's key contention: Meriwether Lewis did not suicide, because Meriwether Lewis "did not lose his courage nor his head in times of trial." How could a suicide possibly fit into the great tale of the Corps? Lewis was a hero who led a team across thousands of miles of unmapped terrain. How could someone who led such a grand and complicated endeavor possibly kill himself? How could Lewis's problems after the expedition—so minor in comparison to his great achievements—possibly come to suicide? Shouldn't his fame and success, let alone his character, have immunized him against despair?

In a word, no. Believing those things disregards both the relentless haunt of depression and the more complex facts of many adventurers' lives. Depression follows its sufferers into the most successful, golden moments of their lives, and does its angry best to ruin those moments. Adventurers are no more immune to the bitter power of depression than anyone else. Most importantly in Lewis's case, the notion that the expedition was enough to guarantee a permanently happy future completely disregards how Lewis himself perceived the trip. No matter what glories Lewis received when he came home, and no matter what legends may have been spun about the Corps in the last 200 years, the key to understanding that night at Grinder's is how Lewis fit the expedition into his own life story, not how the expedition fit into the mythic story of America.

Still, it is understandable that some historians have tried to sanitize Lewis's death and keep both the man and the expedition aligned with the noble legend of the Corps. It is comforting to imagine unblemished heroes and pure endeavors; but most often that hope simply is not realistic. The most honest and most compelling account of Lewis's story includes elements of the legend, but interlaces them with difficult, yet completely human, threads.

There is a backstory to Meriwether Lewis's journey that is just as fundamental to his fate as the route he traced on the map. This tale has to begin with Thomas Jefferson, because both Lewis and the expedition west were molded by Jefferson's hands from the beginning.

The journey is remembered today as the "Lewis and Clark Expedition," but Lewis was, from the start, the very willing vehicle through whom the elderly Jefferson lived out his own dreams of adventure and empire. Legend might paint the journey of the Corps as a brave wilderness adventure by a small band of independent frontier men, but Jefferson's power and passion made the expedition far more politically and psychologically complex. The president's profound, direct involvement in the expedition meant that this was one of the most imperially driven adventures in history. Lewis may have traveled in buckskin rather than lace, but his adventure had far more in common with Isabella, Ferdinand, and Columbus than it did with Davy Crockett or Daniel Boone.

In voice and in spirit, even when thousands of miles away, Jefferson was always the leader of the expedition, and this fact is key in understanding the place of the journey in Lewis's life. At its core, Lewis's pilgrimage is ultimately a father-and-son story, with Jefferson in the role of a father on a grand scale. Lewis's fate ultimately turned on whether he believed he had lived up to his father's nation-sized dreams.

Jefferson had been writing about those dreams since well before the American Revolution. Far from being a simple exploration of wilderness, the journey of the Corps was first conceived by Jefferson as a spearhead of democratic thought, seeding a nation of free states and equal men across North America. Jefferson grandly imagined an "Empire of Liberty," and its creation as the manifest responsibility of the United States.

As one of the strongest voices of the philosophy of Enlightenment, Jefferson also justified the move west as a spearhead of science. The notion was pure Enlightenment: Human knowledge was supreme. Mapped land was better than wilderness; animals and plants were somehow more real if catalogued; "primitive" peoples could be "civilized" if they were properly studied. For nearly two decades, Jefferson promoted the idea of sending large teams of explorers and scientists who would map and record the whispered wonders of the western wilds.

But beneath these claims of advancing liberty and science, Jefferson was also a savvy pragmatist. Believing that "an abundance of land [is] the mainstay of a prosperous republic," and feeling pressure from his constituents looking for farmlands, Jefferson saw an urgent need for the Union to grow. He understood well the threats from the other countries that had dreams of expansion for their own colonies in the Americas. The first nation to actually set foot on—and especially map—the great wilderness in the core of the continent could much more effectively claim dominion.

Such a claim, of course, disregarded the rather obvious—and difficult—fact of the native presence in the American West. At the time of Jefferson's election in 1801, an American traveling southwest through "Spanish" territory, or northwest through the Oregon Territory claimed by Spanish, French, English, and Russian interests, would be very unlikely to see another white man of any nationality; but he would be certain to see any number of nations of Indians. With the possibility of coming across Europeans vying for the same terrain, and the strong likelihood of encountering Indians who would defend their lands, any expedition, Jefferson understood, would have to be primarily a military one, ready to defend its right to claim the West in the name of freedom.

All of these complex and extravagant challenges and agendas for Jefferson's expedition clarified the job description for the leader the president needed for the voyage west. As Jefferson himself described the best candidate: " . . . a character who to a compleat science in botany, natural history, mineralogy & astronomy, joined the firmness of constitution & character, prudence, habits adapted to the woods, & a familiarity with the Indian manners & character requisite for this undertaking."

Jefferson knew just the man for the job.

———————————

Meriwether Lewis was born in 1774 in Albemarle County, Virginia, where his family's tobacco plantation stood within sight of Jefferson's Monticello. Jefferson was well acquainted with Lewis's father William. The Lewises stemmed from a long line of elites in the region. The first Lewis arrived in America in 1635; an uncle of William Lewis married a sister of George Washington; another was a member of a frontier settlement expedition led by Thomas Jefferson's father. Meriwether Lewis's mother, Lucy Meriwether, came from equally rich stock—in fact, from much the same stock. There were eleven marriages between the two families prior to Lewis's parents' union. William Lewis's grandfather was one of Lucy Meriwether's great-grandfathers; William and Lucy were thus cousins.

Many people, including Jefferson himself, have asked whether Lewis's end might not have been predestined by the closed bloodlines of the family. Jefferson wrote that the clan was "subject to hypochondriac affections. It was a constitutional disposition in the nearer branches of the family." (By "hypochondriac," Jefferson was referring to depression in the common language of his day rather than the current meaning of *hypochondria*. Jefferson clarifies what he meant when he later described Lewis's disposition as "melancholy," and when he wrote that he had seen "sensible depressions of the mind" in the man.)

Some Lewis biographers have suggested that when describing depression in the family, Jefferson was speaking not only of Lewis's father, who had a history of melancholic episodes, but also a half-brother from Lewis's mother's second marriage, who was in an asylum for depression on several occasions. If this was the case, it suggests that both sides of Lewis's family, the Lewises and the Meriwethers, may have carried a susceptibility to depression. The illness does run in families, and intermarriage would facilitate expression in each generation.

There were also more direct factors in Lewis's life which might equally explain some of the eventual turns, both positive and negative, in his story. Lewis's father William, like most of the men of his time, fought in the Revolutionary War and was away in battle for virtually all of Lewis's childhood. Then, during a rare leave with his family when Meriwether was five, William Lewis succumbed to pneumonia. Although Lewis's mother soon remarried to a man Lewis liked and respected, Lewis always saw himself as a boy who had lost a heroic father. That loss, many of his biographers have suggested, explained why he became so readily and deeply attached to Thomas Jefferson.

Another factor in Lewis's life that led to the Corps was the power of wilderness as an emotional anchor for him, even from a young age. As a child in Virginia, Lewis was said to be happiest when he was in the woods. This was only reinforced when his stepfather, John Marks, took him to Georgia, most of which was true wilderness at the time.

The stories of the eight-year-old Lewis in the hills of Georgia are a vivid part of his "mountain-man" legend. The boy was said to have gone hunting alone at night, to have shot a bull in full charge, and to have single-handedly stopped an Indian raid on a family cabin. On the basis of Lewis's own writings about the peace and purpose he found there, it is perfectly reasonable to see the wild as the place he was most at home—perhaps, as Jefferson suggested, the *only* place Lewis was ever truly settled.

Lewis was also marked by a uniquely brilliant mind that kept him distant from the world around him. When he was thirteen, his mother started making efforts to get him formally schooled, so that he might take over the family plantation. Lewis was eventually educated back in

Virginia, away from his family. But by age eighteen, he was pulling his mother, once again widowed, and his siblings back to Locust Hill, where Lewis took on the responsibility of running the family business.

The young man did a fine job with the responsibilities of the plantation, but he also struggled with a restless soul. He called life on the plantation a "miserable tedium," and he was clearly not ready to settle for a permanent farming future. His discontent was strong enough that the same year he moved back to Locust Hill, Lewis applied as a candidate for Jefferson's first expedition up the Missouri River, years before the journey of the Corps. There is no record of how Jefferson felt about Lewis's bold proposal, save that he understandably turned the inexperienced young man down. Although Jefferson refused him then, their relationship was re-established, and the episode cemented Jefferson's appreciation of the young man's spirit.

Within two years, Lewis escaped the confines of the plantation despite his responsibilities. With great—if not completely genuine—apologies to his mother, he leapt at the opportunity of the Whiskey Rebellion to leave his family, join the Army, and head to the frontier to protect the Republic.

Lewis flourished in both the structure and the thrills of the army. While desertion and discipline problems were endemic during the messy fight against the rebellion, Lewis showed himself to be a soldier's soldier, and he rose easily through the ranks, re-enlisting when his commission was up and the rebellion was stifled.

"I am quite delighted with a soldier's life," he wrote his family, and he was soon an officer, becoming a captain by the age of twenty-five. The army also proved a perfect place for Lewis to indulge his need for travel and adventure. During his six years of commission, he rambled all through the frontier lands between the Ohio and Mississippi Rivers, and gained rich knowledge of backwoods living and of the command of men.

But there was also a downside to Lewis's military years: the heavy drinking that was so much part of an officer's life. After several incidents of trouble, Lewis was disciplined in 1795 for challenging another officer to a duel while drunk. Ironically, the charges, which could have spelled the end of Lewis's military career, resulted in the best possible turn of fate: Lewis was transferred out of his unit and into the command of William Clark. The two served together for only six months, but Clark proved one of the strongest friends of Lewis's life.

Lewis's military career ended when an even grander role was offered; just days before he took office as president in 1801, Jefferson wrote to ask if Lewis would be interested in a position as his secretary. It was the beginning of Lewis's grooming for the expedition.

"The joy" of working for "a man whose virtue and talents I have ever adored, and always conceived second to none." That was how Lewis described Jefferson's offer in his letter of resignation to his company commander, and that was how he lived for the next three years, absorbed in Washington life and in his constant connection to Jefferson.

There is every indication that Jefferson felt just as positively about his time with Lewis—to the point that Lewis is described by several historians as "the son that Jefferson always wished he had." The president brought the young man completely under his wing: Lewis dined with Jefferson nearly every day, sat in on all his parties with the great men and women of the time, slept in a nearby room in the White House, ran his political errands, and even delivered Jefferson's first State of the Union address to Congress.

But however good a job Lewis was doing as his aide, Jefferson had a more significant task in mind for him. Jefferson's new office finally gave him the leverage to put his ambitious plans of western exploration and expansion into action—especially after a book published in 1801 forced his hand. In 1793, Alexander Mackenzie, a Scot posted to a fur trading post in northwestern Canada, followed the Peace River into the Rocky Mountains of present-day Alberta, determined to find a passage to the West Coast. Mackenzie had only a small team of companions—a fellow Scot, a half-dozen French-Canadian voyageurs and two Indians—but this number had proven sufficient four years earlier when Mackenzie had traveled to the Arctic Ocean from the same spot. On his westbound journey, in just a little over two months, Mackenzie crossed the Rockies, gained the Fraser River, and reached the Pacific. Mackenzie was not sufficiently literate to write his own account of the trip, but his ghostwritten journals went to press just as Jefferson began his presidency.

Mackenzie's success undermined Jefferson's aspirations to be the "first" to chart a course across the continent to the sea (of course,

Mackenzie was hardly the first himself, as natives had been making the journey for centuries). To suit his own ambitions, Jefferson reframed Mackenzie's efforts as a failure. First, he insisted, Mackenzie had not been able to follow a continuous water route, and Jefferson was still convinced of the existence of the fabled "Northwest Passage" to the Pacific that would open up trade in a way that Mackenzie's land route never could. Second, Mackenzie had not, in Jefferson's view, advanced much knowledge about the West, as he was hardly a scientist and had not focused on the natural history of the journey.

But the real problem was that Mackenzie was not an American. It was an American journey that Jefferson's plan for an empire of liberty needed. Very shortly after they read Mackenzie's book together at the White House, Jefferson announced that Lewis would be leading a trip to the West. Lewis started his crash course in the Jeffersonian version of exploration; his secretarial days were over, and the most exciting chapter of his life was suddenly open.

The degree of the president's direct involvement in the planning of the expedition seems inconceivable today. Jefferson took Lewis on as a student, teaching him all he could about the sciences of biology, botany, geology, and astronomy. When Jefferson faced the rare subject he could not personally teach—such as medicine and celestial navigation—he sent Lewis off to experts around the country. Jefferson had a strong hand in every aspect of the details of the journey as well, right down to planning the route and the equipment taken, as well as issuing directions for relating to natives on the way.

Not all of Jefferson's teachings, however, were entirely realistic or of ultimate benefit to the expedition. In 1803, everything west of the Missouri was a land in shadow to Europeans, but that had not stopped people from dreaming up great tales about the wilds. Jefferson proved to be as vulnerable as anyone else to some of these myths.

At the most basic level, because Jefferson was adamant about the existence of a water route to the Pacific (despite information to the contrary from natives), he held that the trip should take no more than a year (when in the end it took well over two). Adding to the underestimation of the journey was Jefferson's odd conviction that the Blue Mountains of Virginia were the highest on the continent. He was certain that the mountains of the West should therefore be no more difficult to cross than the Blues, despite Captains Cook and Vancouver's awestruck descriptions of great snowy peaks they had seen from the Pacific. Jefferson and Lewis were also convinced, with little evidence, that the western mountains were a single ridge. They were confident that even if a portage were necessary, it could be completed in a day.

Jefferson accepted other, more extravagant myths as well: that woolly mammoths and other giant prehistoric animals still roamed the plains; that there were active volcanoes scattered across western deserts; that there was a mile-long mountain of pure salt in Indian country; that a lost tribe of Israel would be found near the mountains; and that one of the Indian tribes was a fair-skinned race said to come from Wales. Jefferson believed that a large part of the expedition's mandate was to prove the existence of these great wonders, and Lewis took the responsibility of confirming Jefferson's beliefs very seriously.

The scope of the expedition and the weight of Jefferson's ambitions must have placed enormous pressure on Lewis, but there is little hint of strain or dissatisfaction in his writings about the period of planning, no record of the restlessness, temper, melancholy, and drinking that plagued him in other times of his life. Instead, the thrill of the preparation and the race to begin the actual travel was described by Lewis as "among the most happy of my life." He seemed completely aware of the importance of the journey he was about to undertake, and of the dangers involved, but the challenges electrified him more than any other adventure he had been a part of.

Despite the daunting responsibilities, Lewis was convinced that he would return with all his mentor Jefferson asked for. Lewis asked his old friend William Clark to join him as co-leader of the voyage, and finally, after a number of false starts and seemingly endless troubles getting gear ready, the expedition cast off into history down the Ohio River on August 31, 1803.

In this age, when an ascent of Everest can take a matter of weeks, the Poles can be reached by snowmobile in days, the great deserts are pocked with oil rigs, and so much of the world is overmapped, the scale of Lewis and Clark's journey can be hard to comprehend. It was in the league of Magellan or Drake rather than Hillary or Scott, measured in years and miles instead of weeks and feet. The Corps traveled for 864 days and covered more than 8000 miles—more than half the distance previously uncharted—by the time they returned to St. Louis in late summer, 1806. The Corps dragged along a huge raft of provisions upstream, but almost everything that kept them alive day-to-day they caught, shot, picked, or bargained for along the way.

In contrast to Alexander Mackenzie's small expedition, Lewis and Clark's Corps was an army, with thirty-four full members, including Lewis, Clark, Clark's slave York, the fabled Indian slave girl called Sacagawea, her son who was born on the journey, and twenty-four temporary members, mostly Frenchmen hired to pole the boats up to the first winter camp with the Mandan tribe in present-day North Dakota. (The records of the Corps do not, however, count the natives who joined along the way, guiding and aiding the journey.)

For much of the trip, all the way to the headwaters of the Missouri, the Corps traveled upstream against a thick current, moving slowly in their sluggish keelboats and canoes. The men often walked on the river shore, because they could manage a faster pace. They were occasionally able to sail, but more often they paddled, poled, or put men on the shore to haul the heavily laden boats with coconut-fiber lines. The somber Lewis preferred to walk, sometimes traveling thirty miles in a day, often alone as he collected specimens and artifacts to send back to Jefferson.

Lewis's collecting was arguably the greatest success of the expedition. He described 178 plants and 122 animal species previously unknown to science, and kept meticulous notes about animal behavior, weather patterns, and geology, all heavily illustrated. The maps made by the team—mostly by Clark—were accurate and complete enough to be a template for a century of exploration. The expedition journals are also the first anthropology of many native tribes, and though they have been understandably criticized by some writers as racially narrow-minded, they offer a fascinating window into cultures encountering one another for the first time.

If Jefferson hoped that Lewis would bring back a vivid-enough portrait to facilitate a public interest in the West, he could not have been more pleased with Lewis's record. The collected writings of the Corps amounted to more than 1.5 million words, written collaboratively by Lewis, Clark, and other members of the Corps, making their journey, as historian Thomas Slaughter points out, "the most heavily documented exploration in history up to the twentieth century."

But the numbers alone do not capture one of the most compelling aspects of the journals: the immediacy and poignancy of the writing, which richly paints the wide-eyed wonder of encountering big wilderness for the first time. The amount of detail captured in the journals is remarkable, but so is the innocence and the sense of thrill that runs throughout the thirteen volumes, particularly in Clark's writing, with its primitive spelling and poetic descriptions. Clark's take on the team, from March 30, 1805, also illustrates how matter-of-fact the journals can be:

> *[The party] are helth. Except the—vn. [venereal disease]—which is common with the Indians and have been communicated to many of our party at this place—those favores bieng easy acquired. all the party in high Spirits they pass but fiew nights without amuseing themselves dancing possessing perfect harmony.*

When the Corps had high spirits, it was almost always when the land readily met their needs. The expedition certainly had the chance to see the American West at its most pristine. They enjoyed, especially on the Great Plains, an Eden of hunting so rich that some members contracted scurvy from filling themselves so completely with meat from buffalo, beaver, venison, waterfowl, and bear. Their descriptions of the game of the Plains have the flavor of the tales of the great African safaris, with seas of buffalo, and dramatic battles with predators.

There is no question that the journey was an epic adventure, and in many ways an enormously successful one. Eight thousand miles of wilderness was mapped out. Despite the length of the journey and the feared hostilities, the only death on the trip came through disease. Trade with the Indians and peace with the other colonial powers looked possible. Hundreds of plants and animals were discovered and named just as Jefferson had dreamed, and the journals of the Corps were a passionate advertisement for western expansion.

On September 23, 1806, the Corps, in Lewis's words, "descended with great velocity" back into St. Louis. The grand adventure was over, and Meriwether Lewis ascended into American myth. His future, by all measures, should have been blessed, and yet within three years he was dead by his own hand.

Why?

In the last ten or twenty years, a very different view of Lewis's story has begun to be written, one that far more clearly accounts for how the mythic hero ended up where he did. In this revisionist view, the key to Lewis's fate is that he started to believe that the expedition, on a number of levels, was as much a distressing failure as it was a heroic success. This is a view painfully familiar to anyone who has struggled with the devious machinations of depression: *Happiness is naïve; beneath any superficial accomplishment lies a truer, deeper failure; your flaws will be outed; the dark days of the past will inevitably repeat themselves.*

The modern assessment of Lewis looks at the journey of the Corps through the relentlessly critical eyes of a depressive. Dispensing with the mythic spin, the first question for Lewis and the revisionists was the deepest one: What *had* the Corps really accomplished? Lewis had not discovered a water route to the Pacific. Opening trade with the Indians was going to involve complicated—and, as history would show, violent—negotiations. None of Jefferson's mythic Welsh Indians, lost tribes of Israel, mountains of salt, or woolly mammoths had been conjured up. No matter that these targets were built on completely unfounded notions; Lewis was letting Jefferson down, and increasingly over the next few years, in Lewis's mind this became an unforgivable disgrace.

Most importantly, Lewis knew that it was a stretch to claim he was the first across the continent. He not only read Mackenzie's book more than a year before he left the East, but he also had to disregard the fact that he ran into 150 whites—British, French, and American—during his travels up the supposed "wilderness of the Missouri." Well beyond the point where he wrote he was entering the "untravelled wilds," he met a Chinook Indian woman who had the name of a white trapper branded on her arm. And he knew that at least thirteen previous British and American traders had reached the West Coast before the Corps, including a few who had already penetrated well into the eastern reaches of the Columbia River.

Although it was completely in keeping with the times, Lewis also clearly struggled with how the expedition myth excised Indians from the story for the sake of maintaining the myth of being "first across the continent." The journals facilely whitewash the fact that natives had been making the crossing from buffalo hunts in the Plains to the coast for millennia. Even when Lewis acknowledges that native guides deserved full credit for getting the team over the Rockies, he persists in decrying their dirtiness, "savagery," and troubling morals. It is obvious that the Corps simply could not have completed their journey without the food, shelter, and advice they received from the Indians. Yet, in return, the Corps offered the Indians trinkets, beat those who did not heed their orders, slept with their women, stole a canoe to get back up the Columbia, and effectively held one Mandan chief hostage for three years—all the while promising a great, mutually beneficial partnership with their "new father" in Washington.

And yet in several places in his writings, Lewis shows apparently genuine respect and compassion for the natives, and regret for the way he may have participated in mistreating them. While other explorers of the time managed to dance around their contradictions with galling hubris, the inconsistency appears to have troubled the ever-moral Lewis deeply.

Though Lewis was a resolutely military man who saw the need to run the expedition with an iron hand, it is also clear that the demands of the command were an increasingly uncomfortable burden for him. In the face of conflicts that were completely natural given the stresses and length of the expedition, Lewis was occasionally explosive and vicious, striking men, court-martialing them, and even ordering whippings. The men described him as moody, withdrawn, and inaccessible, and he went through long stretches—months at a time—when he completely stopped writing in his usually beloved journals.

There's been great debate about whether these gaps in the journal reflect Lewis slipping into episodes of melancholy despite the balm of the wilderness (or whether there were simply missing journals—the rationalization of the anti-suicide camp), but there is far less disagreement about his state of mind when he finally returned to civilization. Whatever happiness Lewis had found on the trail began to fade as soon as he drew up to the St. Louis wharf.

Lewis faced awkward personal burdens almost immediately after the trip. The expedition, though it had been given essentially a *carte blanche* by Jefferson, returned to a mountain of debt. Lewis's inability to settle the expedition accounts was increasingly troubling to him, as is shown in angrier and angrier letters he sent to Jefferson, decrying the pressure that he was feeling from the new administration in Washington to justify the expense of the trip.

The obvious compensation that Lewis did more readily get—fame—was also not without its problems. When the American press and the public realized that the Corps had not perished on the journey as had been predicted, Lewis became the darling of society; but everything about the man's history suggests that for Lewis, the celebrity came with a substantial price. Several of Lewis's biographers described him as "hating cities," yet his return as a hero meant that cities were exactly where he was going to find himself: in Philadelphia, in Washington, in Boston, at balls, at lectures where he would be talking about the "happiest moments of [his] life" in the past tense.

Lewis's appointment as governor of Louisiana in 1807 was equally a double-edged sword: It was a position of honor and responsibility that was meant to be a great reward, but the reality of the job was that Lewis found himself drowning in bureaucracy and petty politics, drifting further and further from the life that gave him his only happiness. To understand how he felt about the job, one needs to look no further beyond the fact that it took Lewis thirteen months after his appointment to travel to the territorial capital in St. Louis.

When he did arrive, Lewis was soon overwhelmed with the burdens of the office. The Territory was a mess of competing interests and historical conflicts. The promise of the opening of the West that Lewis symbolized was turning out to be a nightmare of warring natives, dishonest traders, and financial disaster. Hailed as the great hero, Lewis quickly made vicious enemies among the bureaucrats, one of whom slandered and ridiculed him very publicly.

Lewis seemed to completely lack both the political skills and the energy for the job, and he began drinking heavily once again. He also started to show questionable financial judgment, incurring huge debts on dubious investments, often on the backs of supporters as close as William Clark. Soon, Lewis's government expense vouchers, some of which were still unpaid bills from the expedition, started to be denied by the new president, James Madison. Lewis was precipitously heading downhill, and the fame and memories of the expedition were doing nothing to stop the fall.

And then there were the journals. Lewis was aware that the expedition's place in history relied on the swift publication of the journals, but from the time of his return from the West until his death, Meriwether Lewis did not write a single word. He made repeated promises of delivery to printers, publishers, and especially Jefferson, but until his death he never added anything to the hand-written, elk-skin-bound volumes he carried to the Pacific and back. He claimed to be working on the books, claimed to be editing and consolidating, begged for more time, borrowed more money, made a hundred excuses to Jefferson, and then stopped writing his friend and mentor entirely by 1808, avoiding all contact and correspondence and descending further into his troubles. (Because of Lewis's failure to write about it—and, even more so, due to his suicide—the expedition effectively disappeared from history for generations. History texts in the United States contained little more than a paragraph or two about the Corps until the 1950s, when the story was resurrected.)

Finally, throughout the spring and summer of 1809, Jefferson—no longer President but still championing the expedition as his great legacy—angrily demanded that Lewis produce something. Jefferson was furious that far less complete, less accurate, and only marginally literate serialized versions of the journals by other members of the Corps had started appearing. Lewis finally relented to Jefferson's pressure and committed to returning to Washington to finish writing. He left his home in Louisiana, but was visibly disintegrating as he headed down the Mississippi that hot September. Twice, eyewitnesses claimed, he tried to take his life on the boat trip and had to be closely monitored. By the time he arrived at the fort that stands at the present-day site of Memphis, Tennessee, he was wildly incoherent, drinking, snorting potent snuff, telling wild stories, and regularly taking opium for a variety of vague pains that had been troubling him since his return from the expedition.

When Lewis landed at the fort, the commander was sufficiently concerned by Lewis's "mental derangement" that he ordered an escort to accompany the governor as he left the river and started the long, difficult trip to Washington. But even the deep forests along the Natchez Trace could not soothe him this time. Five days later, Meriwether Lewis rode into the clearing at Grinder's Stand.

A portrait, by J. Russell & Sons, Southseas Photographers, of Captain Robert Falcon Scott.

CHAPTER 2

ROBERT FALCON SCOTT

A Struggle for Existence

SOMEWHERE IN THE ENDLESS DAYS OF COLD AND WIND, they realize it is impossible to make it back to their base, but they all agree there really is nothing to do but continue. No matter how hopeless it might be to go on, Captain Scott insists that to simply lie down and die is inconceivable. But the thought still haunts each of them privately: Would it not be easier to give in to the inevitable? Wouldn't it be so much simpler just to sleep?

Teddy Evans, the friendly joker who impressed everyone with abilities far above his rank, is the first to go. He falls briefly into a crevasse and his spirit seems to stay behind in the hole. Scott writes that Evans is "nearly broken down in brain." He falters in his tracks, his feet freeze, and he lags behind; he seems unable to pull his weight in the evening camps. Finally, he collapses in a coma in the snow and has to be left behind.

Then the quiet one, Lawrence Oates. Feet swollen and infected, he is the first to voice thoughts about giving up, asking the others to simply leave him so that he no longer slows them up; but they will have none of it. Oates makes it easy for them: a loner in life, he chooses the same path in death. He walks off into the blizzard, telling the others he "may be some time." Scott calls him a "gallant gentleman" for "try[ing] to save his comrades" by sacrificing himself.

And then, only eleven miles from the end, the storm. Scott, Henry Bowers, and Edward Wilson are pinned in their wind-whipped tent, knowing that they "must be near the end," but they decline the peaceful solution of the opium pills that Wilson passes out. Scott insisted there should be no taints on their deaths: "It shall be natural," Scott writes. "We shall march . . . and die on our tracks." But they do neither. Bowers and Wilson fail in their sleep, and Scott is left alone until his own death, penciling himself into legend in twelve remarkably coherent letters.

"Had we lived, I should have had a tale to tell," Scott wrote, "of the hardihood, endurance, and courage of my companions which would have stirred the heart of every Englishman."

There have been few tales of noble sacrifice told as often as that of "Scott of the Antarctic" and his men succumbing in the very last few steps of their return from the South Pole. The enduring appeal of Scott's story is no surprise: The arc of his journey traces the path of the mythic hero's trail almost perfectly. Scott was a valiant young man "plucked from obscurity," ordinary enough that anyone could imagine him- or herself in his place. An older mentor passed on the myth of a holy grail—(in this case, it was the geographer Clements Markham, and the quest was for the South Pole)—that Scott took on as a personal crusade. After defeat on a first expedition south, Scott fought for the right to pursue the grail again and returned for an epic pilgrimage, only to discover that the grail had already been stolen (by his nemesis Roald Amundsen). He then valiantly led his men back through murderous conditions, failing on the threshold of salvation. Finally, posthumously, he was crowned a golden hero by an adoring public who saw his sacrifice as even more glorious than victory.

The difficulty with this reading is that it is mostly myth, a hagiography that dehumanizes Scott by refusing to shine light into any of the shadowed corners of his life. The mythologizing prevents the mortals among us from truly connecting with Scott and learning about ourselves through him. The fuller picture of Scott—not only remarkably strong and resolute, but also troubled, despairing, out of his league—is a far more complete and embraceable one.

Just as Meriwether Lewis was saddled with the destiny of a nation by Thomas Jefferson, at the turn of the twentieth century "Con" Scott was asked to "show the world the unconquerable spirit of the British peoples" by Sir Clements Markham, president of the Royal Geographic Society. It would prove an equally grave burden.

Like Jefferson, Markham was an older man incapable of living out his dreams personally, obliged to cultivate a protégé to realize his legacy. Markham's obsession was Antarctica, and he invested the then-uncharted ice with as much mystique, and pursued it with as much vigor, as Jefferson did the American West. A voracious and accomplished traveler in his prime, Markham aged into a role with the Royal Geographic Society (RGS) as a tireless champion of the nobility of hardships in pursuit of the scientific colonization of the world. There was no place, he assured people, that was more formidable, and less understood, than Antarctica—and no place where Britain had a greater right to plant its flag.

On the eve of the demise of the British Empire, Markham invoked what he called the "manifest destiny of the British Crown" to name, populate, and control "all points of the [Southern] hemisphere." In Markham's eyes, Antarctica could be the last cold toe of the Raj; not a consolation prize in the face of the shrinking empire, but the greatest victory of all. It was an objective, Markham went so far as to say, that the men of the Empire would be "willing to give their lives for." It was a stirring call, and Markham expertly used the pulp press to get the British people clamoring for heroes.

Markham played just as active a role in the British polar campaign as Jefferson played in the West—lobbying Parliament and raising funds, dictating the style and membership of the expedition, and especially cultivating its leader. In Markham's eyes, that ideal man would simply be a younger reflection of himself: a hardened Navy man, ready to follow orders and lead the expedition the way Markham himself would have run it.

Before his discovery by Markham, Scott was invisible: just another privileged sailing boy schooled under the lash of the Royal Navy. Born in 1868, he came from two families with long Navy lines, including an admiral (his mother's brother), and it was clear that he would be a Navy man himself. Scott was on board his first ship, the *Britannia,* and very much out of his childhood, at thirteen.

The early start away from home was not unusual, but it does seem to have troubled Scott more than it did most cadets. Many of Scott's biographers have anchored the complexities and contradiction of the man's later character in this early uprooting. Throughout his life, Scott fought contradictory tides of self-condemning sadness and exhilarated confidence. He enjoyed several devoted friendships, but was paralyzed by shyness that was perplexing even to him. He often seemed at the mercy of his moods: calm and compassionately rational at one instant, explosive and ill-tempered at another.

It is not a stretch to look for the reasons for Scott's adult turmoil in his abruptly ended childhood. The colors of Scott's struggles are very similar to those of many children who have been removed from homes and placed in harsh and lonely circumstances. Scott's biographer Elspeth Huxley suggested that the young man was particularly sensitive to the disruption given that he was "shy and diffident, small and weakly for his age, lethargic, backwards and above all, dreamy." He was also intellectual and bookish, and had been raised surrounded almost completely by the delicate women of the Scott household. None of these things served him too well in an adolescence aboard training ships, which were notoriously male, rough, and brutally hierarchical. As Huxley points out, below decks Scott must have had to suppress his softer sides. He often seemed to compensate for any public hint of weakness with an almost masochistic ability to endure suffering.

Scott compensated for his weaknesses so well that he won notice, first by his commander, and eventually by Clements Markham. Markham watched the eighteen-year-old midshipman win a sailing race in the Caribbean, and wrote after Scott's death, "From that moment I was completely smitten with the young man's wit, charm and ability to command his peers." The moment was the beginning of the Scott legend—and the myth-making. Markham claimed that he knew immediately that Scott was going to lead his Antarctic expedition; however, several writers have argued that Markham is guilty of mythologizing when he claims this clairvoyance, as there was no "Antarctic expedition" anywhere near the horizon at the time of his first brief meeting with

Scott. Whatever Markham's sense of Scott's potential, there were still many more difficult years for the young sailor before Markham accidentally ran into Scott again and truly started sculpting his immortality.

In his twenties, Scott was nothing like the mythic figure he became in exploration history. Instead of pursuing great expeditionary dreams, Scott was buckling under the weight of everyday life. His father went bankrupt and then died, leaving the family teetering on the edge of poverty. Scott's older brother Archie, who had borne the brunt of the financial burden of supporting the family, died of typhoid fever not long after his father passed. Scott was saddled with responsibilities that made it almost impossible to have a life of his own. He was ashamed of his situation—especially his poverty—to the point that he became profoundly depressed.

Again and again in his private diaries, Scott plaintively despairs about his "dark future" and writes of how immobilized he becomes under the strain. His description of his misery and paralysis is a perfect sketch of a clinical depression: "This dreary deadly tightening of the heart, this slow sickness that holds one for weeks. How shall I bear it. I write of the future; of the hopes of being more worthy; but shall I ever be—can I alone, poor wretch that I am, bear up against it all."

The weight of his sadness was enough to make him physically ill for several years (so much so that he suffered fainting spells) and hinder his rise in the Navy. It was only because he accidentally bumped into Markham on Buckingham Palace Road in June 1899—only the third time they ever met—that we know of Scott at all today.

When he ran into Markham, Scott had made little advance in the Navy for several years, had barely been able to provide for his family, and knew nothing of Antarctica. But Markham had stirred enough public interest in the nobility of his expedition to encourage hundreds of applications by sailors, and there Scott saw his golden opportunity: Sailing south would get him a commission, relieve his financial burden, get him back in the company of the Navy men with whom he was most at ease, and give him a purpose that would help him drown out the self-condemning voices in his head. When Markham offered the opportunity, it took only a couple of days for Scott to quell his inner doubts; then he settled under Markham's reassuring hand. Scott would be going to the South Pole in only three years, and there was an enormous amount to be done. Just as Meriwether Lewis had discovered during his years getting ready for the journey of the Corps, for Scott, in the role of golden protégé, there was no longer any time, or place, for despair.

The years of planning Scott's first trip south—the *Discovery* expedition of 1901–04—were a chaotic flurry, though mostly for Markham, who struggled to find funding and fought to balance the demands of the various agencies and societies who were backing the journey. Markham's own plans for the trip were clear—it needed to be run by his devoted charge—but it was not easy to sell Scott as the leader. Markham's opponents argued that this was far too expensive and complex a trip to entrust to a man who had never been near ice. Scott's behavior did not help matters. Once again, Scott's fragile sense of self got in his way. As he had in the past, Scott compensated for his self-doubt by turning to rigid discipline—of himself and others—and he was derided as "arrogant," "ruthless," and "ambitious for it." He was responsible for selecting the crew of the ship, and while he easily picked some men, he fought against the selection of others if he was not sure they shared his drive or would obey his commands. And though he was able to attract excellent candidates, and earned fierce loyalty from some of his men, he was seen as aloof and cold by most.

The most complex relationship Scott had on the journey was a troubled association with one of the other greats of Antarctic history, a conflict that would color the rest of both men's lives. Ernest Shackleton, who later rose to glory as captain of the epic polar voyage of the *Endurance*, came on board *Discovery* as one of the few Merchant Navy men, and his civilian status set up animosity with the vulnerable Scott almost immediately. Scott's self-confidence with his men depended in part on his reliance on Navy order, discipline and rank, and many writers have suggested that Scott had concerns about his ability to control the less-disciplined Shackleton. Shackleton's threat to Scott increased when the captain saw how popular Shackleton was. The Irishman was spontaneously appealing, where Scott always struggled to fit in with the men. Scott's fear of Shackleton proved to be astute: Not only was Scott's leadership on the ship measured against Shackleton's natural charisma, but Scott's place in Antarctic history would forever be measured against Shackleton's.

In many ways, though, history has been as unjustly critical in judging the difference between the two men as Scott was in judging himself.

While Shackleton is often cast as the most selfless, humane leader among explorers, and Scott as one the most callously ambitious, this is a shallow analysis that does a disservice to both men. When needed, Scott could be as inspirational as Shackleton, and Shackleton was easily as ambitious as Scott, and just as Machiavellian. Still, the contests between the two men's egos, mostly through Scott's doing, arguably shaped the outcome of the *Discovery* expedition more than any other factor, and the ongoing open animosity between the two men played a huge role in the future of Antarctic exploration.

December 31, 1902. 87°15' S. Three hundred miles further south than anyone had ever traveled, Con Scott was faced with an exasperating but inevitable decision: His first expedition to the South Pole would have to be abandoned. After one winter of acclimating to Antarctica, three reconnaissance probes into the continent, and now two months of travel on this final chance at the Pole, Scott and his two companions were exhausted, suffering scurvy and near-starvation. There had been raw conflict on the journey, in large part because Shackleton, despite Scott's wishes otherwise, had been the most logical partner to accompany Scott on the grueling haul to the Pole. Though the two had moments of superb performance together, tension often erupted openly. Very contrary to the manners of the day, there were incidents of threats and cursing that even drew in the third, usually imperturbable member of the sledging party, Edward Wilson.

Yet it was scarcely better to turn around than it would have been to continue. The terrain, and the snow and wind conditions, made every step work, and it took thirty-five days to make their way back to the ship, much of it hauling the very sick Shackleton on a sled. All three men ended the journey close to death.

Historians have battled for years in their analysis of *Discovery*'s epic failure. Some criticize the minimal experience of the team as the fatal flaw, but this suggestion ignores how few men had experience in the South at the time. Others lay blame squarely on the plans laid by Markham and Scott, pointing out that the two men committed to style and schedule decisions that were openly advised against by the few veteran polar travelers of the day.

Others, however, have suggested that the deeper, truer problem of the expedition showed itself more clearly after the assault team stumbled back to *Discovery*: Scott's self-confidence. Instead of heralding the team's survival, Scott sent Shackleton home as soon as the team arrived back at the ship, claiming the Irishman was too sick to survive another winter of scientific observations. Scott then publicly voiced his opinion that Shackleton was "unfit" for polar exploration, and dumped most of the blame for the failure to reach the Pole on Shackleton's illness.

But if Scott intended to raise himself above Shackleton in the public eye by banishing the man, the plan backfired. As the first member of the team to come home, Shackleton received the lion's share of acclaim, and this gave the Irishman a considerable advantage in funding his own return south. The dismissal also fully engaged Shackleton's own formidable ego: He made it very clear that he felt he had been slighted by Scott, and became obsessed not only with beating Scott to the Pole, but with leading the victorious expedition himself.

Scott's own interest in going back for the Pole was far less clear. Thanks in large part to Markham's spin machine, Scott also returned to Britain a hero after *Discovery*'s third wintering, but Scott recognized that in some people's eyes he was a hero only in the dubious sense that he had survived by the skin of his teeth. That criticism was difficult for the self-doubting Scott to resolve. After all, he *had* failed. Perhaps, he worried, his self-condemnations were valid. While Shackleton pushed relentlessly, and very publicly, for another expedition, Scott accepted a Navy posting and gave no sign of a desire to go back to Antarctica.

It was only when Shackleton made it clear in 1907 that he would be heading south in the summer of that year that Scott's hand was forced. In his first salvo at Shackleton's ambitions, Scott arrogantly insisted that only he had the right to use the staging area around the present McMurdo Base. Even if he was not intending to start an expedition there himself in the immediate future, Scott said, it would only be decent of Shackleton to stay clear of this most natural starting point. Shackleton obeyed Scott's injunction, and despite that hurdle (which added many miles to his journey), mounted a magnificently successful expedition. With a very strong international team (a slap in itself at Markham and Scott's rigid nationalism), Shackleton reached the Magnetic South Pole and came just 113 miles from the Geographic South Pole. Shackleton, to Scott's despair, was knighted for his efforts. That was enough. Scott was kicked into action to mount his own second expedition—to beat Shackleton.

The pressures, it seemed, could not have been greater. Markham's pull with funders was waning and the old man understood that the new expedition of the *Terra Nova*, scheduled to depart in 1910, would be his swan song. The public thrill for yet another trip south was fading, and that made it harder to pitch the trip as the greatest adventure to a press which now understood that Antarctic adventures involved endless months with no drama to report.

The only upside to the story came in the quality of men ready to accompany Scott. The portraits of glory and hardship cultured by Markham captured the hearts of more than 8000 applicants for just a handful of positions, and Scott was able to bring a remarkably strong team together.

In spite of all the thrills and flurry of planning, Scott was more haunted than ever by his "dark thoughts" in the months leading up to the second expedition. He complained that he "just wanted it over," that he was troubled by nightmares and anxieties about the journey, and that he worried for his wife. His moods were swinging wildly, and many sources noted that he seemed to have little consistent heart for the trip.

The finances for the expedition of the *Terra Nova* continued to be so uncertain right to the end that Scott was obliged to stay behind and continue to appeal for money when the ship finally left port on June 10, 1910. Scott was not able to join his crew until he arrived mid-August in South Africa. Despite finally being relieved of the task of begging for money, and despite being back aboard ship, Scott found little respite in the hurried journey across the Indian Ocean to Australia. He was one month behind schedule by the time he landed in Melbourne, and there he received shattering news: The formidable Norwegian explorer Roald Amundsen had turned the quest for the Pole into a race.

Amundsen's involvement came to Scott in a famously curt telegram— "Am going south. Amundsen." The note changed everything, once again bringing Scott's uncertainties and dark doubts to the surface, just as Shackleton's presence had done before. Scott became petulant and was clearly threatened, scrambling to claim that if Amundsen was a sportsman, he would let the British attempt the Pole first.

Amundsen, as always simply and fiercely pragmatic and driven by a formidable ego, laughed at the suggestion. He dismissed the claims of "destiny" and "scientific priorities" by the British as foolishness that they relied on to hide weakness. He ridiculed Markham and Scott's insistence that relying on manpower, rather than sled dogs, was the "noble way to travel," and he was blatantly competitive in a way that shocked the British.

Believing he had been beaten to the North Pole by the American Richard Peary in 1909, Amundsen openly declared that he had "resolved upon a coup" to take the South Pole from under the feet of the British without "feeling any scruples." This was a battle for supremacy, Amundsen insisted, not a cocktail party, and he laughed at Scott's laments that the Norwegian had sparked a "shabby rivalry." Amundsen simply stated that he would get to Antarctica first, would not bother himself with the pretense of science, would run out dog teams to place food caches in the initial part of the route, and would prepare for a spring departure earlier than the British seemed able to manage. He'd then run to the Pole, and be writing his memoirs by the time the British found his flag. It was an audacious claim, but it turned out to be completely warranted. On December 14, 1911, Amundsen and four teammates coasted to the Pole, pulled by nearly 100 dogs, weeks ahead of the British schedule.

Back in the British tents, Scott's rigid attitudes had played right into the Norwegian's hand. When he arrived in Antarctica, rather than engaging in a competition according to Amundsen's rules, Scott committed even more strongly to completing his plan as intended, faithful to Markham's ideals of polar travel.

Scott's insistence on following this ethos—relying solely on manpowered polar travel despite its inherent risks and hardships—is one of the keystones on which some base their judgments that Scott was "mad." Several writers have questioned whether Scott's ethic was not only illogical and antiquated, but also perhaps hinted at a self-destructive, or even suicidal, inclination in the man.

It is not a completely illegitimate argument. Scott had a history of depressions in his life, and was clearly despondent and even panicked at several points during the journey of the *Terra Nova*. However fearful Scott might have been about being beaten by Amundsen, and no matter how he recognized that a Norwegian success might ruin his good name, Scott did nothing to change the likelihood of his own team's victory, or to protect his men. Instead, he kept course and walked his men into a battle that seemed not only futile, but had a high likelihood of being fatal.

Yet so readily judging Scott disregards a context that may have played an enormously influential role in his actions. Yes, it does seem that Scott had a number of deeply-rooted personal issues that affected his choices, but he was also born into a culture of adventure that ennobled suffering, sacrifice, and even death, just as much—if not more—than it did success. Through the eighteenth, nineteenth, and twentieth centuries, British adventure was a story written in blood. If Scott suffered a self-destructive streak, he came by it honestly: a disturbing number of the saints of British exploration perished in their endeavors. If Scott was suicidal, it seemed that the nation behind him not only understood but celebrated the willingness to walk that line. If there was madness in the man, wasn't there also a touch of madness in his nation's deification of self-destruction? Amundsen certainly understood the pattern when he wrote this blunt assessment of Scott's decision to walk to the Pole: "Never underestimate the British habit of dying, the glory of self-sacrifice, the blessing of failure."

In the end, Scott's desperate march to the Pole seemed to perfectly embrace that British habit: in equal measure heroism and fatalism, faith and resignation. Barely a month after Amundsen had enjoyed perfect traveling conditions, Scott's dwindling team fought terrible snow conditions, raking winds, and perilous temperatures. Whatever faint hope they might have had for victory fell heavily when they discovered Amudsen's flag at the Pole on January 17, 1912.

At some point in the acrid march homeward, as broken men started to fall, Scott may have understood that there remained only one way to salvage victory from the increasingly tragic tale.

Late March, 1912. 79° S. Eleven miles from the One Ton food cache. No matter what came before—the contradictions, the self-doubts, the sadness, the anger—at the end Scott drew close to the mythic version of himself. In the endless, bitterly cold weeks from the Pole back to the sea, Scott was able to write a graceful and heroic ending to his story, one that fit perfectly with the myth that Markham had so dramatically constructed. The self-punishment that he was so used to turned into a strength, giving Scott the ability to go on while others fell. All the dark fears that he had harbored for years were relit with righteous purpose:

the agonizing death that had haunted him always on his journeys south could give purpose to an entire nation. Even the martyring of all of his men could be reshaped, into that "fine conception which is realized when a party of men go forth to face hardships, dangers and difficulties with their own unaided efforts."

Alone in his tent, chilling toward death mere miles from a life-saving depot, with the bodies of his last two teammates lying beside him, Scott is at his very best. Philosophically heroic in his last letters to his family and friends, the families of his men, and his country, he tries to forgive others, rationalize the failures, and insist on the ultimate nobility of his expedition and its outcome. "For my own sake," he wrote, "I do not regret this journey, which has shown that Englishmen can endure hardships, help one another, and meet death with as great a fortitude as ever in the past."

Inside his journal, Scott wrote "Send this diary to my wife," then scratched out "wife" and changed it to read "widow." He died alone sometime in the hours or days after this last diary entry on March 29: "It seems a pity, but I do not think I can write more. RFS. For God's sake look after our people."

Solomon Andrée (© Grenna Museum / The Swedish Society for Anthropology and Geography).

CHAPTER 3

SOLOMON ANDRÉE

We Cannot Fail

ON AUGUST 5, 1930, THE CREW OF THE NORWEGIAN sealing vessel *Bratvaag* motored out of a thick fog that had been haunting them for days in their journey around the tortuous north coast of the Svalbard Archipelago, high off the northern reach of Scandinavia. In the gray middle distance to the east, the *Bratvaag* captain, Peder Eliassen, caught sight of a brilliant snowcap of an island, and he roused the crew to find a landing. Eliassen knew he had come upon the isolated and rarely visited Kvitøya ("White Island") and thought that the scientists who had chartered the ship would be pleased to get ashore, as walruses blanketed one of the few stretches of bare rock visible.

Even from the ship, it was clear that Kvitøya was a bitter place, sealed under a permanent glacial dome nearly 600 feet thick, except in two bays where black gneiss and shattered granite lay bare. "This was the home," one of the scientists wrote, "of the great white silence, and it was not possible to feel other than slightly depressed by the deathly quiet." The *Bratvaag* anchored between great icebergs that had calved off the glacier. The crew explored briefly, then spent the evening preparing for a day of hunting by the sealers, and exploration by the geologists and biologists.

The next day brought the first taste of sun in weeks. The sealers and the captain were soon in their boats, pursuing the walruses to a cove on the other side of the island. Eliassen returned alone in just a few hours, somber and carrying a sodden, tattered book in his hands. "We have found Andrée," he said. Every man knew whom the captain was talking about.

The crew scrambled back to the site of Eliassen's find. There were the remains of a camp and a boat, there were journals and letters, and there were bodies: headless, bone-gnawed corpses, obviously savaged by polar bears. Hundreds of miles from where it had been expected, the sealers had stumbled onto the answer to one of the great mysteries of adventure—the fate of Solomon August Andrée and the crew of the polar balloon *Örnen* ("the Eagle"). The sealers mapped Andrée's campsite, collected all the artifacts they could find, including film plates that would prove to hold some of the great images of Arctic exploration. Then they solemnly wrapped the corpses, and took Andrée and his men home. The *Bratvaag* crew had solved one part of one of the puzzle—the final fate of the *Eagle*—but there was still much more of the difficult story to learn.

Born in 1854, Solomon Andrée grew up in what was then the small village of Gränna, in the picturesque lake country of southern Sweden. Andrée was one of seven children. His father was a pharmacist; his mother came from a prominent clerical family which added both modest wealth and strong—if rigid—values to the boy's upbringing. His mother, commenting to the newspapers when her son started his rise to fame, said of Andrée that he was "uncommonly big and strong," with "mental development rather ahead of his years," but also "perhaps, a stubborn and defiant child." The Andrées raised their children close to the woods and tried to instill in them a love for the outdoors, but it was Andrée's fascination with the logic rather than the aesthetics of nature that charted the course of his life.

Andrée had a brilliant mind, though even in his youth he felt constrained by the broad classical education his father had arranged for him. He dismissed interest in the arts as frivolous, and disdained the spiritual teachings his mother tried hard to pass on to him. From early on, Andrée embraced an entirely different religion: an unwavering faith in the capacity of science to explain all things. His faith began, according to his mother, with an early habit of asking difficult questions about everything; and his devotion to science was consecrated with his admission to the Royal Institute of Technology in Stockholm at a very precocious fifteen.

Andrée entered academic science at a heady time. Industrial applications of the scientific method had been reforming Europe to the core through the 1800s—changing not only manufacturing, but also altering politics, economics, architecture, art, literature, and the structure of the family. Like many of his contemporaries, Andrée saw the Industrial Revolution as proof of the power and truth of science. For men like Andrée, the tenets of science were a scripture profound enough to guide every aspect of life. Every unknown was a problem that simply had to be thought through; every puzzle, no matter how complex, could be measured and reduced to a formula that could be worked out, given enough time. Science could not only explain nature, Andrée argued, it could master it and better it.

And it was not only mechanical things that Andrée believed would yield to science. He was a rabid social Darwinist, adamant that all things were ultimately amenable to logic: nature, art, behavior, even social issues. Though focused on physics in college, he also announced plans to publish a series of papers examining the possible applications of science to everything from marriage to athletics through education and liberty. He wrote prolifically, and even won an award for his plans for reforming the education of young girls—by including, not surprisingly, more science in the curriculum. Andrée would eventually serve for many years in the Swedish Patent Office as its Chief Engineer—a perfect place for his firm, critical mind—but not before taking a trip that set his life on a completely unexpected path.

In 1876, the twenty-two-year-old received support to attend the Centennial Exposition in Philadelphia. On the journey across the Atlantic, the ever-curious Andrée was mesmerized by the consistent patterns of wind currents on the sea. He correctly deduced that the air flow would be even stronger, and more consistent, the further one rose from the surface. It was only a small leap for Andrée to connect this principle to a fascination he had had since childhood: the relatively new adventure of ballooning, and the challenging new science of aeronautics. By the time he reached New York, Andrée was convinced of the feasibility of crossing the Atlantic by balloon.

That he had never seen a balloon, let alone flown one—nor had any experiences in adventure of any kind—was completely irrelevant to the man. Designing and flying a balloon, he believed, were problems of physics and nothing more: Do all the calculations, and there was little need for worry. To better understand the nature of the challenge, he tracked down the very experienced American balloonist John Wise and arranged to go up for a flight. Andrée had a portentous introduction to the realities of ballooning when he watched Wise's balloon explode in a fireball while still on the ground; but the experience did little to shake his mechanistic convictions. Wise's accident, Andrée insisted, was simply due to a resolvable miscalculation of the variables.

From Andrée's point of view, as his interest was the *science* behind ballooning, there was no point rushing into the sky himself. He had no time for the thrill-seekers who were leading ballooning at the time, nor for the "adventures" that he saw as little more than follies attributable to failures in planning. His goal was not a daring exploit, but rather a sober conquest of gravity through intelligence and precision, and that would take thinking at the drafting table instead of floating about. In the end, Andrée would take another seventeen years before he had refined his calculations enough to step inside a balloon.

In that long gap, circumstance shifted the geographic focus of Andrée's "experiment" from the Atlantic to the Arctic. By the 1880s, the United States and several European nations were involved in a fevered competition to plant their flags at the Poles, with particularly bitter rivalry over the North, in which the competition for records of latitude were sometimes measured in single-digit miles, and minutes of degree. Just as they would soon begin to do in Antarctica and on Mount Everest, several nations in the contest started to claim that they had an historic "right" to the North Pole, and insisted others were unworthy suitors. This was especially the case with the Scandinavians, who not only claimed the Pole as part of their spiritual heritage, but also tried to argue that it lay within their geographical borders.

Such nationalism meant little to Andrée. His allegiance was to science, not to any flag. He saw a flight to the North Pole as a perfect opportunity to test his balloon theories in a very challenging environment; if he could capitalize on currents of national fervor to raise the funding for his project, all the better. It was simply a matter of timing that he was setting out toward the Pole rather than crossing an ocean to try to prove the truth of his calculations. In the late 1880s, the patent engineer with absolutely no credentials in adventure, and zero experience in a balloon, started his hunt for patrons and funds.

If there were any doubts about this sedentary man's fitness for Arctic conditions, Andrée waylaid them when he joined the scientific team of the Meteorological Institute of Stockholm for a winter on Svalbard, the desolate archipelago that would play such a pivotal role in his life. Andrée gained a reputation for a stubbornly fierce commitment to his research projects, heading out in 100-mile-per-hour blizzards to take weather readings while everyone else stayed hut-bound, and sealing himself into a completely lightless hut for months to test a theory about light deprivation's effect on skin color. Andrée convinced himself, and a few others, that he was the man for the Pole.

———————————

If there is one characteristic of Andrée's personality that rises above all others, it is the cold rigidity of his will. He set his goals admirably and let nothing get in the way, yet to many people, he seemed arrogant and contemptuous. In almost all accounts he appears as a caricature of the emotionally detached scientist, humorless and unmovable, disdainful of people and their weaknesses. In photographs he glares soberly, with close-set, sad eyes, an always-stern mouth, and the huge walrus mustache that was the look of the time. Although he was said to be fiercely loyal to friends, he had few of them, and he was adamantly and openly opposed to romantic relationships. Dismissing "simple" human needs, he wrote, "In married life one has to deal with factors which cannot be arranged according to a plan. It is altogether too great a risk to bind oneself to a condition of things where one individual would be fully entitled to demand the same place in my life that I myself have occupied."

Once Andrée fixed his eyes on the Pole, he was obsessively committed. In 1893, nearly forty, he finally collected the funds to buy a balloon and ride in one for the first time. He made nine solitary flights in *Svea*, chronicling every ascent in painstaking detail, drily noting the minutiae of wind, weather, the performance of the balloon, and the effects of his own actions on the flight. It is clear from the logs that Andrée viewed the flights as rational tests, rather than emotional experiences. Even when Andrée had moments that must have been terrifying— being thrown by winds far off course across the Äland Sea, where he had to bail out and spend a cold night marooned; or crashing several times when his draglines snagged on the ground—his reports are almost bizarrely laconic and emotionless. The near-disasters are written up as irritating miscalculations to be resolved with a slide rule rather than as rousing escapades to be recounted at a gentleman's club.

In Andrée's eyes, nine flights in *Svea* provided more than enough data to script the true test of his theories. In February 1895 he announced to the Swedish Academy of Sciences his plans to fly to the North Pole, and then repeated the same grandiose claim internationally that summer at the Geographical Congress in London. Both audiences were reportedly "stunned" by the Swede's "brashness," and more than a few people dismissed him entirely. Even if they admired Andrée's science and his creative invention of new techniques and equipment, many listeners were skeptical that the only attribute a polar victor needed was an ability to add up numbers. If experienced explorers like Fridtjof Nansen and Roald Amundsen were getting beaten back by the unpredictable Arctic, how was this odd-mannered middle-aged mathematician going to survive, let alone win the prize? Newspapers were no more charitable: One, Vienna's *Neue Zeitung,* sulphurously suggested that Andrée was either a "fool or a swindler."

And yet Andrée's self-assurance managed to win over a number of sponsors, including Alfred Nobel and the King of Sweden. Against all the odds, he sailed north toward Svalbard in 1896 with an army of carpenters, welders, engineers, cooks, and a new balloon. Crafted to his rigorous guidelines, the *Eagle* was probably the finest airship of the era. She was buoyed up by 170,000 cubic feet of hydrogen held captive by more than 3000 pieces of heavily-varnished bright orange Chinese silk and laced together by over nine miles of stitching. The gondola beneath the balloon held room for three men, and included bunks, a cooking area, and even a darkroom for the immediate development of photographs.

Most importantly, the *Eagle* also included a revolutionary steering mechanism developed by Andrée. Based on his experiences with *Svea,* he rigged up a system of three steering sails and several draglines—nearly 3000 feet of heavy coconut-fiber lines that could either act as ballast, or be dragged along the ground to change the direction of the balloon. Andrée insisted that, stocked with gear, the *Eagle* could easily stay aloft for a month. He was so certain he had the details right that the balloon's maiden voyage, and its first inflation, would be the 600-mile trip to the Pole.

Though he wrote that he would have preferred to go north alone, Andrée understood that he was not going to be able to both pilot the balloon and make all the scientific recordings he planned, so he invited two companions. Nils Strindberg (whose famous family included the playwright August Strindberg) was a young scientist with considerable experience in skiing, and nearly as much—or as little—experience as Andrée with ballooning. The second member chosen was Nils Ekholm, who had invited Andrée on the scientific expedition to Svalbard years before. From the beginning of his involvement, Ekholm expressed doubts about the viability of the endeavor, and his skepticism created considerable friction when rubbed against Andrée's brazen convictions.

In the end, neither man was given the chance to prove he was right. After two weeks' steam to Svalbard, the large construction team prepared the launch site on the rocky shore, building a huge cylindrical hangar and hydrogen-generating plant while the balloonists set *Eagle's* complex rigging. The team celebrated the first inflation, but then waited two and a half months for a wind that never came. Andrée's perfect *mechanical* planning had left ludicrously little room for the whims of nature. The team left the hangar standing, then limped back to Stockholm, where Fridtjof Nansen was being celebrated for yet another new Arctic record: reaching only slightly more than 200 miles from the Pole. Receiving a medal from the King, Nansen used the opportunity to ridicule Andrée and his scheme, publicly pronouncing him an "idiot."

Another public attack on Andrée came from a more hurtful source. His balloon-mate Nils Ekholm turned on Andrée in the scientific community, claiming that the *Eagle* was poorly designed and could never hope to make the journey. He insisted that Andrée was being foolhardy, and that his "calculations" were nothing more than arrogant, and ignorant, guesses. Despite the criticism—or perhaps because of it—Andrée rallied against both these influential critics. He shot back that Nansen had not reached the Pole himself, and that Ekholm knew nothing about ballooning—so why pay attention to them? He then found himself a new partner, a fit young mountaineer and skier named Knut Frænkel, and announced that he would return to Svalbard the following summer.

Andrée and his men boarded their ship on May 18, 1897, anchored by the balloon-house (which was still miraculously standing) on May 30, and were waiting for the launch—and the necessary south wind—by July 1, nearly a month before they had been ready the previous year. After another frustrating wait, on July 11 nature nodded in Andrée's favor. Following a burst of frantic action, Andrée called out "Cut away everywhere!" and the *Eagle* was finally freed from the earth for the first time.

And yet, by the following day, Andrée himself was already asking the question that would be debated by hundreds of others for decades: "Shall we be thought mad, or will our example be followed?"

History, it would turn out, would judge Andrée both ways: as madman and exemplar, fool and hero. The brief, tragic flight of the *Eagle* has been condemned as a naïvely conceived disaster of an expedition, but the struggle of the crew to survive has also been called one of the greatest of adventure tales. Andrée's plan to drift to the North Pole was ridiculed by many laypeople, scientists, and adventurers, both before the flight and after, but the core of the plan was the model for four other attempts to balloon to the North Pole before the discovery of Andrée's last camp thirty-three years later.

Judging the man apart from the plan is more complex, less readily shaded in black and white. While Andrée has often been discarded as "a pompous fool," "tragically flawed," and even "a lunatic," he's also heralded by an equally ardent crowd—which includes one of the gods of polar travel, Roald Amundsen, and most of Sweden—as one of the great heroes of exploration.

The difficult ambiguities of the man make it hard to measure him. He could be completely rational and meticulous, yet capable of remarkably short-sighted decisions; apparently mechanical and emotionless, but the leader of one of the great acts of spirited endurance and camaraderie in the history of adventure; almost singularly intellectual, yet as fiercely physical as the greatest outdoor heroes when put to the test.

The lay judgment of "madness" in Andrée is intriguing. Some of the writers who have labeled him so seem to be castigating him for little more than his decision to risk the journey at all—but this judgment places Andrée in the company of many esteemed adventurers who have risked everything for the sake of their goals, and invites the question of how he would be measured differently if he had succeeded in his quest. He seems the perfect example of a man who would have been doubly glorified *because* his plan was so improbable.

Others have focused on Andrée's idiosyncrasies—particularly his obsessive attention to detail and his social brusqueness—as though they were not just odd, but different and distinct to the point of being symptoms of a diagnosable disorder, (perhaps a schizoid personality disorder). It would not be an illegitimate stretch to label him so, but other writers, looking at Andrée's endurance and perhaps respecting his eventual fate, have been kinder, insisting that the oddities were no more than the marks of any man of science or anyone obsessed with a grand scheme.

Virtually all his biographers, however, have ended up questioning Andrée's solitary, alienated nature. He pushed many people away, never married, apparently never courted and, until his mother's death just before the first expedition of the *Eagle,* was deeply bound to that fragile, troubled woman—all of which made him seem peculiarly removed from the world.

The slipperiest question, though, is whether Andrée's unbending faith in science constituted a form of madness itself. His complete trust in the power of science to account for all the variables led him to blindly ignore dangerously possible outcomes that did not fit into his calculations, and to dismiss the kinds of intuition that adventurers often rely on to keep them alive.

And yet if Andrée was "mad" for having such a faith in science, our entire modern technology-worshipping culture is vulnerable to being judged the same way. There are hundreds of examples where our collective faith in the science behind transportation, pharmaceuticals, and other industries has been no less fatal.

What seems exaggerated in Andrée's case is the degree to which his faith was inviolate, how he dismissed the value of experience versus calculation, and refused to listen to others who might have moderated his certainties. When Andrée wrote in his journals "We cannot fail," he seemed to have been not only suggesting, like Meriwether Lewis and so many other adventurers, that he was troubled by the pressures of obligations to creditors and sponsors; instead, he seemed to be proclaiming that, despite all evidence to the contrary, he could not fail because he *could not be wrong.*

Just how wrong Andrée was became apparent immediately.

At 1:46 PM on July 11, the *Eagle* rose out of the Svalbard balloon

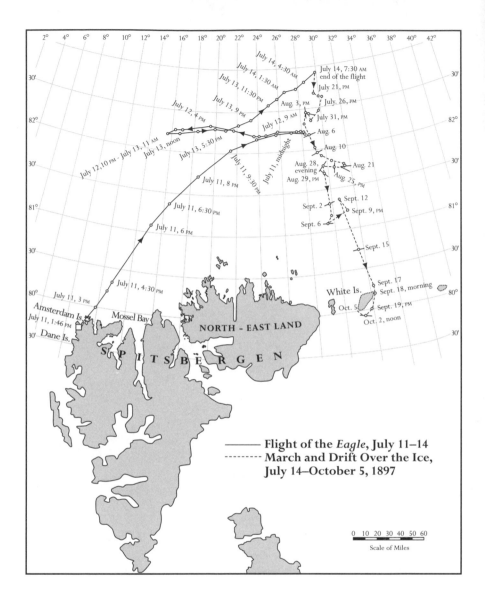

2° 4° 6° 8° 10° 12° 14° 16° 18° 20° 22° 24° 26° 28° 30° 32° 34° 36° 38° 40° 42°

30'

July 14, 4:30 AM

July 14, 1:30 AM

July 14, 7:30 AM
end of the flight

July 13, 11:30 PM

July 21, PM

July 13, 9 PM

Aug. 3, PM — July 26, PM

July 12, 4 PM

July 12, 9 AM — July 31, PM

82°

July 12,10 PM - July 13, 11 AM   July 13, noon

July 13, 5:30 PM

Aug. 6

July 11, 9:30 PM

Aug. 10

30'

July 11, 8 PM

July 11, midnight

Aug. 28, evening

Aug. 21

Aug. 25, PM

Aug. 29, PM

July 11, 6:30 PM

Sept. 12

81°

Sept. 2

Sept. 9, PM

Sept. 6

July 11, 6 PM

Sept. 15

30'

July 11, 4:30 PM

Sept. 17

80°   July 11, 3 PM

White Is.   Sept. 18, morning

Amsterdam Is.   Mossel Bay

Oct. 5   Sept. 19, PM

July 11, 1:46 PM

NORTH - EAST LAND

Oct. 2, noon

30'   Dane Is.

S P I T S B E R G E N

————— Flight of the *Eagle*, July 11–14
‑ ‑ ‑ ‑ ‑ ‑ March and Drift Over the Ice,
July 14–October 5, 1897

0 10 20 30 40 50 60
Scale of Miles

house and moved northeast over Virgo Harbour, lurching up and down
as it found its buoyancy point, turning slightly as the wind caught the
sail vanes, dragging the uncoiling guide lines just as it should. Suddenly,
though, the balloon dropped precipitously, and the crew had to frantically throw valuable ballast bags overboard to stay aloft—a choice that
everyone knew would seriously compromise their later ability to control the balloon. The airship bounced across the water, then started to
rise once more, far more dramatically than expected.

The ground crew soon discovered why: The rolling of the drag-lines over the shore had unscrewed the safety release mechanism that attached the lines to the balloon, and all three lines had fallen free—meaning that the *Eagle* had just lost half its ballast and all its steerability. It rose to 2000 feet, then descended close to the ground once again at the last point of land. To the ground crew, it appeared as though Andrée was contemplating aborting the trip at the last possible moment, but instead of giving in to that only sensible decision, Andrée maintained his altitude and drifted off at the mercy of the wind.

The journals and photographs discovered by the crew of the *Bratvaag* thirty-three years later on White Island showed that the months that followed were a heart-wrenching saga of will in the face of remarkably bad fortune. At the start, Andrée's confidence seemed unshakeable despite the loss of ballast and dirigibility that were just the beginning of a string of errors in his technical predictions. By 8:00 PM that first day, borne on the wings of a strong southwest wind, the crew of the *Eagle* encountered their first pack ice. The team fought desperately to try to splice together the remaining bits of their draglines in the hopes of regaining control of the balloon, but by 10:00 PM it was clear that their destiny was essentially out of their hands. Despite the likely disastrous situation, Andrée threw a message buoy over the side, with a bluff note that insisted, "Our journey has so far gone well. . . . In the best of humours."

It was less easy to be nonchalant the following day when another of Andrée's miscalculations of nature became painfully clear: The *Eagle* ran into heavy mists which started settling on the surface of the balloon, forming a carapace of ice that dropped the ship quickly. The crew threw even more of their invaluable ballast overboard, but by noon Andrée recorded "bumpings every 5th minute," and then within a few hours, "touch every minute" and "paid visits to the surface and stamped it about every 50 metres." By the late evening, Andrée was lamenting the bone-jarring thumps against the rough ice and remarked how difficult it was that they could get no sleep with "everything dripping."

Overnight the *Eagle* slowed to a sodden crawl along the ice, and Andrée slipped into a troubled rumination on his fate: "We think we can well face death, having done what we have done." It is clear from the diaries of the other two men—especially Strindberg, who planned to return to his fiancée—that they were not quite so willing to accept Andrée's readiness to die so as not to be "forgotten by coming generations."

This last comment, from a long, reflective night alone on watch by Andrée, is the only definitive record of any kind of fatalistic egocentricity in the man, but it might well be the clearest picture of the tickings of Andrée's mind. He seems to understand full well—despite the bravado of that first, and later notes, which claim absurdities such as "all is well on board"—that his fate is likely sealed, but he seems disturbingly content to martyr himself to that fate.

The flight of the *Eagle* came to an end on July 14, after several grinding snags on the ice, a fire in the gondola, and violent motion sickness in all the crew; and after it became clear that the icing of the balloon was irreparable. After sixty-five hours and just seventy-five miles in the air, the *Eagle* fell on its side and the crew set about preparing for a terribly uncertain march, carrying everything they thought they might need.

The scale of Andrée's hubris about the journey was never clearer than when the men took stock of their supplies. Andrée had been so convinced that the *Eagle* would easily fly over the Pole in a matter of just a few days, and land somewhere in the vicinity of the Bering Straits, that the crew were almost completely unequipped for a land journey of any length. Because Andrée calculated that the crew were going to spell each other sleeping in the balloon, the *Eagle* carried only one sleeping bag. The tent they had was nothing more than a shell of balloon silk. The only thing that seems to have been well-conceived was the foresight of bringing guns and many rounds of ammunition, and a wealth of treat foods and alcohol that Andrée planned to use for a polar victory celebration.

The most crucial order of business after the crash landing was to decide what direction to take, but this was no simple matter. The three men were fully aware that they had landed in a scatter of chaotic, moving pack ice, serrated with pressure ridges and split by shifting channels of open sea. It was 200 or more miles to any land they could reach by ice, with the very real possibility that the inevitable flow of the pack ice might drift them away from any target faster than they could move toward it.

The eventual decision to strike out east toward Franz Joseph Land was in the end little more than a guess—a reality that must have infuriated the obsessively calculating Andrée. After several days paring down and packing up their gear, the team set out on July 22 with 400-pound sleds. Within only minutes, Strindberg had lost his sled in a pool of water; it stayed under only for a moment, but long enough to ruin several pieces of equipment and a letter and photograph from his beloved fiancée.

The going proved utterly miserable, with the men falling regularly into water, pushing and pulling the sleds over the tortuous ice ridges through a constant drizzle, praying for the sight of a seal to augment the thin food supply, constantly on the lookout for polar bears—which became, tragically as it would turn out, the team's primary source of food.

Through the end of July, despite the misery of the travel, it looked like the effort had been worth it. Andrée's calculations showed that progress, if slow, had been positive. But in early August, the worst happened: Their readings started to show that the direction of the pack ice had shifted. Over the next three days, the team lost almost all the distance it had traveled as the ice drifted backwards. The move east was abandoned and the three started heading completely in the opposite direction toward the edge of their floe, over ice barely three feet thick, hoping to beat the drift.

Two days later, another sobering realization dawned when the bearings showed that between their current drift and the earlier meanderings of the disabled *Eagle*, the three men were now almost exactly where they had been on July 12, nearly a month before. Despite it all, the diaries of the three suggest they had slipped into a patient acceptance of their predicament. They pushed on without stopping, they seemed to get along, and they even continued their scientific observations—especially Andrée, whose journals are filled with notes on birds, structures of the snow, and the dismal weather and current patterns.

That the crew continued their trudge was an inspirational testimony to their strength, but it could not last. The work, the weather, the diet, and the terrible emotional burdens all took their toll, and each of the men started to have troubles with their health, both physical and mental. All three were knocked down for days by intestinal bugs. Frænkel and Strindberg both had painfully infected feet. Frænkel began expressing his despondency, withdrawing, and sometimes refusing to move from camps. From the middle of August until the middle of September, the depressing pattern continued: ten-hour days of hauling on ice that more often than not was drifting them back to their starting point of the day.

The journaling by all three men slowly tapered off as each appeared to lose faith that they would be found before the snows fell. By the third week of September, they decided to give in and make a winter camp on their floe, but still prayed that the currents might carry them south.

Toward the end of the month, there was a brief moment of exultation when the men spotted the first land in nearly two months. Far to the south they saw the shimmering ice cap of Kvitøya, and they held a celebration. Strindberg's spirits picked up enough for him to write out the menu for the grand meal in his log:

Seal-steak and ivory gull fried in butter and seal-blubber, seal-liver, brain and kidneys. Butter and Schumacher bread. Wine. Chocolate and Mellin's-food flour with Albert biscuits and butter. Gateau aux raisins. Raspberry syrup sauce. Port wine 1834 Antonio de Ferrara given by the King. Toast by Andrée for the King with royal Hurrah! The national anthem in unison.

It was Strindberg's last entry.

On October 2, the ice floe that the men had made their life raft broke up around their shelter. All Andrée writes about October 3 and 4 is that they involved an "exciting situation." Somehow, by October 5, the crew managed to get themselves onto Kvitøya, despite the fact that they had previously dismissed the desolate island as an unsuitable place to land. Within two weeks, there were no more entries in anyone's journals. On October 7, Andrée simply wrote, "Moving." Ten days later, his last words, in the face of the arrival of winter storms and an obvious failure of the plan to move, were, "Home 7.05 a.m."

In the end, despite Andrée's unbendable faith in the ability of science to control and guarantee all outcomes, it was ironically an error in the oldest, most basic science of all that likely took the lives of all three men. Evidence shows that mistakes in the simplest principles of cooking and shelter killed Strindberg first, then Frænkel, and then left Andrée to die alone not long after.

Forensic processing of the scene has been carried out several times since the discovery of the bodies, and it suggests that the most likely cause of Strindberg's death was trichinosis-infected bear meat (which would also explain the recurrent episodes of severe gastrointestinal distress suffered by all three men). It was clear that Strindberg died first, because his was the body found in the shallow grave that had been dug up by the bears.

(There was a final, melancholic note to Strindberg's story. His fian-cée, whose memory the man credited for so much of his endurance on the ice, married another man after years of hope and mourning. Her un-dying love for Strindberg was so obvious to her new husband, however, that when she finally died in her new home in America, years after the crew of the *Eagle* had been found, her husband had her heart sent back to Sweden to be buried with Strindberg, her one true love.)

After Strindberg, Frænkel appears to have died next, in the make-shift tent that had been strung up against a rock outcrop. Andrée himself was found sitting with his back against the rock, his gun near his hand, as though he was waiting to protect himself against polar bears, the predatory scourge of Arctic explorers, which would have been sure to be circling the camp.

The fact that neither man was in the reindeer skin bag suggests that they were likely awake when they perished, and it has been hypoth-esized that both died either because of a similar problem with the meat, or because they were asphyxiated by carbon monoxide in the improp-erly vented shelter. The balloon fabric they were using for the tent, was after all, thanks to Andrée's expert design, perfectly airtight.

Donald Crowhurst astride a still unfinished Teignmouth Electron, *just days before sailing, October 1968 (Photo courtesy Simon Crowhurst).*

CHAPTER 4

DONALD CROWHURST

The Reward Was Madness

BEACHED ON THE IDYLLIC WESTERN SHORE of the island of Cayman Brac, where it was tossed years before by a hurricane, the broken skeleton of a three-hulled sailboat lies awkwardly on scrub weed and sand, bleaching in the Caribbean sun. Its plywood frame molded and rotting, the unsupported weight of the boat's outer hulls is slowly tearing the fragile fiberglass shell apart, leaving raw edges. The boat has been scavenged: stays, windows, pulleys, hatches, screws picked clean long ago, the cabin ransacked.

There are few things that seem as lost as a boat dying on land. The *Teignmouth Electron*—you can just see the ghost of the name on the main hull and the stern—has the feel of an abandoned dream: no sails, no mast, threaded through with wires that connect nothing to nothing. It is easy to feel that the wreck deserves to be freed, swept back out to sea again where it might drown with dignity. And yet, despite its forsaken appearance, this boat has never really been abandoned: The *Electron* still has friends who remember the illustrious ambitions of its owner, and can tell his troubled story. Nearly forty years later they still come to Cayman Brac to see the ship, take a photograph or a souvenir piece, and try to make their own sense of one of the most uncomfortable stories in adventure history.

As heavy as the weight of nationalism borne by early explorers could be, changes in the world of adventure mean the pressures on modern explorers can be far more complex. One of the most striking revolutions in modern adventure has been the switch from the large expeditions mounted and supported by national governments, which ran until the late 1950s, to smaller trips led by individuals who scramble to gain experience, establish their credentials, and find teams and sponsors.

While national ambitions can be heavy loads to shoulder, private aspirations to climb a mountain or cross a desert can become obsessive, unrelenting burdens in their own way, pushing people to make choices they feel little control over and no freedom from. And when a grand personal dream goes public and others get drawn into it, a plan can easily develop a troubling gravity, growing much bigger than it was ever intended to be and spiraling out of sensible reach. In some cases, adventurers have had to enter into business deals with sponsors that compromise the integrity of the mission, while creating entirely new kinds of obligation to succeed. There may be no better example of a dreamer losing control of the dream than that of Donald Crowhurst and his plan to sail the world.

The flame that drew Crowhurst seduced many other men and many nations. Through the 1960s, sailors from around the world committed to a series of single-handed ocean races. As Peter Nichols suggests in *A Voyage for Madmen*, in many ways the races were intentional, very symbolic, anachronisms. At the very time that mankind was chasing the moon, several countries—especially Britain and France—left out of the competition for space sought to remind people of their more glorious past and challenge for dominion of the sea just as they always had: brave men carried by nothing more than wind along the most ancient routes. In these last years before the sea was changed by satellite navigation and emergency beacons, the racing sailors were as far from home, and as on their own, as they would have been during the height of Europe's battles for the oceans 200 years before.

Newspapers and sponsors were thrilled. The races were easy to spin, and the public adored the sailing heroes. They tended to be men of the classic heroic mold, as independent as mythic cowboys, burnished by the sun and sea, taciturn but intelligent and eloquent when they did speak, quietly but ferociously competitive. And when Francis Chichester's return from his round-the-world one-stop solo in *Gypsy Moth IV* drew a quarter of a million fans, it also became clear that sailing stories could be a goldmine.

In 1968, *The London Sunday Times* published plans to sponsor a race for the greatest unclaimed sailing prize: the first non-stop, single-handed circumnavigation of the globe. Hot on the heels of Chichester's lionization by the press (and knighting by the Queen), the announcement drew scores of entrants with a broad mix of skills and motives. It might as well have been an advertisement that read: "Become a hero."

Donald Crowhurst's early life was as firmly rooted in Britain's past as the race was. He was born in India in 1932, the son of a high-level bureaucrat with the North Western India Rail Company, birthed into the privileges of the Raj— servants, a small estate, the finest schools.

Of course, at the twilight of the empire, those comforts were little more than a façade, a memory of what could have been rather than what really *was,* and this was especially true in the Crowhurst home. Donald's family crumbled just as readily and predictably as the empire did, perhaps because their characters echoed the same flaws that spelled the failure of the Raj. His father was an aggressive bully who condemned his son at every turn; his mother was a profoundly sad woman, weighted down by the dissatisfactions of her descent in life.

Perhaps the most telling reflection of Crowhurst's family is captured in the earliest published photograph of them all together. In the garden of the family home in northwest India, Alice Crowhurst slumps in a chair, grimacing and barely touching the infant precariously balanced in her lap, while John Crowhurst turns away, enduring the camera with a pained smile on his face. It is an image of a family that has lost its connecting threads.

So much of Donald Crowhurst's energy in his adult life seems to have been aimed at regaining those easy privileges in the world, and yet so often, his story ended up turning into failings and disappointments that only confirmed the distance from those golden days.

In fact, disappointment colored Crowhurst's life even from its first moments. His mother, he understood, always wished that he had been a girl rather than a boy, so much so that she kept him in unfashionably long hair, and sometimes in girls' clothes, until he was nearly seven. The cross-dressing, if that is what it was, created an odd bond between Donald and his mother, but soured his relationship with his brusque, explosive, hard-drinking father. There was always a gap between the boy and his father, and the pain of his father's criticisms played themselves out in Donald for the rest of his life. His father's harsh voice stayed within Crowhurst as a serious, self-reproachful shadow that he battled and overcompensated for again and again.

Independence and partition in India forced the Crowhursts back to Britain, a move that was a hard slap for everyone in the family. Alice Crowhurst's misery grew even more sodden, Donald was lost in the new world, and a business venture failed so badly for John Crowhurst that it effectively killed him. The senior Crowhurst's heart failed within a year of returning to Britain, bringing his wife and son to the brink of poverty. One of the last remnants of the family's life of privilege—a posh private school for Donald that the family had barely been able to afford while his father was alive—was suddenly swept out from under him, ending the boy's hopes for an education at one of the finer universities and an easy return of the family's reputation.

But Donald rebounded against the hardship with the flair that became his signature: He showed up at his new, less prestigious, public school with a roar, as a larger-than-life personality, always the bravest boy, always taking the biggest risks. He won people over readily, impressing others with his brilliance and his bravado, making some people—including sometimes himself—believe he could do anything. If he could not go to Cambridge as planned, he would get a diploma from a technical college. He had always been fascinated with mechanisms and gadgets, and he was brilliant at figuring things out. A technical diploma might not have the same cachet as a university degree, he decided, but it could still open doors for him to become the great inventor that he knew he could be. He might not be rich now, but he told people that he soon would be.

Throughout his life, Crowhurst seemed to be walking a razor's edge between an ambitious, talented, serious side, and an extravagant, frenetic, careless one. He had great plans for himself, and could apply himself for a time, but he always struggled to restrain his impulsivity. There was a touch of mania in his style, a melodramatic fervor that grew into a disturbing problem in later years; but Crowhurst was also a master at getting others to forgive him.

There certainly were times when Crowhurst needed forgiveness. He demolished a series of careers—first in the Air Force, where he showed promise as a pilot, but enjoyed the myth of himself as a dashing airman too much. He drove his prized sports car too fast, drank too much, and dragged other airmen into silly pranks that kept getting him into trouble and eventually cost him his commission.

Undeterred, Crowhurst joined the Army as an electronics technician, but was soon up to his old pranks again, getting arrested several times for drunken driving and finally getting caught by the police while hotwiring a car. Crowhurst tried to flee, and as he had already had his license suspended for drunken driving, that foolish decision cost him his second career in the military.

Like many men who feel they have been unjustly denied a university education, Crowhurst could be loudly and pretentiously intellectual, challenging others to contests of knowledge and pushing philosophical arguments on helpless bystanders in the local pub. There was little question that he was brilliant, but his insistence on demonstrating his intellect or boasting about his great future plans could be infuriating to anyone on the receiving end of Crowhurst's need to prove himself.

As irritating as he could be, Crowhurst could also ingratiate himself to anyone, convincing several people of the genuine promise of his smiling buoyancy and his great schemes. He courted his wife Clare with as much verve as he approached every one of his ambitions, walking up to her out of the blue at a party, the first words out of his mouth telling the stunned girl that she was going to marry him. With Clare as with everything, he pursued until he got what he wanted; the two married within months.

Crowhurst detested the petty details of life holding him back, hated it when people seemed not to recognize his talent. He had great plans for his first job out of the Army with an electronics firm, dreaming that he would be given room to pursue his many ideas and inventions, only to find himself stuck in office drudgery. Crowhurst could not possibly last long in such a job but instead of simply quitting, he ended the disappointments of this career in flames as well: He crashed a company car, told management what he thought of the firm, and was fired.

True to form, Crowhurst insisted the blow was nothing more than a hidden opportunity and the criticisms leveled at him nothing more than jealousy. Within the space of a few short years, he found a new job, quit that, and then took the step to start his own firm. Electron Utilisation, Crowhurst was certain, would be the avenue to finally bring his ingenious creations to the world.

As with so many moments in his life, however, there was a shadowed side to Crowhurst's success launching the firm. Crowhurst had the money for the startup of the company only because of a terribly difficult event in his family. Since the death of her husband, his mother Alice had been struggling, and Donald and Clare finally had her come to live with them and their young children. One morning in 1962, Alice Crowhurst called her son to her room and swallowed a handful of pills right before his eyes. She would be hospitalized and institutionalized for the rest of her life. It was a terrible tragedy, but it was the resulting sale of his mother's home that allowed Crowhurst to finance his company.

His mother's problems, the stresses of starting the new firm, and his self-imposed pressures to succeed all took a toll. Crowhurst crashed yet another car, in circumstances that led several writers to question whether he might be showing a more intentionally self-destructive bent. He also stumbled in several business decisions (all of which revolved around Crowhurst convincing himself that the business was doing better than it actually was). In the thick of these troubles, Crowhurst started becoming visibly moody, and occasionally violent. Acquaintances were distressed to see him acting oddly, pursuing strange thoughts that included some occult practices that seemed bizarrely out of character with his resolutely logical mind.

The disintegration that Crowhurst showed under these stresses was the first clear harbinger of his eventual fate. He first deteriorated and turned inward, hiding from the world, tinkering with brilliant, though often impractical, electromechanical inventions. He then grew steadily more expansive and grandiose in his thinking, until he came up with the plan that would not only make his company great, but would, he believed, finally guarantee him the future he deserved.

Living near the Somerset coast in southwest England, Crowhurst had fallen in love with the sea. A small sailboat (whose name, *Pot of Gold*, was as good an insight into Crowhurst's dreams as anything else in his story) was his sanctuary. As the writers Nicholas Tomalin and Ron Hall point out in their wonderfully complex and insightful book, *The Strange*

Last Voyage of Donald Crowhurst, the boat and his little workshop were perhaps the only places in Crowhurst's life where he could leave behind the bluster and truly be himself, without the constant need to please others, or the worry of being judged.

Crowhurst managed to combine both his loves—invention and sailing—in the first product for his fledgling electronics firm, a handheld navigation device that he called the Navicator. It was probably the most grounded of all Crowhurst's unique inventions, but it still required a strategy to win in the competitive marketplace. Instead of basing this strategy on a cautious business plan (never his forté; a close acquaintance called him "hopeless" in business), Crowhurst stayed in character, deciding that he himself would be the plan. Seeing the attention that Francis Chichester's one-port voyage was starting to garner in 1967, he announced that he would do Chichester one better: He would take his Navicator and sail around the globe nonstop. *That* would prove his brilliance to the entire world.

The announcement was the beginning of the tightening spiral that mapped out the rest of Crowhurst's life.

Crowhurst's plan became the singular, obsessive focus of his life. He came out of his despairs running in six directions, racing to catch up to others who had already announced similar aspirations in Chichester's wake. Four men were making plans in 1968—Bernard Moitessier, the Frenchman who had so inspired Claudine Juedel with his purification-by-the-sea mysticism; John Ridgway, a British Special Air Service captain who had rowed across the Atlantic two years earlier and was pitching the proposed circumnavigation as a public test of his will; Robin Knox-Johnston, a down-to-earth, meticulous merchant mariner from Britain; and Bill King, a hardened British navy veteran, at fifty-seven the oldest in the pack. Every one of them was scrambling to find the funds and the right boat for the journey, but none of them ran with Crowhurst's manic energy or eccentricities.

Crowhurst's first strange strategy was to belittle Chichester. Though he had once seemed to worship the man, when he announced his own sailing plans, Crowhurst told people that the journey in *Gypsy Moth* had been nothing special, except that Chichester was, at sixty-seven, an old man. It was not a wise public-relations move given Chichester's popularity, and when Crowhurst saw the public's disapproval of his insult, he quickly changed his tune and began courting Chichester as a patron. Crowhurst brazenly proposed that he be given *Gypsy Moth* for the attempt, and actually managed to draw in some influential people, though not Chichester himself. He was finally rejected by the society that owned the boat, but his proposal had managed to get his name into the public eye.

Crowhurst was more successful in seducing another supporter. Stanley Best was a businessman who had helped keep Electron Utilisation afloat when Crowhurst had run into financial trouble. Despite continuing troubles in the company that were severe enough to prompt Best to ask for his money back, Best, much to his own surprise, found himself agreeing to finance Crowhurst's circumnavigation. "He was," Best later said, "the most impressive and convincing of men."

It might have been a spectacular testimony to Crowhurst's ability to persuade, but Best's involvement was actually a double-edged sword almost from the beginning. Crowhurst worshipped the man, seeing Best as the perfect example of the kind of self-made millionaire he himself dreamed of becoming. To prove his worth to Best, Crowhurst overextended himself enormously, telling Best that his investment in the venture would be far less than it turned out to be, making grandiose claims about his ability to win the contest (insisting, for example, in an utter lie, that he had "thirty years sailing experience") and providing spurious calculations to "prove" why he would win the race.

But the weight of Best's support was relentlessly grinding. In Crowhurst's mind it sealed an obligation that would prove almost impossible to meet.

Crowhurst enslaved himself to his own claims in more public ways as well. He was one of the first competitors to join when the original, casual competition was turned into a formal race by the sponsorship of *The Times*. The announcement by the prestigious newspaper meant the winner would now receive a substantial prize and guaranteed exposure, but it also meant that there were now the additional pressures of formal rules. Contestants could leave Europe at any time before midnight on October 31; there would be prizes for both the first ship home, and for the fastest journey. However valuable the exposure might be for Crowhurst, it was readily clear that building or buying a boat by October was going to be exceptionally difficult, and it was obvious that Crowhurst would not be one of the first sailors to start the race.

Despite this, Crowhurst wrote brash letters to yachting magazines describing why his design for a three-hulled boat would win the race, despite the fact that his boat was not close to being built, that he had never touched a trimaran before—let alone sailed one—and that stable single-hulls were the racing norm for good reason. (Some writers have argued that Crowhurst's choice of the trimaran was based on the thought that he would be more visible and memorable in an unusual boat.) While the clock on the final date for departure allowed by the rules of the race ticked speedily on, Crowhurst also told anyone who would listen about all the remarkable gadgets he was inventing that would guarantee him victory. (These included electronic pumps, hydraulic devices to right his boat in the likely event of a capsize, a "computer" capable of controlling the sails—several of which were ideas well before their time.)

In so many ways, both in retrospect and to curious onlookers at the time, Crowhurst's dream seemed painfully doomed. Although he was a competent weekend sailor, he had never been out onto true blue water. He had a wife and four children, and a struggling company to run, and all of these were thrown aside in the chaotic flurry before the race. He was in debt up to his throat, and the only hope of paying for his commitments lay in actually winning the race—which everyone except Crowhurst agreed was a near-impossibility. His boat was nothing more than a drawing well into the summer, and he had forced a construction schedule so tight that he had to have two yacht-making shops working full time on pieces that would be glued together for the first time at the last minute.

Still, Crowhurst's bravado won him considerable attention. Although there were other marginal, ill-prepared characters drawn to the race as well, Crowhurst was the most visible, and the one most able to obscure his oddities and improbabilities. He was flamboyantly public—to the point that the boat builders complained they saw more of him on TV than in the shop, which delayed production considerably but thrilled Crowhurst. He was unabashedly self-promoting and full of hyperbole, dismissing the other competitors' chances as slim compared to his own. Crowhurst's friends were worried about his unrelenting pace and his increasing explosions of anger, but they also agreed that he was more alive than ever. He seemed to have unlimited reserves, bouncing back after even the hardest days, dealing with hundreds of details and relentlessly chasing possible sponsors for the voyage.

With his family history of depression (in both Alice and John Crowhurst, according to Crowhurst's son Simon), and his own history of bouts of despair mixed with periods of euphoria, there is every indication that Crowhurst was suffering from some form of clinically diagnosable mania throughout the lead-up to the race. It also appears that he had long suffered a thinly-veiled depression before. His grandiosity, capacity for self-delusion, impetuousness, boundless energy, explosiveness, and overextensions all meet the criteria for a bipolar (or manic-depressive) disorder. Also supporting this likely diagnosis, several of Crowhurst's acquaintances add that, as the deadlines for the race approached, his typical energy was overlaid with anxious instabilities in his moods, and disturbance in the process and content of his thinking.

Right to the last minute everything was chaos. The boat, which had been christened the *Teignmouth Electron* (from Crowhurst's company name and Teignmouth, the southern coastal village where the boat would be launched) was popped together with barely enough time for one test run. Crowhurst's various inventions were still little more than scattered wires and transistors. Key parts were missing from the rigging and bilge pumps. There were angry run-ins with the builders, whom Crowhurst had saddled with an almost impossible schedule, made worse by his own distractions and inattention to important details. Throughout it all, Crowhurst kept appearing in the media, cultivating a romantic appeal as the dark horse in the race and embellishing his history with dramatic, mostly fabricated tales of his "experience" at sea.

The *Electron*'s maiden voyage, which was meant to be a three-day sail to test the boat and its systems before Crowhurst finally joined the race at the end of October, was an unqualified disaster. It was meant to take three days, but dragged into two weeks in the English Channel in a mess of rough seas, problems with the boat, poor handling, and dawdling by the captain. Crowhurst was violently seasick throughout the journey, the boat proved very difficult to handle, and there was conflict with the crew from the boat builders who were along to gauge the performance of the craft. Three times on the journey, Crowhurst clumsily fell overboard. But at the end, despite the struggles and several pieces of strong advice, Crowhurst announced to the world that the boat was ready to win the race.

At the last minute, however, Crowhurst's convictions seemed only skin-deep. People who knew him well worried that he was terrified by the corner he'd backed himself into. The boat was not ready. It leaked. Several components had been jerry-rigged. None of Crowhurst's great gadgets were actually finished; there were strings of wire all through the boat, ending in space. It looked to many as though the journey was doomed from the start, and there were repeated hints that Crowhurst might have thought the same himself (though his son Simon still insists adamantly this was not the case).

Crowhurst squeaked under the final deadline for departure, October 31, by only six hours. Some of his competitors had left months earlier, and some had even already dropped out, though they had been sailing in much more reasonable weather than Crowhurst was going to face leaving so late in the season. In the last few days, even Crowhurst's formidable shell showed obvious cracks. He was exhausted, walking about muttering to himself, and was gathering scorn from the locals who were increasingly starting to see him as a masochistic and embarrassing oddity rather than as the self-anointed "Ambassador of Teignmouth." Only three resolute supporters showed up at Crowhurst's final supper before departure.

That evening, Crowhurst finally broke open wide, sobbing until morning, telling his wife that he knew he should not go, and that he had failed. By dawn, however, Crowhurst had convinced himself that he had no choice but to go. He could not, he decided, live with the shame or with the financial consequences of backing out.

In a cold autumn drizzle, Crowhurst was towed out to sea. He raised his sails only to discover in one last public humiliation that the mast had been stayed incorrectly, preventing a full unfurling; a rigger from the builders had to come out to the *Electron* to sort the mess out. Finally, from out in the harbor, Crowhurst shouted to the small crowd of mostly skeptical onlookers, "I'll be glad when I'm on my own without help from you lot!" and then vanished into the mists.

———————————

Perhaps it was the loneliness. Of all people in the world to sail off, without any contact with another human being for months and months, Crowhurst seemed most unlikely to cope. Beneath almost all of Crowhurst's complex drives, there was apparently a need to be defined by others—through approval, through comparison, through opposition—as though he simply did not exist except in relation to others. Most of us would have an exceptionally difficult time living in the prison of a small boat—the cabin of the *Teignmouth Electron* was only nine by eight feet—let alone dealing with the endless work, the monotony, and the moments of unalloyed peril. But for a social man, especially one who worried about betraying any weakness to himself, it must have been excruciating.

On November 15, 1968, Crowhurst recorded a tape for BBC Radio (part of a media deal that his public-relations manager had worked out for him) in which he laid out some of the challenges dogging him, even this early in the voyage. Still sitting off Portugal, he had made almost no progress, had been faced with a number of failures in the boat's design and construction—most problematically, a failure of his generator—and he had started to experience the despair that tracks most long-distance sailors. At times in this recording he seemed unusually open, with more than a hint of anguish in his voice:

> *Conditions in a small boat are so peculiarly devastating that it's amazing people go to sea in small boats at all. Everything on this boat is wet. I mean* wet, *not damp. Condensation is on the roof, it drips in your ear when you're trying to sleep, every hole is a potential leak, and the noise . . . is continuous and often deafening.*
>
> He goes on: *The thing about single-handing is it puts a great deal of pressure on the man, it explores his weakness with a penetration that few other occupations can manage. If he's lazy, he'll be twice as lazy when he's on his own, if he's easily dispirited it'll knock the stuffing out of him in no time at all, if he's easily frightened he's best staying at home—I wouldn't mind a dose of it myself right now.*

This was a brilliant bit of self-awareness and disclosure, and seems a perfectly honest accounting of his struggles, revealing his desire to be almost anywhere else, with the weight of the race off his shoulders. But within the space of a breath, Crowhurst could also revert to the mythic hero that he worked so hard to cultivate in the media, reasserting his convictions that he would be the one to win the race, predicting his future rounding of Cape Horn in good speed with echoes of all the great sailing tales he had read.

His logbook for the same night stayed on the original despairing course of the tape recording, but without the gloss-over. He was surgically self-critical, and methodically staked out all the corners of his predicament, even acknowledging that the only chance he had of winning the race would be if everyone else dropped out. But then, after several bleak pages, he made exactly the same leap that he had made, sobbing beside his wife, two weeks earlier: He *must* continue. Even if "I have an equal chance of making the trip or drowning," even if—here Crowhurst the masterful optimist crept in to reframe the failure as an opportunity—even if he might be able to go back and announce that he had plans for the fastest journey of all *next* year, it still would not be enough. "To turn up at a UK port and say 'I'm back folks' is not feasible."

Instead, at that crucial moment, Crowhurst started to incubate an alternate plan to achieve what he called "some form of salvage." The first step, he wrote, would be to make a landing where "I can communicate with Mr. Best." Perhaps he could save face by landing at Capetown, where his competitors Chay Blyth and Ridgway had already abandoned their attempts. Perhaps he could "Get Mr Best's support for having a go next year." Then, quickly, as though he had finally resolved his dilemma, he ended the entry with an admonition: "Philosophizing is irrelevant, however, and must stop. I have things to do!"

The realization that a dream has ended can be unbearable to some, shattering self-confidence and eroding faith in their ability to control their destinies. When the burden of letting down very public promises is added, the weight can be crushing. For Meriwether Lewis, it was enough to drive him into a suicidal despair; for Robert Falcon Scott, it impelled him to accept a rewriting of his life story as one of sacrifice rather than victory.

Although Crowhurst's story ultimately ended with equal finality, he first chose another, far more hazardous path to overcome the blunt realization that he had failed. Rather than give up and try again the next year, or go home and find a way to pay back Stanley Best, Crowhurst elected to deceive the world and falsify a circumnavigation. He convinced himself that if he did all the right math, and was cautious and patient in making his claims, he might be able to salvage all he had worked for, hold onto his hopes for a brilliant future, and save the reputation of his family.

There have been a surprising number of similar decisions in adventure—for example, by world-class mountaineers such as Tomo Česen and Caesare Maestri, both of whom claimed fraudulent ascents, and by polar explorers such as Frederick Cook and Richard Peary, both of whom made illegitimate claims to have reached the North Pole.

In all of these cases, the choice of fraud was soon, as Crowhurst's son Simon put it, "a solution worse than the problem." Once these men took the first steps toward falsifying the records of their journeys, this decision shadowed every moment of the rest of their lives. For all of these men, and perhaps especially for Donald Crowhurst, the lie quickly grew into a dangerously unmanageable psychic burden.

On November 26, after only three and half weeks at sea, Donald Crowhurst was meandering, at the slowest speed of any of the competitors in the race, into the south Atlantic. Though he was cautious in the scale of his fabricated claims at first, by December 6, he was fully committed to the ruse. With some complicated mathematical trickery, Crowhurst began plotting out a fabricated course. On December 10, Crowhurst announced via his radio that he was not, in fact, in dead-last place in the race, but had set a record speed for a twenty-four-hour single-handed sail.

Crowhurst dove into the deception with the sudden burst of energy he had shown in many other endeavours. Where he had been almost slovenly in his navigation before, he set about the sham journey with the kind of precision and enthusiasm that he brought to every new task. He had to: the ruse required reverse position calculations and deviations to avoid shipping lanes that would have challenged the best navigators in the world. Crowhurst had to begin keeping a second logbook for the real journey, while filling his official race log with details about the weather in the false locations that he monitored off the radio. As he purportedly crept up on the pack, he was obliged to construct precise details of imagined days of faster and faster sailing. Ironically, in deceit Crowhurst showed his brilliance more clearly than ever before in his life.

By Christmas, he made 550 more imaginary miles than real ones. In reality, Crowhurst was drifting in completely the opposite direction of the race, making his way to Brazil when he was meant to be entering the Indian Ocean. Through January and February, he floated with no aim

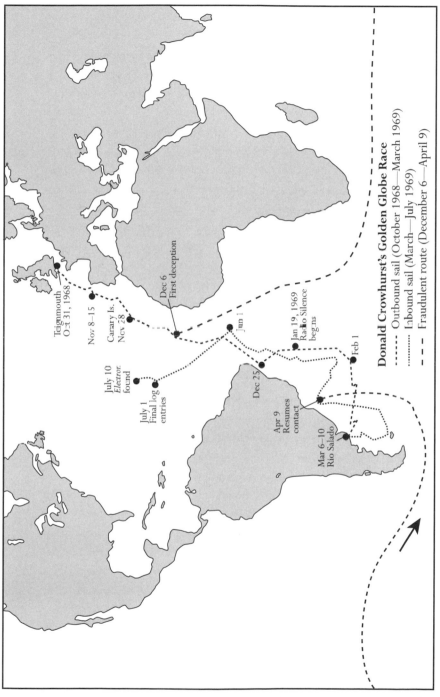

Donald Crowhurst's Golden Globe Race

· · · · · · Outbound sail (October 1968—March 1969)
········· Inbound sail (March—July 1969)
— — — Fraudulent route (December 6—April 9)

Teignmouth
Oct 31, 1968

Nov 8–15

Canary Is.
Nov 28

Dec 6
First deception

Jun 1

Jan 19, 1969
Radio Silence
begins

July 10
Electron.
found

July 1
Final log
entries

Dec 25

Feb 1

Apr 9
Resumes
contact

Mar 6–10
Rio Salado

other than avoiding being seen along the South American shore. He made no outgoing radio contact for nearly two months, but avidly listened in on other broadcasts, collecting data for his log and learning how the world was processing his silence. If anything, his performance only improved in the vacuum; back home, his press agent took radio silence as "proof" that Crowhurst must be racing through the radio shadow south of India, or that he still had troubles with his damaged generator. The agent's spin was every bit as creative as Crowhurst's own, and ultimately put even more weight on Crowhurst's weakening shoulders.

For several months, Crowhurst's busyness prevented too many of the kinds of "philosophical" indulgences that filled his early logs. Instead of ruminations about his place in the world, there were few direct hints about Crowhurst's feelings about his growing hoax in his writings. He even got casual about his success; in early March, he took an enormous risk and actually landed in a small port north of Buenos Aires. There, he repaired the *Electron,* and finally had a brief chance to connect with people. He reportedly had a grand time, laughing and getting drunk, and he must have left with some regret.

Crowhurst calculated that it was time to get serious about the possibility of a return home. By early April, he decided that he had been out of contact long enough to plausibly claim to have rounded Cape Horn. He emerged from radio silence with a vague message on April 9 which suggested that he had been making remarkable time (so remarkable that Francis Chichester began voicing doubts about Crowhurst's claims).

The other racers were in an interesting situation themselves; one which Crowhurst had been following avidly, so that he might not overstep reason in his speed claims. The only three sailors who had reentered the Atlantic were Robin Knox-Johnston, the methodical Brit; Nigel Tetley, a British naval officer; and the Frenchman Moitessier. True to mystical form, Moitessier decided to leave the race and simply keep sailing well into 1969. Knox-Johnston had finished the race on April 22, getting the first of the two prizes (for the first boat to complete the voyage), but his time had been slower than expected, and both Tetley and Crowhurst could joust for the fastest time.

In mid-May, Crowhurst came out of hiding in the south Atlantic and began to race home in hot pursuit of Tetley. It appeared to the world that he had a serious chance of setting the record for the fastest circumnavigation of the globe—especially when Tetley's boat was damaged in a storm off the Azores, and sank. At home, Crowhurst's press agent was working furiously to stir up interest in Crowhurst's return, adding even more pressure with telegrams to Crowhurst saying, "TEIGNMOUTH AGOG AT YOUR WONDERS" and similar hyperbole. Finally, Crowhurst's dream of fame was within a few thousand miles' grasp. After the years of waiting, all he had to do to get the name he wanted, and write the ticket for his future, was sail home. But, in the end, he could not.

Instead, in the face of actually having to live his lie for the rest of his life, Crowhurst began to come apart as clearly and painfully as any fractured psychiatric patient. By June, the meticulous calculations in the logbooks that would have won him the race started to be replaced with bawdy and irritatingly adolescent limericks on one page, and complex, troubled philosophical meditations on the next. As Crowhurst biographers Tomalin and Hall pointed out, these seem to be the two sides of the Crowhurst coin: "The bar-room braggadocio and the lone, dedicated boffin."

If there had been any doubt which was the truer face of Crowhurst, the answer was soon resolved. Soon, there was nothing but pain in the logs.

Crowhurst's entries through the waning days of June read like a textbook example of psychotic thinking. His sharp mind suddenly seems to have disintegrated into an undifferentiated labyrinth of confused thoughts, with God, science, his relationship with his father, relativity theory, and social justice all jumbled together, and with a recurrent grandiose theme that he, the great unappreciated intellect, understood it all.

Much of what he wrote was as pedestrian as late-night musings on the nature of the universe by intoxicated college students—if not for the darker reality of an obviously tortured descent into true madness. Crowhurst "computes" God in his "Cosmic Integral" (in which "the sum of man from minus infinity to plus infinity equals zero") and imagines a dialogue between himself and Albert Einstein, in which Crowhurst's reasoning power gains control over the universe by solving mathematical puzzles.

"I introduce this idea," Crowhurst scribbled in his log, "$\sqrt{-1}$ because [it] leads directly to the dark tunnel of the space-time continuum, and once technology emerges from this tunnel the 'world' will 'end' (I believe in the year 2000, as often prophesied) in the sense that we will have access to the means of 'extraphysical' existence, making the need for physical existence superfluous."

Day by day, Crowhurst sank deeper, stopping sailing almost altogether, drifting for days at a time, obsessively writing and speaking into the tape recorder for hours. He constructs a "Theory of Progress" a diatribe of 12,000 words filled with nonsensical mathematical formulae. Much of it is gibberish, barely legible as Crowhurst's manic scrawl shrinks to stuff the pages, but it seems to boil down to two thoughts: He is the messenger of the new era, and perhaps most tellingly:

> *If creative abstraction is to act as a vehicle for the new entity, and to leave its hitherto stable state it lies within the power of creative abstraction to produce the phenomenon!!!!!!!!!!!!!!!!! We can bring it about by creative abstraction!*

In his own twisted way, it seems as though Crowhurst is trying to rationalize his actions. Creative abstraction—lying—becomes, in his self-forgiving model, nothing more than the vehicle to create the new path for the world. And *he* will be the messenger.

Crowhurst was not so self-forgiving for long. On June 28th, the last radiogram he received from the outside world told him that crowds several hundreds of thousands deep would be waiting to greet him in Teignmouth. In his final descent into madness, which seems to have been provoked at least in part by this message, he turned back on his choices, as witheringly self-condemning as he ever was as a child:

> *Nature does not allow / God to sin any sins / Except one—/ That is the sin of concealment / This is the terrible secret of the moment of the soul / needed by a natural system to keep trying / He has perpetrated this sin on the tormented.*

By July 1, the words were little more than fragments of thoughts, separated by measurable gaps, because Crowhurst has marked time codes beside each one.

> *10:10:10—System of Books reorganize perfectly / Many parallels.*
> *10:19:10—Evil is the choice of interpretation of symbols.*
> *10:23:40—Cannot see any "purpose" in game*
> *10:25:10—Must resign position in sense that if set myself impossible task then nothing achieved by game*

Then he stopped chronicling the times of the entries:

Now is revealed the true nature and purpose and power of the game
offence I am
I see what I am and I see the nature of my offence

And later still, on the last page of the diary, dated July 1:

I will only resign this game if you agree that the next occasion this
game is played it will be played according to the rules that are
devised by my great god who has revealed at last to his son that
not only the exact nature of the reasons for the game but has also
revealed the truth of the way of the ending of the next game that
It is finished
It is finished
It IS THE MERCY

Then, at the bottom of that final page

11.17:00—It is time for your move to begin
I have not need to prolong the game
It has been a good game
that must be ended at the
I will play the game when
I choose I will resign game
11:20:40—There is
no reason for harmful

And the words stop.

———————————

On July 10, 1969, the Royal Mail vessel *Picardy* found the *Teignmouth Electron* floating 1800 nautical miles west-southwest of England. She appeared to have been abandoned. Donald Crowhurst's body was never found.

part 2: the bent

For better or worse, we are most often creatures of the collection of habits, experience, and biology that we call personality. In most people, this predetermination is rarely an issue. Their personality meshes with the world well enough that they can perceive, act, and relate fluidly and happily. They are neither so vulnerable that the world feels unjustly dangerous to them, nor so rigid that they try to force others to meet their out-of-sync needs or share their discordant beliefs.

There are exceptions, however, where someone's personality structure is clearly odd or grating, to the extent that it causes trouble for the person or for others, and these "personality disorders" can be found in the world of adventure just as they are anywhere else.

Of the many varieties of personality disorder classified by psychiatry, the two types that are the most salient in a book about the line between "normalcy" and "madness" in adventure are the narcissistic and the sociopathic disorders.

Narcissists are so self-absorbed, and their egos so dominant, that they perceive the world as revolving around them. *Everything* about their behavior and thoughts is constructed around, and justified, solely by their needs and desires. Other people become merely agents—or enemies—of their needs.

An interesting twist when considering narcissism in this context is that adventure is, almost by default, an unusually self-absorbed activity. It *is* self-centered to take months off to ski to a Pole, or to risk your life for the sake of a mountain summit, possibly leaving a widowed spouse or orphaned children behind. It *is* egotistical to endanger teammates by dragging them along, no matter how willingly, on your dream to cross a desert, especially if aspirations of your own glory are bound up in the dream. Adventurers *can* seem self-important when they publicly crow about their risk-taking as the height of human achievement. And yet only the harshest critics condemn all adventure as narcissism. Most writers—and certainly most adventurers—appreciate that in the majority of cases the willingness to take risks and then talk proudly about it is a healthy exultation of the human spirit. Rather than being a pathological self-glorification that denigrates the unadventurous, there is constructive risk-taking and exploration that can serve as inspiring, universal affirmations of our strength and willpower. Where to draw the line between healthy and troubled egos, however, is sometimes a puzzle.

The question of sociopathy in adventure is even more complicated. The sociopath is a narcissist of more extravagant colors; so self-centered as to believe that other people's rules, conventions, and values simply do not apply to him. In the worst cases, this disregard for other people's rules and values gives the sociopath permission to harm others; this extreme is not seen very often in adventure, though it has been argued that some adventurers have shown self-centered immorality by, for example, risking the lives of locals for the sake of an expedition.

But there are lighter shades of sociopathic behavior, and it is in those grayer areas that the judgments of the "madness" of certain adventurers have been made. Some explorers and adventurers, with their willingness to take risks and their disdain for the restrictions of everyday life, can seem like extreme or marginal characters, living entirely by their own rules, thumbing their noses at less "interesting" lives. Whether this is just an intriguing difference or a disorder is one of the questions to consider in the stories that follow.

The characters in the next three tales have been, fairly or not, accused by history of having pathologically distorted personalities. It would be patently foolish to try to suggest that any adventurer is completely free of ego, but in most cases, the great beauty of adventure is that it offers something so much grander than the individual that it puts the scale of a person's ego in perspective. Most sensible people with thoughts of "conquering" anything through adventure lose them quickly in an ocean storm, or on the middle of a 6000-foot alpine wall. In the healthiest cases, the beauty, the power, the danger, and the grandeur of adventure are paths that transcend ego, not confirm it; but in the stories here, the characters' egos were arguably almost the entire focus of their adventures.

In the case of the Arctic explorer John Franklin, several historians have judged him to be so blindly self-absorbed that he dragged nearly 150 men to their deaths for the sake of his own glory. The ace pilot of the 1930s, Jean Batten, was said to be so self-involved that she ruined the lives of many around her—and ultimately ruined her own. The mountaineer Aleister Crowley was called a profoundly immoral hedonist, both within and beyond his adventures.

Whether any of these tales constitute something more troubling than the simple, singleminded obsession of adventure is the puzzle at the heart of all these stories.

Sir John Franklin, c. 1825. (National Archives of Canada)

CHAPTER 5

JOHN FRANKLIN

The Man Who Shouldn't Have Been There

SIR JAMES GRAHAM, FIRST LORD OF THE BRITISH ADMIRALTY, sat stunned. The news that Dr. John Rae had carried home to London in the autumn of 1854 could not possibly be true, but no matter how scandalous the accusation might be, Rae insisted there was no other explanation. Sir John Franklin, Britain's "Arctic Hero," had led all 127 of his men to "a fate as terrible as the imagination can conceive."

Rae's chilling claim was that one of the greatest expeditions ever mounted by the British Empire, Franklin's 1845 search for the fabled Northwest Passage, had not ended in a great storm as had been imagined. Instead, Dr. Rae claimed that slowly, over the course of four years, Franklin's men had endured a horror of disease, starvation, and then finally, "the last resource," cannibalism.

Although Rae had not personally witnessed the scores of bodies at the site of Franklin's last stand, he brought relics that confirmed the remains were Franklin and his men. Rae told graphic tales of what Inuit hunters had seen when they stumbled across skeletons along the shore of the Great Fish River: white men, laying where they had died, in boats, huddled in tents, surrounded by the odd gear they had been hauling—monogrammed silverware, Franklin's medals of honor, books, and British coins. And most importantly, Rae described the discovery of a cooking pot, filled with boiled human bones.

The firestorm of incredulity and denial that followed Rae's claim was hardly surprising. The Franklin expedition had been one of the most heavily funded and lavishly equipped in the history of the Empire. Sir John was a bona fide hero, knighted for his heroic survival of another great Arctic expedition twenty years before. Many writers, Charles Dickens among them, insisted that civilized men, no matter how desperate, would never have acted the way Rae claimed Franklin's party had.

The British public proved no more willing than Dickens to have one of their great heroes turning savage, and it was only a short time before Rae was slandered. His evidence was ignored and then largely forgotten, while Franklin was returned to his pedestal, sculpted more nobly than ever. For nearly 100 years, Franklin was resurrected not just as a hero, but as that even more-favored son of the Empire, a tragic martyr.

But the story was far from finished.

———————

The issues raised by Rae were too important to ignore. Revisited by historians willing to suspend moral judgments and accommodate all the known facts, the halo around Franklin was simply too fragile to last. By the end of the twentieth century, the "Conqueror of the North" had been redrawn by several writers as a hapless fool trying to relive (dubious) youthful glory, who was out of his depth in the Arctic, and pushed by a drive to be remembered that was murderous in its effects. History's vacillating treatment of the Franklin story offers one of the most interesting insights into the changes in how we measure our adventure heroes. It is also a telling exploration of the complex role that ego plays in some heroes' stories, and a fascinating proof of how readily vanity feeds itself.

Still, at the heart of any measure of Franklin, there needs to be some compassion for Sir John as a man of his time. If his ego seems treacherously inflated today, he did come from a time and place in which the egos of men like him were nurtured to expand. If he turned to adventure to further feed that ego, it was a natural turn: adventure was where the public was applauding the loudest. If he found himself surrounded by tragedy on his adventures, Franklin, like Scott, lived in an era of remarkable acceptance and even sanctification of tragedy. And if his ambitions seemed far greater than his skills, it may well have been because he had several others' ambitions fueling the fires of his journeys.

Like most of the great British explorers of the era, Franklin was a Navy man, born into relative privilege. His father was a knighted magistrate, serving in a small town in central Britain, when Franklin was born in 1786. Franklin joined the Navy very young, starting as a first-class mate on board the gunship *Polyphemus* at fourteen. He was immersed almost immediately in the cult of patriotic sacrifice that would color so much of his story, serving in Nelson's fleet in the Battle of Copenhagen less than a month after boarding ship. There Franklin saw 255 fellow sailors killed and nearly 700 injured in this marginal British victory. He described it as "an honor" to have witnessed this carnage in service to the King.

Barely two weeks after that battle, Franklin's career in exploration launched when he was transferred to the scientific vessel *Investigator,* bound for a survey of Australia. Even this gentler mission was shadowed with illness and death. Eighty men and boys left Britain, but only twenty returned two and a half years later. The rest were lost through drowning, scurvy, and dysentery. The next five years were scarcely less harrowing for Franklin, marked by a shipwreck, the Battle of Trafalgar (during which several of Franklin's deck mates were killed), and the Battle of New Orleans (in which Franklin himself was seriously injured).

Again and again, Franklin performed well enough to be noticed. One commendation read, "He was in battle fearless and in danger brave," and these words impressed Franklin himself (he quoted them often) as much as his commanders. As Britain slipped into peace for the first time in several generations, and looked for new ways to (in the words of Franklin biographer Albert Markham) "employ her men and money on equally glorious matters," Franklin was a natural candidate to lead the new ventures.

The avenue for glory contrived by the Admiralty came with a genuine pedigree of ennobled tragedy. Since the early 1500s, European powers had been convinced that a water route to the riches of the Orient and the American West lay in the far north; and since the late 1500s, Britain had acted as though it held the sole right to chart this fabled Northwest Passage. Expedition after expedition was sent into the jigsaw of straits, islands, and dead-end sounds west of Greenland; over the course of three and a half centuries, hundreds of men disappeared, or perished of scurvy. In the shadow of those deaths, the North was anthropomorphized as the great white nemesis of the British Empire.

By the early 1800s, the dream of a practical commercial path through the ice had been largely extinguished, but in the hands of a visionary spinmaster committed to the mystique of the North, the search for the Northwest Passage was reinvented as the proving grounds for British dominion over the sea. The Second Secretary of the Admiralty, John Barrow, pushed for the conquest of the Passage as the noblest challenge the country could face, though it was already understood that such a Passage, if it existed at all, would be virtually useless for trade, given how rarely it would be free of ice. Still, playing the role for Franklin that Jefferson had played for Lewis, and that Clements Markham would for Scott, Barrow single-handedly sculpted a no-cost-too-high, no-loss-too-great crusade that thrilled the British public and effortlessly seduced men like Franklin.

The renewed search for the mythic Passage took place at a time of remarkable confluence of events and ideas about exploration. As there was no material or imperial gain associated, the quest conceived by Barrow would be the first real example in history of adventure for adventure's sake. It also reflected the dramatic change in the targets of adventure: instead of searching to lay claim to resource-rich tropical Edens, the men called "Barrow's Boys" chased forbidding, but majestically beautiful, wastelands. In a perfect fit for a nation which had proved its steel in war, the fight for these dangerous new dominions was spun as a celebration of bravery in the face of risk. Britain's hugely popular "penny press" eagerly sold sensational stories of heroic sacrifice to an audience that had been primed by bloody tales from the war years.

Challenging the hostile lands was also scripted as another kind of test: proving the power of technology over nature. European nations saw wilderness as a forum to show that their men and their machines were superior to those of any other country, and they launched magnificent, extravagantly equipped vessels to push to the boundaries of the map.

Perhaps most importantly, Britain was sunning itself in the brilliant light of its own ascendance. The spread of the Empire to India, the success of the colonies in Canada and Australia, Britain's victory in the Napoleonic Wars, and the apparent invincibility of its Navy, all contributed to an imperial hubris about the British ability, and right, to go wherever it wanted in the world, on its own terms. The idea that the "civilized,"

British way was the right way to move through any terrain was the cornerstone of the psychology of British exploration, and ultimately its fatal flaw. It was also Franklin's.

In 1818, Franklin got his first taste of the North, commanding one of two ships ordered to attempt to sail to the North Pole by a route almost due north of Britain. It was a typical John Barrow expedition: highly improbable, led by men with little experience in the environment (neither Franklin nor the other ship's captain, David Buchan, had ever encountered pack ice before), heavily and lavishly equipped, and proceeding with blunt force. In this journey, the two ships simply tried to ram through the ice barrier again and again, moving longitudinally but not changing strategy, as though Providence would eventually guarantee a breach just because it admired the British pluck. In the end, Franklin got no further north than had any of the explorers of the previous century.

Somehow, however, the expedition was written up as a success, if only because it "proved" the impossibility of sailing to the Pole by a due-north route, and because, in Franklin's eyes, it showed that he had the "snuff for the North." The fact that the seamen had stayed on the ship the entire voyage, and had barely engaged the landscape at all, didn't seem to worry Franklin; he saw himself as an Arctic explorer, and so did Barrow.

In 1819, Franklin received a commission to lead a land-based expedition to map the Arctic coast to the east of Canada's Coppermine River, which was guessed to be the southern border of a possible Northwest Passage. Franklin was assigned to travel to Hudson's Bay, arc northwest to the Arctic Ocean, and then over the course of two years attempt to chart the edge of the continent.

The expedition was a disaster of planning and execution. It took more than three months to sail from Britain to Hudson's Bay, and four arduous months more to drag grossly overloaded canoes (the team wrestled more than four tons of equipment) 700 miles to their first wintering at Cumberland House, high in northern Saskatchewan. (More precisely, the local voyageurs, of mixed native and French blood, did the hauling. Like most explorations of the age, Franklin's expedition mirrored the class structure at home, and the officers did little of the physical work themselves.) A late spring at Cumberland and repeated obstacles throughout the summer slowed the expedition's progress the following year, allowing only 1000 miles of travel. The team was forced into another winter well below their target on the Arctic coastline, the blame for which the British were more than willing to pass on to the support team.

But finally reaching the coast in 1820 only worsened the situation. Franklin and his men were so blindly committed to their imperial goals that they completely disregarded the natural patterns of the land they were charting. Though they managed some constructive mapping, they missed the caribou hunt that would have fed them during the harsh winter that descended on them heavily. Their canoes were destroyed by the rapids and the ocean (which the voyageurs had accurately insisted the British had no business paddling in birchbark canoes), and so they began the winter almost completely without food.

The expedition began to disintegrate in the terror of the winter. Officers and men were starving, forced to eat little more than lichen and, in a desperation that Franklin would become infamous for, even eat their shoe leather. The team had to split, sending the stronger men south to seek help from the Indians. Scurvy set in, mentally and physically breaking the men. Conflict rose to the point that one of the British was murdered by one of the voyageurs, who was then executed by the officers. In the end, four of the five British members of the expedition lived to return home, but only two out of twelve voyageurs lived. Several voyageurs died because the British had simply abandoned them to starve where they fell.

The lessons from the expedition should have been profound, especially the basic truths that the Arctic was a treacherous place; that the strategies and certainties dreamed up in warm London rooms need to be skeptically questioned; and that the people who had lived in the Arctic for centuries knew best how to survive in that climate.

In fact, exactly the opposite conclusions were drawn: Franklin's record of the disaster insisted that he believed he and his men were the strongest forces on the team, and that it was the locals' stubborn resistance to discipline that nearly killed them all. Franklin also arrogantly insisted that it was British technology and fortitude that got them through the winters. Today, it also seems self-evident that the British would have been far better off if they had followed some of the practices of the indigenous people who had offered so much help. But to be fair, this self-righteous preference for doing things in a "British" or "civilized" way was hardly a flaw in Franklin alone; it was a delusion that repeated itself again and again in European exploration history.

Thanks to masterful public-relations campaigns led by Barrow, and a voracious public appetite for death-defying feats, Franklin returned to Britain as a hero instead of a fool. There were commemorative plates and stamps issued in his honor and he received an honorary university degree. Despite the loss of so many of his men, and a smirking reputation as "the man who ate his shoes," Franklin was immediately given a commission to return again to the Arctic, this time to the west of the Coppermine. There was never any evidence that Franklin felt remorse or responsibility for the deaths of his men, but until the recent revisionist looks at him, neither was there a suggestion that anyone else felt he *should*.

The 1825 expedition descending the Mackenzie River system, was, surprisingly, far more successful—though some have argued that this success owed more to luck with the weather, and easier terrain, than any improvement in planning. Franklin was knighted in the aftermath, became known as one of the great men of the Empire, of the North, and of science. Though Franklin himself had previously described his shoe-eating expedition as a "disaster," he now redrew it as a heroic pilgrimage. Proud Britons were more than happy to accept such glorification as a reflection of their own strength.

But even this golden expedition suffered a serious taint. There were rumors of cannibalism—now accepted as likely true—helping his men survive the winters on the Coppermine, and even allegations of murder. The outrage that followed these claims had exactly the same flavor that followed Rae's claims thirty years later—and exactly the same result: Franklin was exonerated. He was a hero, his defenders insisted, and good, Christian heroes don't eat people. If any men had eaten human flesh, it must have been those damned natives.

———————

Like Meriwether Lewis, Franklin found some of glory's rewards hard to live with. The 1825 expedition earned Franklin the questionable prize of the governorship of Tasmania. The commander was a disaster in the position. All through his 1837–43 term, his incompetence fuelled the wrath of the government administrators. Franklin alleged the bureaucrats were "jealous of his fame and popularity," and he might not have been entirely wrong. For all his faults, this "simple, plodding, run-of-the-mill Navy officer," as one writer dismissed him, was loved by the citizens. Newspapers of the time, however, generally agreed with Franklin's critics. They labeled his governance "an imbecile reign," and headlined his recall to Britain as "GLORIOUS NEWS!"

When Franklin returned to Britain he was an overweight, bitter man with an unraveling reputation, barely anchored to a glory nearly twenty years past. In the eyes of those who have judged Franklin to be dangerously narcissistic, his decline in status from great explorer to failed politician was key. It was unacceptable to the often pompous and self-aggrandizing man, impelling him to return to the North to seek a final chance at immortal glory despite the possible costs. The critics paint Franklin as a pathologically callous man who intentionally ignored his fatal record as an explorer and arrogantly risked the lives of hundreds of men when he sought command of Barrow's new quest for the Passage, scheduled to leave Britain in 1845.

But dismissing Franklin solely as a morally blind narcissist ignores other key elements in the man's story. Another group of Arctic historians—Owen Beattie, Pierre Berton, and Kenneth McGoogan prominent among them—have focused their criticism of Franklin on his competence, rather than his ego. In their view, Franklin was as inept an expedition leader as he was a governor, with a history of poor planning, worse decisions in the field, and a tragic blindness to the need for change.

It is not impossible to reconcile the two views: Although narcissism is certainly seen in the talented, it more often seems to be a compensatory tool of people who live on the edge of their abilities. The largest and loudest egos are often found in people who seem least likely to deserve them, whose proclamations of talent are designed to prevent the world from discovering weakness. Like many people of this type, Franklin's life seems to have been an unfortunate story of rising into positions above his abilities because he so actively chased the limelight.

Still, Franklin's story is arguably also a candidate for the "Burdened" section of this book, for there were also many other people, and other factors, that were as complicit as his ego in the weave of his life. Though he bears ultimate responsibility for the tragedies of his expeditions, Franklin's place as a leader was hardly his doing alone. This was especially true of his final, most tragic command of all.

There is no question that Franklin himself saw a need for a swan song to restore his reputation after the downfall in Tasmania, but the first stone in Franklin's path back North was laid by his formidable second wife, Lady Jane Franklin. Lady Jane's own ego was easily the equal of her husband's, and she had played a deft hand in shaping his final expedition. Lady Jane would not stand to have her husband's image (or, by proxy, her own) tarnished. So she pushed the 59-year-old Franklin to seek a command that would bring redemption, and she used her own political connections to ensure he would be given the commission. She not only solicited support for Franklin among the powerful, but she also worked behind the scenes to eliminate some potential rivals.

Selling Franklin as a polar leader was not easy for either Franklin himself or for Lady Jane. Franklin was so out of shape that it was said he could barely walk a mile, and he was openly ridiculed by several of his colleagues as something of a buffoon. Even John Barrow was initially unwilling to accept Franklin, until three preferred candidates turned down the job. It was only after he reluctantly offered the helm to Franklin that Barrow began to portray "Sir John of the Arctic" as "the ideal man" for a return attempt.

Franklin had stronger supporters in the Navy, though not necessarily for the best reasons. Several men who championed him were his age peers, and many writers have suggested that such men voted for Franklin simply because they wanted to see one from their own era enjoy a victory over the young. Historians have also hypothesized that there were equally as many people who endorsed Franklin's command because they simply felt pity towards a man who would "die of disappointment" if he didn't get a chance to redeem his name.

And then there was the question of the hubris of the nation behind Franklin. For this ultimate endeavor, Barrow mustered all the resources that Britain could throw at the Passage. To quell concerns about Franklin's suitability for the rigors of the voyage, the Second Secretary insisted that the two luxuriously outfitted ships of the command, the *Erebus* and the *Terror,* would have so few problems that Franklin's condition simply wouldn't be a concern. The planning was so perfect that he would not be going ashore, so why should age or fitness be an issue? There were so many men, and the vessels were so good, Barrow insisted, that "victory was guaranteed." The ships, armored to break the ice, were filled with huge libraries, polished silver tea sets, fine china, and mahogany furniture, and stocked with food to last three years. Why not have the man who had led more expeditions North than anyone else captain the ship?

For all his limitations, Franklin was not alone in his ill-preparedness for the Arctic; only one of the officers on either ship had any ice experience at all. But the British were so confident in the expedition's might that they made no plans for rescue. In fact, even before the ships had left port, the Admiralty and the press focused their attentions on planning Franklin's glorious return celebrations. This would be, the papers crowed, the most acclaimed, most certain British victory of all: not just over other men, but over nature herself.

What was not accounted for, yet again, in this sanguine prediction was the Arctic itself. Records show that Franklin sailed into the worst northern ice in nearly 700 years. Exactly what happened is a tale that continues to unfold even today.

––––––––––––––

John Franklin and his two ships left port on May 19, 1845, with 134 men on board. We know from his letters home that Franklin dropped six ill sailors in Greenland, and was last sighted by a whaling ship on June 25. Then he vanished into the ice, with no clues to his course. There were no bones, no shelters, no flags.

Franklin disappeared so completely that it would take more than thirty expeditions over more than a decade—by the Navy, by private interests seeking the posted rewards, and several trips funded by Lady Jane—before it was universally accepted that Franklin and his crew had died miserable deaths. The press, the government, and faithful public all remained so convinced of Franklin's and the ships' ability to withstand any hardship, that for years they continued to talk as though Franklin and his crew would simply pop out of the Bering Straits with another valiant tale to tell.

When conclusive evidence of Franklin's fate was finally unearthed in the late 1850s, it was clear that the *Erebus* and *Terror* had become monuments to Franklin's corrosive ambition, but also to the lethal hubris of his time.

Exactly what happened to Franklin, and when, remains one of the great mysteries of exploration, but various bits of the expedition that have been discovered around the eastern Arctic over the years have lit some of the shadows of the story.

In 1850, the crew of the *HMS Assistance* discovered evidence of Franklin's first winter camp on the shores of Beechey Island in the high eastern Arctic. Nearby, they also found the first bodies—three sailors who had perished during the winter and spring of 1846.

Nine years later, one of the expeditions funded by Lady Jane found a sequence of messages in a cairn on the shores of King William Island, in the complex archipelago of icy islands south of Devon Island. The first note, written in May 1847, described the first wintering, and vaguely outlined futile attempts to find a northern channel through the islands.

The second note on the same page, written by a junior officer eleven months later, was far bleaker. Franklin's ships, it explained, had been icebound since September 1846, and had to be abandoned when it appeared that, once again, the ice would not break up in the cold spring.

The second wintering had been a deadly one, with twenty-four men lost- -including Franklin himself, who died in June 1847. The final note indicates that the crew intended to strike out overland for the Great Fish River, where their bodies were eventually discovered seven years later by John Rae.

Forensic archeologists have shown that the initial deaths of the men, both on the ships and on land, came from a range of predictable and completely preventable sources: Scurvy, tuberculosis, and lead poisoning from the newly invented tinned foods that the expedition carried. By the last days of the expedition, however, the men were falling to starvation, desperation, and the aimlessness of their futile overland haul. The misery of their final days is almost inconceivable.

Recent historians have laid much of the blame for the chaotic disintegration of the expedition squarely on Franklin, and it is not a completely unjust accusation. The historian Pierre Berton points out that a better man than Franklin would have recognized his weaknesses and understood that he was a "man who shouldn't have been there." Instead, Franklin's bottomless need for acclaim, his self-aggrandizing trust in certain victory, and his blind disregard of the wisdom offered by more experienced local travelers caused the deaths of 147 men in the course of his Arctic career.

And yet this blunt assessment of Franklin's story took a very long time to be made. We might excoriate the man today for what seems to have been fatal hubris and incompetence, but in his day and long after, Franklin was consistently forgiven and cast as a martyr, if not a saint, of the British Empire. Though there's no evidence whatsoever that Franklin intended to sacrifice himself for any cause, the need for heroes to emerge from the fiasco was insistent enough that Franklin's misery (for the expedition was always written with Sir John as the central, if not the only significant character) was recast for generations as a gallant submission to Nature, carried out in Britain's name.

In one of the most intriguing twists in the psychology of adventure, the rewriting of Franklin's story as a glorious "sacrifice" made him the model for the most heroic version of adventure for more then 150 years. Instead of being held up as proof of the dangers of unbridled hubris, or as a warning of the risks of stepping beyond one's abilities, Franklin became the poster child for the nobility of sacrifice. Though they were worlds apart in talent and rightful place in adventure history, the line gets drawn, even today, from Franklin through Scott to George Mallory on Everest, tracing one consistent theme: that death in the service of adventure is as honorable as success in reaching the goal.

However chilling the premise might be, and however it might understandably invite accusations of "madness" by outsiders to adventure, the glorification of dying for adventure is hardly an incomprehensible notion. The theme of perishing while reaching for a dream lies at the heart not just of the best adventure literature, but of many of the great stories and myths of all cultures. And if, as writers such as Francis Spufford and Beau Riffenburgh have suggested, the real psychological purpose of adventure is to give us heroes rather than summits or Poles or Northwest Passages, then arguably the purest heroes are those so committed to their adventure that they died for it.

Franklin's story shows us, however, that our desire for such superhuman will can be so strong that we may be willing to forgive dangerous motivations and questionable behavior, and see heroes even where they don't exist.

Jean Batten waves to adoring crowds in Sydney, 1934. (Fairfax Images)

CHAPTER 6

JEAN BATTEN

A Terrible Beauty

In mid-October, 1982, an elderly woman, obviously English-speaking but quite fluent in Spanish, checked into a budget tourist apartment complex in a rough suburb south of Palma de Mallorca, the hectic capital of the lovely sun-and-sand island off the northeast coast of Spain. She took a simple, bare studio for the winter, and furnished it with little more than she carried in her one small suitcase. She was quiet, reserved but polite with the other guests and staff—not standoffish, but also never particularly friendly. As people had said of the woman all her life, she was beautiful: elegant, head-turning even at 73.

Most days, the woman would sit on her balcony overlooking the busy street below. She also took long walks alone, to the market for the food she cooked alone in her room, through the winding streets of the town, or into the tropical woods behind the hotel. Just a few weeks after she arrived, hotel staff were concerned when the woman said that a stray dog had bitten her on the leg on one of her walks through the woods. The staff suggested that she see a doctor, but the woman dismissed their advice, saying she would clean and bandage the small wound herself.

Within days it was obvious that the bite wound was far more serious than the woman was ready to admit: The puncture reddened. The leg rapidly started to swell, and then lost all mobility. Bedridden, the woman continued to emphatically insist that she did not want medical attention. A couple of weeks passed, and the woman remained immobile, obviously ill and eating almost nothing but, according to the hotel maid, not looking especially sick. So it was a complete surprise to the housekeeper when she entered the plain white room on the morning of November 22 and discovered the woman unconscious and fevered. The maid ran to get help, but by the time she had returned, the woman was dead. An autopsy later showed that the infection, which could have been so easily treated, had spread to her lungs, finally drowning her.

The Spanish authorities were left puzzling over how to deal with the woman's body. They had no way of contacting any friends or relatives; no one had come to visit during her entire stay at the hotel and she had called no one, even when she was gravely ill. Without access to the woman's funds, the authorities were finally obliged to bury her in an unmarked pauper's grave. It was nearly five years before a journalist's relentless pursuit of a story uncovered that the woman in the hotel had been one of the great adventurers of the twentieth century and, if only for a brief sunlit moment, one of the most famous women in the world.

Although she died in anonymity, for much of Jean Batten's life nothing seemed more important than the pursuit of fame. In the 1930s, and then again in a fleeting burst in the 1970s, Batten went to extraordinary lengths to carve her name into the records as the finest female pilot in history.

If Batten was not exactly, as she liked to tell people, born to fly, she was certainly bred to—and was just as surely bred for fame. Just a few weeks before the girl was born in Rotorua, New Zealand in 1909, Batten's mother, like the rest of the world, was captivated by the thrilling new adventure of flight; but Ellen Batten channeled that thrill into a dream of greatness for her daughter. Even though Batten came into the world a sickly and fragile child, her mother made sure lofty aerial ambitions were in the child's mind from the beginning.

Where other mothers might fill cribs with flowers or toys, Ellen Batten pinned a photo of Louis Blériot, the newest hero of aviation, to her daughter's cot. In this image, the Frenchman who had just completed the first flight across the English Channel stood victorious beside his homemade monoplane, the absurdly fragile *Blériot XI*. "Almost the first thing her baby eyes saw," Ellen Batten told reporters years later, "was that picture of his ramshackle machine."

Everything Ellen Batten did as a parent, she would later say, was designed to give her daughter a chance at distinction, to make sure that the girl was independent and completely free of the restraints Ellen herself felt shackled by—especially the restraints of being a woman in the early years of the twentieth century. From the moment Jean Batten was born, her mother said, she knew the girl was destined for great things. Ellen Batten would do everything she could to cement that promise.

In his remarkably insightful biography, which gives us almost all we reliably know of Jean Batten, Ian Mackersey showed that Ellen's commitment involved an obsessively singular focus on her daughter. At the expense of her relationship with Jean's older brothers, who grew to feel they had no place in their mother's life, and with her husband, from whom both Ellen and Jean were soon estranged, Ellen Batten turned all her attention and affection to her daughter. She began to mold Jean with as much controlling attention to detail as she brought to every aspect of her own life.

Ellen herself was a complex and formidable character, very used to drawing attention. Others commented on how strikingly beautiful and elegant the tall, graceful woman was. She was talented in many spheres, intelligent, and ahead of her time in her feminism, pushing boundaries wherever she could. Before and after marriage, she organized suffragist rallies, captained a rowing team, rode her own horse through her small provincial town, and gambled on horse races.

But she was also a twist of contradictions: flamboyantly extraverted at times, but almost reclusively private at others; open-minded in principle, but more often remembered for how stiffly formal, repressed, and haughty she seemed; feminist, but staunchly feminine in dress and bearing. Ellen was obsessively attentive to appearances, going well out of her way to create an immaculate image for both herself and her daughter. But it was an image that flew in the face of the more difficult truths of her life, especially the failure of her marriage and the often-desperate state of her finances. Ellen, with Jean following in her footsteps, spent much of her life creating a perfect public mask and a myth of unblemished happiness.

The scope of Ellen's efforts to sculpt her daughter's life was impressive, though disturbing. She passed on rigid notions about health and diet, rules about cleanliness and hygiene that bordered on compulsive, and especially, admonitions about womanhood. There was nothing that a woman could not do, Ellen Batten taught, but at the same time many things a woman *shouldn't* do. She gave the young girl a conflicted legacy of independence within her own rigid constraints of "proper" behavior. Jean could do whatever she wanted, provided she never embarrassed herself or her mother, and as long as she always showed her best side to the world. A woman, Ellen adamantly maintained, could have just as adventurous a life as a man, as long as she never showed a moment's weakness; she must fiercely guard her privacy about "delicate" matters, and be always properly dressed and made-up.

These conflicting messages were a profound force, creating one of the more enigmatic, and fascinating, characters in adventure history. Jean struggled all her life to balance the contradictions of her mother's encouragements and rules. She became an adventurer who took great risks, but also made sure to clean herself up before anyone saw her afterwards. She always strove to be in the spotlight, but hid whenever she could to reduce the anxiety of being somehow seen to fail. She was committed to being completely independent, but seemed fixated on finding a husband who would validate her. Far more importantly, she never sought independence from the most powerful and oppressive force in her life—her mother.

Ellen Batten's dominance in her daughter's life was unwavering—so much so that a family acquaintance described Jean as "a prisoner" of her mother. Ellen's control never seemed to have been met with the kind of rebellion that might have been expected in a healthier clan. Instead of eventually striking out, as most children would, Jean worshipped her. The two were inextricably intertwined as long as Ellen lived, rarely out of each other's sight for more than sixty years.

No other relationships would come close to theirs, for either woman. Jean's father, for the limited years when he was involved in Jean's life before he was permanently banished from the lives of both women during Jean's late adolescence, played only a small role in facilitating an adventurous spirit in his daughter. He took her on forest hikes and rides on his motorcycle. "Through him," Jean wrote in her unpublished memoirs, giving her father a rare nod, "I first discovered the intoxicating effect that speed had on me." He also taught her rudimentary compass skills. But it was her mother who pushed Jean toward the skies.

Ellen began with the picture pinned to Jean's crib, and throughout Jean's childhood kept her daughter immersed in aviation. She took Jean down to watch flying boats at the local harbor, and often went to the local flying school where, to Jean's recalled thrill, she sat in the cockpit of a plane. When Jean was ten, Ellen started showing her stories in the newspapers of the heroic airmen who were starting to attempt daring ocean crossings, and were becoming famous, and rich, in the process. If Ellen wanted to make her daughter famous, and perhaps get the recognition she believed she had missed herself, there was no better way to do it than by encouraging her daughter to fly.

There has never been a time in history in which adventure has been more in the public eye than during the great years of aviation. From the end of the First World War through the end of the 1930s, newspapers ran almost daily front-page stories about air races to cross the continents and the oceans, in faster and faster times, sometimes for huge sums of money. There has also never been an adventure "sport" with a higher fatality rate; many stories which made the news told of the crashes of the pathetically dangerous aircraft of the time, and a tragic number of the great pilots of the time lost their lives in very public disasters or disappearances.

The other most striking thing about the period, which must have appealed enormously to Ellen Batten's feminism, was the relative equality that women enjoyed in the young sport. The number of female pilots—*famous* female pilots quite the equal of men—was much greater than women's penetration of other risk pursuits.

The first woman to fly the English Channel, Harriet Quimby, did so only three years after Blériot's historic Channel crossing. During the true "golden" decade of aviation following Charles Lindbergh's flight across the Atlantic in 1927, female pilots were in the newspapers nearly as often as men. Amelia Earhart was famous around the world, as was Amy Johnson and many others competing not just for the "first female flights," but for the "fastest" and "firsts" independent of gender. In her biography, *My Life,* Jean Batten listed nine very experienced women who all inspired her dream to become a great pilot herself, many of whom she would meet within the first year she started to fly.

By her mid-teens, Batten was telling her friends that she would one day "be a very famous person," but she understood that her ambitions could not come to life in New Zealand. By nineteen, she informed her stunned father that she had decided on a plan for her life: she would be the first person to fly from England to New Zealand. When Fred Batten said no, insisting that it would be too dangerous and expensive, Jean and Ellen found the money themselves, lied to Jean's father about their plans, and moved to England where Jean could learn to fly without Fred's interference.

Other than a brief return to New Zealand, obliged when Fred discovered their deception and cut off Jean's "allowance," she never moved back to her homeland, and hardly ever spoke to or saw her father or brothers again.

Although it is transparently true that all adventurers are uniquely driven, and that many have to tread on other people's toes to find the space to realize their dreams, what was unique about Jean Batten was the degree to which her drive for fame burned bridges all around her.

Batten chased her ambitions with remarkably little concern for the consequences of any of the treading she did along the way. She wrote in one of her autobiographies, "Once my mind was set on anything, it was quite useless to attempt to swerve me from any purpose or to dampen my enthusiasm in any way"—but even this apparently candid confession disingenuously minimized just how many liberties she would take on behalf of her ambitions.

As always, the best explanation for Jean's cutthroat ways lies squarely at her mother's feet. Ellen Batten spent years nurturing a self-esteem in Jean that went so far beyond mere confidence that she appeared, to many people, to have a staggering arrogance. By the time Jean and Ellen arrived in Britain, Jean was, at least on the surface, thoroughly convinced that she was an absolutely unique person, destined for a greatness that no one should ever be permitted to obstruct. Ellen taught her daughter to understand that whatever Jean wanted she was entitled to have, no matter what it took to get it.

Jean and Ellen Batten's stories suggest that both mother and daughter showed all the signs of narcissistic personality disorder: The feelings of superiority and convictions of entitlement, the obscuring of personal flaws, the exaggerations of personal achievements and reputation, the drawing of attention to one's self in every circumstance, the obsessive over-valuing of appearances (even when rough edges would be forgiven) and the self-centered use of others, especially in the seductive way Jean mastered. Jean might have ultimately achieved her (and Ellen's) ambition to become one of the great figures of twentieth century adventure, but she did so at tremendous cost to others, and ultimately, with considerable personal pain as well. Jean cut a swath through her relationships—in family, love and business—that left her profoundly lonely most of her life.

Like her mother, Jean was a strikingly beautiful woman. Every biography and newspaper report on the woman seems to mention this appraisal within the first few lines, to a degree that feels blatantly objectifying and sexist—until you begin to understand how carefully and consciously Jean constructed the attention to her beauty.

From the moment in 1930 when Jean first stepped onto the field at the Stag Lane aerodrome in London—perhaps the best place to learn to fly in the world at the time—she showed such self-confidence and charisma that she instantly won many people over, especially men. Flight instructors stumbled over themselves to teach her. The other younger pilots rushed to try to date her, and Jean—as she would all of her life—capitalized on the opportunities. She masterfully farmed a series of suitors and sponsors who would effectively pay for all her plans but receive little in return.

We would know very little about the role of these various men—or about many other, deeper truths of Jean Batten's life—without the research done by Ian Mackersey and his wife Caroline.

Mackersey, himself an amateur pilot, became intrigued by Jean's story when she stepped briefly out of self-exile in the early 1970s, and reminded everyone who she had once been through a series of grand public appearances. Mackersey developed an obsessive devotion—not to Jean, but to more deeply understanding the idiosyncrasies and contradictions in her story. Like many people who came into contact with the story, Mackersey saw that the image that Jean had so carefully cultivated in her public displays and her autobiographies—1934's *Solo Flight* and 1938's *My Life,* reissued as *Alone in the Sky* in 1979—did not tally with so many of the facts of her life, or with the opinions of so many people who had to deal with her.

Jean's own books—even her unpublished memoirs, to which the Mackerseys had access—were exactly what one would expect from a narcissist: face-saving hagiographies that bordered on fiction. In them, she never acknowledged that her parents had split, or that she never talked again with her brothers after the 1930s. Nor did she admit that the beginning of her flying career was filled with troubles resulting from truly marginal skills; that she suffered several embarrassing crashes in her career; that she had had conflicts with several other pilots; or that she tossed aside a string of men who had funded her dreams. Jean either completely wrote her funders and her lovers out of her story, or blithely suggested that those few who stayed in her story should join everyone else in her world and feel honored to have witnessed her grand destiny.

Despite her initial troubles mastering the basics of the cockpit, Batten's obsessive commitment helped her to truly become quite a remarkable pilot. She developed a reputation for a willingness to take risks that terrified other pilots, and seemed to have a sixth sense for blind navigation. By 1932, Jean had not only earned her pilot's license but had become admired in flying circles for having a coolheaded faculty for extracting herself from difficult situations.

Difficult situations were the norm in the world of 1930s aviation. The aircraft—such as the deHavilland Gipsy Moth biplanes that Batten flew to fame—were delicate wood-and-linen tinkertoys, cramped, primitive, and prone to technical bugaboos. The Moth had a wingspan of only thirty feet and was pushed along by a 120-horsepower motor, with a maximum cruising speed of barely eighty-five miles per hour and a range of only 250 miles. The pilot had to squeeze her way into the cockpit behind the noisy two-stroke engine, and try her best to wrestle the plane against the whims of wind and air currents.

These planes had to fly frighteningly close to the ground to be kept in control, and navigation was rudimentary at best, often limited to a compass bearing, hints from a primitive airspeed indicator, and a great deal of luck and dead-reckoning. Pilots heading out across the open ocean followed their noses, guessed the amount of lateral wind drift, and prayed.

Many very experienced pilots crashed or disappeared, but this did not dissuade Batten. When she saw the acclaim Amy Johnson received for a groundbreaking solo flight from England to Australia in 1930, Batten decided the risks were worth it. She went in search of an airplane.

In her autobiographies, Batten refers to "a pilot" with whom she struck an arrangement to jointly purchase the Moth in which she would start her run to fame. The anonymous pilot was, according to Ian Mackersey's research, the second in Batten's long chain of lovers supporting her dreams. She secretly began seeing this man while she was still with the man who funded her pilot's training—and who apparently still expected to marry her (though marriage, according to the Mackerseys, was never in Batten's plans).

The wealthier new lover could afford to buy Batten her first plane, but ended up being treated much as the first had been. Although Jean suggested in her books that she had shared ownership in the Moth with the partnering pilot in exchange for fifty percent of her story rights, she never repaid the man and virtually ignored him once she secured a new sponsor—even though she had considerable wealth later in life, and he had crippling financial troubles.

On April 9, 1933, when Batten finally left on her solo flight from England to Australia, her departure was followed by a passel of reporters, who commented on how "pretty" the twenty-three-year-old looked, posing by the Moth in her "fur-lined flying suit," "powdering her face" and amiably chatting with the reporters. Ellen Batten accompanied her daughter to the airfield south of London, and clearly enjoyed the spotlight just as much as Jean did.

Jean climbed into the open cockpit, which was stuffed with provisions for the flight: the food which Batten would have to eat with one hand while she held the constantly chattering joystick with the other; the layers of clothing she would have to shed once she hit the scalding 100-degree days over the deserts of the Middle East; the flashlight she could shine on the instrument panel—and the ground—if she got stuck flying in the dark. While Jean waved and started the Moth lurching down the runway, Ellen held court with the reporters, spinning the myth about the perfect family behind the perfect daughter.

Batten was not only chasing Amy Johnson's record of nineteen days to Australia, she was sharing the sky with several other notable pilots. There were at least eight other planes trying record-breaking crossings the day Batten took off, including three other women and two pilots who were missing (both of whom, it turned out, had fatally crashed).

Batten started her flight with only 130 hours of airtime behind her, but she already had a strong reputation for meticulous planning. She had made some well-conceived adjustments to the plane, especially adding a second fuel tank which would allow the long-distance hops necessary for the trip. She also had the foresight to add a second propeller to the fuselage; breakdowns and minor crashes were almost inevitable.

The records set by the pilots of the 1930s were completed in stages, often involving frighteningly drawn-out leaps across open water, or through mountain passes, both of which pushed the planes and the pilots to the maximum. The small planes were so vulnerable to drafts and currents that the stick had to be continuously controlled, giving the pilot no chance to relax or to stretch out in the cramped confines of the cockpit.

But Batten quickly showed herself up to the game. She logged a very impressive first day out of Britain, flying just a hair under 1000 miles to Rome in ten hours. This was a strong showing by any pilot, let alone a relatively inexperienced woman who had to fly out the last drops of fuel in her tanks, manually pumping the reserves, blistering her hands in the process.

If there had been any doubts about Batten's capabilities before that first day, they washed away in the acclaim she received in the international press on her arrival in Rome. In less than a day, she went from being an unknown to being a force to reckon with. The media loved the image of the smiling debutante sliding demurely out of her plane, perfectly made-up in the white flight suit that was to become her signature.

The following days, from Italy to Greece and then east, offered Batten a more honest taste of the realities of distance flying—running blind in the early-morning, bitterly cold dark over the Adriatic, forced to guess where she would find Turkey; facing down severe turbulence near the Taurus Mountains that would have shaken the most seasoned pilot—but Batten later wrote that she was thrilled by the experience. She endured terrifyingly violent winds in sandstorms that "made all the wires ripple" and forced two landings in the Iraqi desert. The second time, she dropped out of the storm, then landed by moonlight in the middle of absolutely nowhere. Batten awoke in the morning to find herself surrounded by Bedu tribesmen, whom she allegedly charmed as easily as she did all men. In Batten's dramatic tale of the event, she soon had the Bedu helping her turn the plane, spin the propeller and watch, enthralled, as she bounced down the desert and into the air.

The press ate up the thrilling details, but this first Batten adventure was soon earthbound. Approaching Karachi, Pakistan, over the great western deserts, Batten ran into yet another sandstorm, and this time the winds threw her into a rough landing in less forgiving terrain. Batten slammed the Moth nose-first into the mud, hopelessly damaging her propeller. It took all her wiles to get the locals to help her get to Karachi and then, true to form, manipulate the local powers to get the plane fixed. After being wined and dined by local royalty, Batten was back in the air in surprisingly little time, only to crash again far more seriously within minutes of takeoff. "In a split second," she wrote, "all my hopes and dreams had been shattered."

Though she would prove to be a master of the theatrical in her writing, Batten's devastation in this instance was not just melodrama. She had destroyed a plane that did not belong to her, and getting another plane to try the flight again—or to simply get home for that matter—was well out of Batten's financial range. It did seem that her dream of flying was over, but Batten's remarkable luck at attracting support soon landed yet another patron, this time the head of a British oil company. Lord Wakefield of Castrol Oil had been following Batten's press avidly, and found "the new girl star . . . stunning." He not only paid for the passage for her and the wrecked Moth back from India, but gave her enough money to buy her own Moth. "Finally," Batten sighed about the plane in *My Life,* "my very own, at last."

She spent a long year readying herself for her next try, tuning the new Moth, finessing the details of her route and equipment, getting momentarily engaged (another fiasco that she would edit out of her autobiographies), and honing her commitment to beat Amy Johnson's record.

Ian Mackersey suggests that her focus was almost suicidally sharp by the time she took off again in April 1934. "She was playing Russian roulette with all the chambers loaded," pushing the limits of the little plane right to the edge with several decisions that many pilots felt were unnecessarily showy. Even Batten eventually acknowledged hubris when she suddenly found herself out of fuel in a storm off the Italian coast, pushing herself so she could claim the fastest time for the first leg of the flight: "I had set off against the advice of weather experts and now must pay the penalty. . . . A watery grave was what I deserved." With more luck than skill, she managed to barely avoid such a grave by "pancaking" the Moth into a radio field just 300 yards from Saint Paul's Cathedral in Rome.

Batten's capacity to blur facts and reshape her image was as clear as ever in the aftermath of the two crashes. While her new Moth was being almost completely rebuilt, Batten spent as much time rebuilding her reputation. In her retouching of history, the crash in India became solely the fault of a mechanical malfunction, and the crash in Rome nothing more than "running out of petrol."

She turned both accidents into "thrilling experiences," over-dramatized the dangers, and puffed up her own handling of the predicaments, claiming that other pilots were applauding her for keeping her head (when in fact they were condemning her risk-taking). By the time she was ready to leave for her third try—the one that would bring her onto the world stage—the adoring newspapers were calling her the "Try Again Girl," skilled, independent, and almost impossibly brave. But other pilots were rolling their eyes.

———————

Judging the self-centeredness of a life like Batten's, lived in the public eye with so many attention-drawing abilities and aspirations, is not a simple matter. Despite best intents, many skilled, ambitious, and acclaimed people appear arrogant and standoffish in public, and can act as though they truly believe their fame makes them better than others. But it is not reasonable to assume that their public behaviors signal a deeply entrenched narcissism. Celebrities—whether in movies or in the world of adventure—sometimes act the way that they do because they are responding to the difficult realities of celebrity. It can be hard to stay grounded when the world constantly elevates you, or to stay open and warm when thousands of people want a piece of you.

But Jean Batten's personality was different from the transient "situational acquired narcissism" that psychologists see in some celebrities. Batten's grandiose self-regard apparently preceded her fame by years and was the reason for—not the consequence of—her rise to celebrity.

This isn't to say—at all—that Batten's fame was unwarranted. She was not one of those celebrities who was "famous only for being famous." Far from it: Batten's third attempt at the flight to Australia proved she was the equal of *any* pilot of the day. After taking off from the Lympne Airfield on May 8, 1934, she stared down desperate conditions, including days of violent storms, mechanical troubles, and near-death plunges, and she won desperate bets on fuel and winds. When she landed in Darwin, Australia on May 23, she had bettered Amy Johnson's record by four days—and had done so in perfect style.

In the aftermath of the flight, the press crowned her the "Princess of the Sky," the public swarmed in crowds tens of thousands deep, and governments—Britain's, New Zealand's and Australia's—scrambled to lay claim to her. The stream of free gifts and hotel rooms, sponsorship opportunities, and cash rewards seemed endless, and Batten swam in the adulation as though she felt she was finally getting what she deserved.

Batten presented in large groups as a public-relations agent's dream: immaculately dressed and groomed, charming and apparently modest, articulate and gracious, the perfect citizen and daughter, saying exactly the right things about family, country, and overcoming challenges. She came across so well that the press coverage from her era was little more than gushes of sycophantic praise (though a few critics also suggested that everything about her was contrived and rehearsed, as though she had been in training for years for this moment).

In smaller groups, or one-on-one, Batten could also show up perfectly—providing the audience had something she wanted. She was a master at seducing support, financing, accommodation, and bookings, though by all accounts she hardly had to use these sharp skills, as gifts kept falling her way. The combination was enough to keep both Ellen and Jean living in sponsored luxury for more than a year in Australia.

But the records and the public personas, no matter how impressive and endearing, rarely tell the whole story of complex characters like Batten. Yes, she was fast and daring and talented in the air, and beautiful and ingratiating in the spotlight, but it was the way that Batten moved behind the scenes that reflects a truer sense of the woman. When she dropped her mask, Batten was an entirely different person. The veneer of gentility vanished, uncovering an abrasive egocentrism. Batten pushed many of the people who offered their help to the limits of their tolerance, overstaying her free welcomes, running up bills, often not thanking or acknowledging patrons, but still asking more and more from them. She treated others like her servants, with a diva's list of demands.

The depictions that Mackersey heard from Batten's acquaintances, flying peers, business partners, sponsors, patrons, and even family members, say it all: She was "rude . . . controlling . . . aggressively bent on winning through at all costs . . . expected to click her fingers and get instant service . . . she put herself up on a pedestal and could only think of herself and her exploits . . . she needed the adulation because she was incredibly immature . . . her life was utterly empty . . . [she had] no real friends, ever . . . you could never warm to her . . . she was cold and self-centered . . . brusque and bossy . . . the most objectionable woman."

One of the most difficult aspects of fame is the pressure for a second act. As any Everest climber or Oscar winner can testify, a single achievement, no matter how notable, does not seal a future. The natural course of events alone can be perilous: Inevitably, someone else will come along and beat the record you just set, obliging you to try again to stay on top. Even Batten's steel-plated ego was not secure enough to rest on the fame of what was effectively her only completed flight.

On April 8, 1935, Batten took off again in her Moth from Australia, bound for England. By flying the route home she was setting a record of sorts—the first woman to solo both ways—but she also had it in mind to beat her own eastbound speed. This time, however, she had what she described as the most terrifying experience of her already fright-filled career. Between Australia and Timor, her engine clogged with dust and she came precariously close to having to fatally ditch at sea. She survived because of her skill, but people who knew her reported that she seemed forever shaken by the experience, as though she had been reminded again that her "destiny" was a devil's bargain.

Batten arrived in Britain seventeen days later—the fastest westbound time by a woman, but three days longer than her eastbound flight—to a much flatter reception than she had received in Australia. Only a handful of people turned out at the airport (you would never know this from *My Life,* in which Batten wrote, "London was seething with excitement.") It was not long, though, before Batten was being celebrated by high society as a "lovely addition" to dinner parties, which she highlighted in her books through long lists of the nobility whom she now counted as "friends."

Still, Batten described the flight to England as a depressing failure. She needed to look for a greater affirmation of her skills. She chose a flight from Britain to Brazil, leaving on November 11, 1935. It was an ambitious plan with a huge ocean crossing that would have challenged any of the best pilots of the day, and required that Batten use some of her newfound wealth to purchase a new, much more impressive plane, a Percival Gull. It could stay in the air far longer than the Moth, and fly at twice the speed, but the trip to Brazil was still a serious undertaking.

In the end, Batten pulled off a spectacular flight. She crossed 2000 miles of open sea, navigating with nothing more than a compass, and thirteen hours later arrived within a half-mile of her target on the shoulder of the Brazilian coastline. The "Carnation of the Sky," as the South American papers called her, had beaten every record for the crossing, by man or woman.

The success opened doors around the world for Batten, and awards and accolades showered down. She received trophies from aviation societies and medals from sporting federations. She made lists of "women of the year," and was made a Commander of the British Empire. The acclaim, not surprisingly, did little to soften her. More and more she presented her achievements as supreme—and as completely of her own making. "I accomplished it all without help, influence and money," she absurdly suggested in an interview. That claim was enough to bring her past lovers and sponsors out of the woodwork looking for repayment, but she brushed them off without any sign of guilt, and never openly acknowledged her debts.

There were signs, however, that Batten's flying and her public behavior were taking a complicated toll, not unusual in personality disorders. Batten was showing signs of anxiety and alienation in public, and it was obvious that, while she pursued the attention, she was increasingly uncomfortable with it. She withdrew to spend time alone with her mother, to the point that newspapers that had been so supportive began to worry about her health and state of mind (though this sympathy came because the press continued to frame her as a vulnerable "petite girl," without understanding that she was also avoiding the creditors and former lovers and patrons she had been battling for years).

But whatever Batten was suffering from during the first half of 1936, these concerns were put to rest when she climbed back into the Gull in October with the grandest plan of all: a solo flight from Britain back to her native New Zealand.

Planned in secrecy and then carried out with almost perfect precision, Batten's flight was a landmark. She rocketed from Britain to

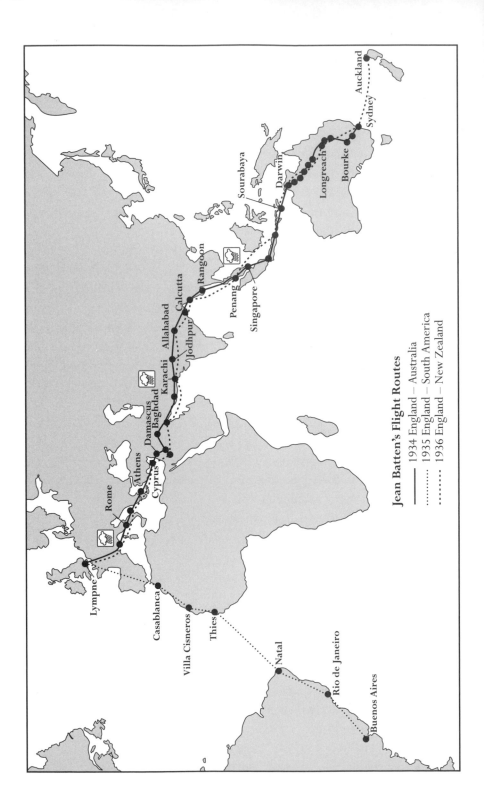

Jean Batten's Flight Routes

1934 England – Australia
1935 England – South America
1936 England – New Zealand

Auckland

Sydney

Bourke

Longreach

Darwin

Sourabaya

Rangoon

Penang

Singapore

Calcutta

Allahabad

Jodhpur

Karachi

Baghdad

Damascus

Cyprus

Athens

Rome

Lympne

Casablanca

Villa Cisneros

Thies

Natal

Rio de Janeiro

Buenos Aires

The agony of Scott's journey, manhauling to the South Pole (Courtesy of the Scott Polar Research Institute, University of Cambridge).

The wreck of the Teignmouth Electron, *Cayman Brac (Photo: Nicky Watson, Caymanian Compass).*

(7.k)

Dear Sir   Monticello Aug. [...]

This will be handed you [by] mr Bradbury, an English botanist, who proposes to take St Louis in his botanizing tour. he came recommended to me by mr Roscoe of Liverpool, so well known by his histories of Lorenzo of Medici & Leo X. & who is president of the Botanical society of Liverpool. mr Bradbury comes out in their employ, & having kept him here about ten days, I have had an opportunity of knowing that besides being a botanist of the first order, he is a man of entire worth & correct conduct. as such I recommend him to your notice, advice & patronage, while within your government or it's confines. perhaps you can consult no abler hand on your Western botanical observations. I am very often applied to to know when your work will begin to appear; and I have so long promised copies to my literary cor- respondents in France, that I am almost bankrupt in their eyes. I shall be very happy to receive from yourself information of your expecta- tions on this subject. every body is impatient for it.

You have seen by the papers how dirty a trick has been played us by England. I consider all amicable arrangement with that nation as desperate during the life of the present king. there is some ground to ex- pect more justice from Napoleon. & this is perhaps favored by the origi- nal defeat he has suffered in the battle of the Danube, which has obliged him to retreat & remain stationary at Vienna, till his army, literally cut up, can be reinforced. in the mean time, the spell of his invincibility being broken, he is in danger of an universal in- surrection against him in Europe.   your friends here are well, & I have been long in expectation of seeing you. I shall hope in that case to possess a due portion of you at Monticello, where I am at length enjoying the never before known luxury of employing myself for my own gratification only. present my friendly salutations to Genl. Clarke, and be assured yourself of my constant & unalterable affections.

33429

Govr. Lewis.   Th Jefferson

Thomas Jefferson's plea, asking Meriwether Lewis to return to Washington and complete the Corps of Discovery journals, 1809 (Courtesy Library of Congress).

to sustain the idea of this great love. It is nearly impossible to imagine how she and her mother could have accommodated a relationship with anyone else. Still, the accident was a crushing blow. Batten stopped flying completely and slipped into seclusion with her mother until well into the autumn of 1937.

It was only when she heard that someone was planning to try and break her Britain-to-Australia record that the competition brought her briefly out of her shell. While the great pilot Jimmy Broadbent flew east, Batten headed off west, back to Britain, in a head-on speed contest that thrilled the public.

Batten treated the race like a cleansing by fire, pushing herself to the point of complete exhaustion, almost collapsing when she completed the stage of flight ending in Italy, but still recovering for a classic Batten arrival in Britain a few days later—clean and perfectly made-up. She not only won the race, but beat her own speed record by three hours.

It would be the last time the public would cheer Batten out of a plane. She was only twenty-eight years old, and she never flew again.

The remaining long years of Batten's life were a slow, painful spiral down; an agonizingly prolonged psychological crash (though with one brief, odd recovery from the dive in the late 1960s). After her last flight, Batten went on a public-speaking tour and began to write her sanctifying books, trying to keep her legend alive. Then, in the mid-1940s, she and her mother completely disappeared from public life. She had so few friends that she was able to vanish without anyone really noticing. The only ones to try to chase her down were a mildly curious media, but even they gave up.

Batten never clarified the reasons for her withdrawal. The best guess about this period is that the weight of maintaining her public persona became too much for her to bear. To both seek the public light and yet struggle with it is an intriguing contradiction, but not unheard of. At the core, celebrities are often uncomfortable with the attention they receive, but have an unresolved need to seek it. This seemed especially true in Jean Batten's case; her motives for seeking fame always seemed tortured, and her relations with others were often forced and contrived. It was a situation bound to flame out, especially when Jean was

Australia in five days, shaving twenty-four hours off the men's world record, in a single-engine time that would stand for forty-four years. She then crossed the Tasman Sea in nine-and-a-half hours, yet another record, and landed to a veritable crowning—Ian Mackersey called it one of the greatest events in New Zealand history. If Jean Batten ever needed confirmation of her place in the stars, she could now see it written everywhere: "The most extraordinary woman in existence," said one paper, while another called her "Her Serene Highness."

Quite rightly, as it would turn out, Batten said that she was at the high point of her life.

———————

Even when considering the most difficult personalities there is still room for sympathy, for appreciating the circumstances that created their rough edges, and recognizing that they suffer many of the same pains and disappointments as the rest of us, even though they may have a stronger hand in bringing those troubles upon themselves. In Jean Batten's case, you can understand, if not forgive, the egocentricity and the treatment of others if you understand the warped symbiosis she had with her mother. Ellen's control of and enmeshment with her daughter was so profound that Jean was never able to function completely as a separate person, and never seemed to develop a realistic measure of her self and her entitlements. She was consequently, as one acquaintance characterized her to Ian Mackersey, "a terribly lonely person."

Other than her relationship with her mother, there was only one other connection that Batten suggests touched her at all, and perhaps she deserves some sympathy for how tragically it ended. This man, whom she had managed to spend only brief periods with between her flights, was tragically killed while a passenger on a commercial flight in New South Wales, Australia in February 1937. For days, Batten flew her Gull up and down the state looking for the wreckage, until it was discovered by another party.

In her first autobiography, written a year after the crash, Batten only refers to the man as her "great friend," and it took considerable digging by the Mackerseys to discover how important a role he had actually played in her life. It was a tragic ending to Batten's "one true love," but sadly, the death may have been the only thing that allowed her

Solomon Andrée's Eagle, *trailing draglines as it descends perilously after launch, July 11, 1897 (© Grenna Museum / The Swedish Society for Anthropology and Geography).*

The crash of the Eagle, *July 14, 1897 (Photo: Nils Strindberg, © Grenna Museum / The Swedish Society for Anthropology and Geography).*

Jean Batten at Rongotai Airport, Wellington (© Alexander Turnbull Library).

Jean Batten and friend at Rongotai Airport, Wellington (© Alexander Turnbull Library).

Aleister Crowley, master of magick (Courtesy Ordo Templii Orientis).

*Aleister Crowley in unusual garb, en route to Kangchenjunga, 1905
(Courtesy Ordo Templii Orientis).*

Preparing Claudio Corti's rescue, on the summit of the Eiger (Collection of the International Commission for Alpine Rescue).

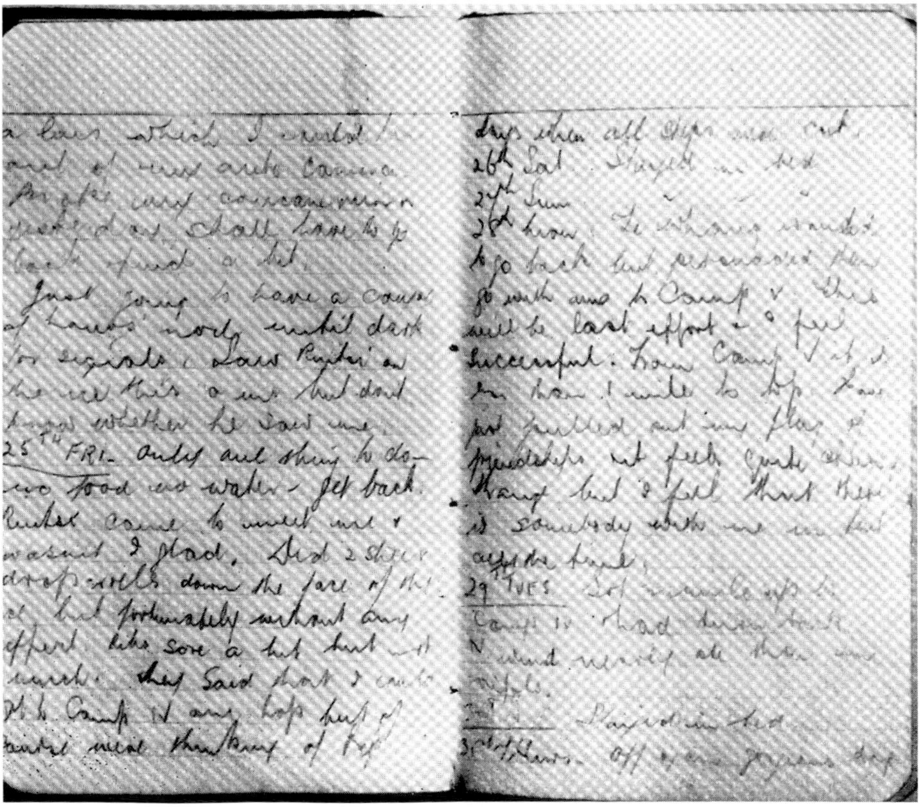

a [illegible] which I [illegible]
[illegible]
[illegible]
[illegible] shall have to go
back [illegible] a bit.
Just going to have a couple
of hours' work until dark
for signals. Saw Rinzi on
the ice this a.m. but don't
know whether he saw me.
25th FRI. Only one thing to do —
no food no water — get back.
Rinzi came to meet me &
wasn't I glad. Had 2 sheer
drop-offs down the face of the
[illegible] but fortunately without any
effect. Ribs sore a bit but not
much. They said that I could
[illegible] Camp III any [illegible]
[illegible] thinking of [illegible]

days when all shops were out.
26th Sat. Stayed in bed.
27th Sun [illegible]
28th Mon. [illegible] wanted
to go back but persuaded them
go with me to Camp V & this
will be last effort & I feel
successful. From Camp V [illegible]
[illegible] I have
just pulled out my flag of
friendship [illegible]
[illegible] but I feel that there
is somebody with me [illegible]
all the time.
29th TUES. [illegible]
Camp [illegible]
[illegible]
[illegible]
[illegible] Stayed in bed.
31st Thurs. Off again, gorgeous day.

The final pages of Maurice Wilson's diary (Courtesy The Alpine Club, London).

Tenzing Norgay and Earl Denman near Darjeeling (Courtesy Graham Denman).

Sage's Ravine, Connecticut: Guy and Johnny Waterman on Johnny's first ice climbing trip (Courtesy Laura Waterman).

no longer getting continuous affirmation from flying. Her disappearance at the top of her game, becoming "the Garbo of the skies" in newspaper headlines, was a far better cap to her legend than the more public dissolution that her behavior seemed to predict would be inevitable.

But withdrawing from the world hardly guaranteed happiness: by all accounts, the next decades were empty and sad, as Jean and Ellen moved between a series of tropical escapes, staying almost exclusively in each other's company. Ian Mackersey's research shows that Jean likely had a series of brief affairs, but basically she lived in hibernation with her mother until Ellen died in her arms in 1966.

Predictably, this was a shattering event, leaving Batten rudderless until she came up with a vain—in both senses of the word—plan: she would become Jean Batten the famous pilot again. After a period of troubled grieving after Ellen's death, Batten had a facelift, dyed her hair, bought a fashionably short miniskirt (at least it was fashionable for a twenty-year-old in 1969; it made the sixty-year-old Batten look disturbingly foolish) and announced her rebirth to the British press.

The press vacillated between treating her with respect and writing her up as an oddity dug out of a dusty attic, but Batten acted as though she had never been gone. Although it was unsettling from a sixty-year-old, and far less successful than it once had been, Batten pulled out the seductive flirtatious act again.

She also showed her other side again, being as icily demanding as ever, just as dramatic, needy, irritating, and rude. She still overstayed her welcome and left people speechless in her histrionic wake. Although her behavior could be disturbing, she also surprised many people by succeeding with it. For years, Batten managed to make a living appearing at public events, and could still rivet a crowd with her stories.

And then, just as she had disappeared in the 1940s—suddenly and with no trace—she vanished again in the mid-1970s. It was only through the persistent interest of the Mackerseys, who had become fascinated with Batten during her brief resurrection, that anyone—including Jean Batten's family—ever learned that Jean had finally disappeared anonymously into the expatriate community in Mallorca, and had found her peace in an unmarked pauper's grave.

Aleister Crowley, likely at Cambridge, c. 1895 (Courtesy Ordo Templii Orientis).

CHAPTER 7

ALEISTER CROWLEY

The Wickedest Man in the World

"CROWLEY. HE WAS INSANE."

When I started casting about for thoughts of who should be part of this book, one vote seemed to be unanimous, at least among mountaineers:

"Aleister Crowley. He was a madman. Crazy."

"He pulled a gun on somebody on an expedition, for God's sake."

"Hedonist."

"Satanist."

"Did you know his body was hacked into pieces when he died and the parts were placed at the corners of a devil worshipper's pentagram?"

"He was a drug-addicted sex-fiend."

. . . And proud of it.

For a time, Aleister Crowley was one of the most accomplished mountaineers in the world: one of the first to touch the Himalaya, the first on giant K2. He was also a published poet and author of some renown, an acclaimed Orientalist, a yogic master, and a ranked chess player, but these would never be the things that he would be remembered for. The reason that Crowley is the subject of a surprising number of biographies, is written into heavy metal songs, and even had his face pasted into the montage on the cover of The Beatles' album *Sergeant Pepper's Lonely Hearts Club Band*, is certainly not his achievements in climbing: He is best known for his self-anointed role as prophet of the dark occult forces and magus of a bizarre pagan stew of a religion. Crowley may have been a thousand complex things, but he was perhaps best at manufacturing the enduring drama of his own legend. Even in the sometimes painfully self-glorifying, edge-walking world of adventurers, he has no equal.

He called himself The Beast—as in the Great Beast 666, the Father of Darkness, Satan. Even more dramatically (always Crowley's forte), he liked to tell people that his own mother was the first to call him that. "My mother actually believed that I was the Anti-Christ of [the] Apocalypse," he wrote, but he made it clear he wore her shame of him like a badge of honor. Shame when she should have been "in awe," Crowley cursed, was just another signature of his mother's "shallow stupidity."

But even Crowley, who usually reveled in drawing a uniformly sinister picture of himself, admitted that his life was not always so dark.

Born into privilege in rural England, Crowley was the only surviving child of a father from a family with a lucrative centuries-old brewing business, and a mother from a devout Christian home. The Crowleys enjoyed inherited prosperity, which gave them servants, fine houses, and the ability to give young Alec, as the boy was then called, the finest schooling alongside the aristocracy of Britain. Crowley wrote that he adored his father and, despite his later rages at his mother, hinted that he also shared a close bond with her. On the surface there was little in Alec's early years that directly forecast his future—but seeds had been planted.

Of all the characters in this book, Crowley left the most detailed record of his early life; but as several of his biographers—and even Crowley himself—have pointed out, the details provided by Crowley do need to be read skeptically. He archly insisted that as he was "trying to explain greatness" in describing his life, "mysterious events which not even I can divine" are part of his story—including some events that seem highly unlikely, and some that clearly never happened.

Crowley claimed, for example, that his birth was marked by religious portents from both Eastern and Western traditions. His mother gave birth near midnight on October 12, 1875, in the quiet resort town of Leamington Spa northwest of London. The day of the birth saw a tremendous, once-in-a-century storm flood the small town, destroying homes and allegedly forcing his mother into premature labor. Crowley called the flood "the heralding," with all Christian significance pretentiously intended.

Crowley also wrote that he was born "tongue-tied like the Buddha." This grandiose claim relied on twisting myth to fit his self-aggrandizing story: There is no record of the Buddha being "tongue-tied," yet this was the "sign" that most prominently stamped Crowley for the rest of his life. Being "tongue-tied" refers not only to the familiar expression; it is also a medical condition in which the fraenum, the connective tissue on the bottom of the tongue, extends to the front of the mouth, making it impossible to speak. Crowley's fraenum had to be cut, leaving him with a speech impediment that drew ridicule when he was a child, and left him sounding odd as an adult. Crowley's imagination alone transformed the unfortunate affliction into a mark of alleged "divinity."

A more realistically vital seed of Crowley's future was the strong religion in the home. Crowley's father Edward had retired from the family business at age twenty-six and had become a fully committed member of the Plymouth Brethren, a breakaway sect of Quakers that insisted on the literality of the Bible and on the immediacy of the Rapture of the Second Advent (the return of Christ that would see all disbelievers cleansed from the earth).

So strong was the Brethren's faith in the Rapture that they insisted that members never show any sign of doubt of the prophesy. The true believer would understand that the coming of God would take care of everything—which meant no mortgages, no life insurance, or plans for retirement. Once he connected with the Brethren, Crowley's father gave up the "sin of brewing ale" and spent the rest of his life preaching his evangelical cause, both in public and in his family.

Critical biographies of Crowley almost universally pin the blame for his adult excesses on the fundamentalism in his home; and yet by all firsthand accounts, including his own, Crowley worshipped his father and had little trouble accepting the stringencies of his religion. Crowley was harbored within the self-contained Brethren community, and its strictures, no matter how constraining they might appear from the outside, were all he knew. The Brethren ways made complete sense to the boy; it was Edward Crowley's death that more truly changed his life.

When Crowley was ten, his father was diagnosed with cancer of the tongue. Instead of getting medical treatment, Edward turned to a homeopath from within the Brethren, and was dead within the year. Crowley described the devastation he felt, and his subsequent problems, in his autobiographical *Confessions* (referring to himself in the third person, as he always did until he was "reincarnated" by the death of his father):

> From the moment of the funeral the boy's life entered on an entirely new phase. The change was radical. Within three weeks of his return to school he got into trouble for the first time. He does not remember for what offence, but only that his punishment was diminished on account of his bereavement. This was the first symptom of a complete reversal of his attitude to life in every respect. It seems obvious that his father's death must have been causally connected with it. But even so, the events remain inexplicable. The conditions of his school life, for instance, can hardly have altered, yet his reaction to them makes it almost incredible that it was the same boy.

The "trouble" that Crowley is referring to was his questioning of the Bible in school, a shocking thing for a Brethren child. In this regard, Alec's acting up seemed pointedly aimed at his mother. In her mourning, (which Crowley acidly called her "Hysteria of Widowhood"), Emily Crowley immersed herself in the more fanatical elements of the Brethren practice, separating herself from friends who were not as rigidly devout as she was, and pulling her already awkward child into even greater isolation.

Like many children who lose a parent, especially at the beginning of adolescence, Crowley sanctified the memory of the lost parent while blaming all the turmoil he was feeling on the one left behind. He increasingly remembered Edward as a perfect, pious, and fair man while he vilified Emily as "a brainless bigot of the most narrow, logical and inhuman type."

His anger at his mother was only the first taste of Crowley's lifelong streak of open misogyny, which was one of the more loathsome aspects of his character, but was completely in keeping with the Brethren's view of women as lesser beings.

Much of the rage underlying Crowley's life seems to revolve around his predicament of hating the church and its effect on his mother, while finding himself inadvertently following many of its root tenets. Condemning the Brethren in his *Confessions,* Crowley sounds as though he might be speaking about his own dilemmas and rationalizations:

> *An irreligious man may have moral checks, a Plymouth Brother has none. He is always ready to excuse the vilest crimes by quoting the appropriate text and invoking the name of Christ to cover every meanness which may delight his vain and vicious nature. For the Plymouth Brethren were in themselves an exceptionally detestable crew.*

Fighting back against his mother and her church would become a mission that arguably dominated most of his life. Through his "boyhood in hell," Crowley battled at every opportunity, and Emily and the church tried everything they could to control him.

Crowley was furious when his mother took him to live with her brother Tom, of whom he wrote: "No more cruel fanatic, no meaner villain, ever walked this earth." Tom and Emily felt the cure for Alec was an even more rigid application of fundamentalist principles, but it was not at all successful: Every action was met with dramatic resistance from Alec.

When Tom's strict controls failed, Crowley was packed off to a Brethren boarding school, the Ebor School, that would seem severe in a Dickens novel. The once-placid boy was soon the worst offender in the ranks, enduring lashings, canings, being shunned—forbidden to speak or be spoken to—and being given no more than bread and water to eat for a full term and a half.

Exactly what it was that he was doing to deserve these punishments is unclear in Crowley's accounts, but several of his biographers have reasonably suggested that Crowley was likely being targeted because of perceived homosexual or masturbatory leanings. The Ebor School, like many Victorian boarding schools, would have been obsessed with the danger of sexuality in its children. (Presuming he had such inclinations is not much of a stretch, as Crowley later wrote that he "jumped into masturbation with as much enthusiasm as anything in [his] life," proclaiming it "a sin worth sinning.") But at the time, Crowley was confused about the reason for his punishment, so he did what many angry adolescents do: upped the ante so the discipline at least seemed justified. "I simply went over to Satan's side," he wrote; "and to this hour I cannot tell why."

Moving to Satan's side meant questioning the literality of the Bible (a near-mortal sin in his mother's eyes) and committing acts that got Crowley into a storm of trouble outside the family as well. He exploded bombs, spiked school meals with mild poisons, and—the hallmark sign of a budding sociopath—tortured animals. The fourteen-year-old Crowley, however, insisted there was "no question of sadism or cruelty" in his "experiment":

> *I got it into my head that the nine lives of the cat must be taken more or less simultaneously. I therefore caught a cat, and having administered a large dose of arsenic I chloroformed it, hanged it above the gas jet, stabbed it, cut its throat, smashed its skull and, when it had been pretty thoroughly burnt, drowned it and threw it out of the window that the fall might remove the ninth life. In fact, the operation was successful; I had killed the cat.*

As he would do many times in his life, Crowley made a leap of logic to rationalize his behavior—especially when it came to explaining how he could manage to honor the religion of his pious father, but at the same time fight against the injustices he believed he suffered at the hands of his mother and the Brethren.

Crowley's justification for his troubled behavior involved convincing himself that by sinning "thoroughly" he was attempting to impel the most profound spiritual awareness and thus draw himself closer to God. It was a convoluted justification that he ran with for the rest of his life.

Crowley was also convinced that in surviving his punishments he was showing himself to be stronger than any of his persecutors. He believed he had to continue to strengthen himself by earning punishments. He wrote that he suffered a "strain of congenital masochism," a trait that almost killed him in his final year at Ebor, when the continued shunning became too much for the boy to stand emotionally.

Crowley was saved from himself only when he was pulled from the school with myriad illnesses, real and psychosomatic. Several of his illnesses, especially asthma and kidney disorders, would trouble him for the rest of his life. It took Crowley more than a year to recover, during which time Emily gave up on a miracle cure from her own brother and took Alec to live with his father's brother Jonathan. This second uncle's conviction that the boy needed physical labor to cure his ills opened the door to the stage of Crowley's life that brings him into this book.

———————————

In the summer of 1892, Emily Crowley traveled with Alec to the Isle of Skye, hoping that the mountain environment might smooth his still-angry edges. But instead of sitting peacefully in nature with his mother, the oddly engaging sixteen-year-old attracted the attention of a group of climbers staying at a nearby hostel. One of the group was Joseph Lister, later *Sir* Joseph, the founder of antiseptic surgery and a keen mountaineer. Lister encouraged a team to take Alec (who by then was calling the rougher version of himself "Alick"—the first of his many rechristenings) out on a traverse of one of the long, exposed, and loose Cuillin ridges. It was a thrilling day that hooked Crowley on climbing.

Another temptation that same summer was to prove equally compelling and more lasting. One of the many tutors his mother hired for him—one of the rare ones that Crowley did not drive away—decided that the boy's problems lay in everything interesting being forbidden. Taking exactly the opposite approach, he introduced Crowley to smoking, drinking, card playing, and convinced him that sex could be pleasure instead of sin. It is unclear whether the man merely arranged sex for Crowley, or *had* sex with the boy, but he clearly had a profound effect: Crowley later wrote, "I shall not easily forget my debt to him." The boy returned from the summer no longer a virgin and committed to pursuing sex with as much vigor as climbing, though rarely without an undercurrent of guilt.

Crowley stumbled into climbing at a time of great change in the sport in Britain. The old guard of the heyday of genteel Victorian alpinism was slowly fading out of the game, but they were rabid in their criticism of a new breed of climbers exploring much more technical rock climbing. Crowley fell in with the latter crowd, and happily adopted their rebellion against what the group saw as the stagnant mediocrity of the old school. Perhaps as an extension of his "congenital masochism," Crowley also gleefully embraced the new climbers' ethos of taking the risk of a climb as a measure of its worth. As the questionable gear and the pushy styles and ethics of the new climbing spelled almost certain death if a fall was taken, real risk was what the new game was all about.

Crowley's natural skill and risk tolerance quickly elevated him above many of the older climbers around him, but it was his unalloyed ego that really set him apart. Being able to present himself as fearless was a heady, ego-inflating intoxication for an adolescent like Crowley. After years of seeing himself as weak and sickly, Crowley suddenly found that he was getting recognized for his natural talent; unfortunately, Crowley handled the attention poorly, puffing himself up to the point that he openly sneered at others' limitations.

When Crowley realized that he was able to keep his head together in situations that kept others off hard climbs, he started swaggering about the climbing community, braying about his successes. Within just a few months of learning the rudiments of the nascent hard-rock game, Crowley was turning on his teachers, declaring them "imbeciles" and claiming that they did not deserve their reputations. Whenever he could, he would try to take the wind out of other climbers' sails. In one instance he scrawled *"Advertisement!"* at the end of a description of a climb that he felt had been unjustly glorified in a climber's hut log. In another, he famously ridiculed the ascent of an easy climb "by a 'lady,'" by repeating the route with his dog. Crowley's snide and typically misogynistic entry in the log read: "First ascent by a St. Bernard bitch."

As he would for the rest of his life, Crowley drove people away shaking their heads in amazement and irritation. But as he baldly claimed in *Confessions,* he believed he had been given a mission: Crowley intended to show people what real climbing was. "I must admit that my methods were sometimes calculated to annoy;" he wrote, "but I had no patience with the idiotic vanity of mediocrity."

Crowley's conceit was not entirely unwarranted, however. From very early on he was climbing harder and more boldly than were the people around him, trying new techniques and pioneering the use of equipment that would not be universally accepted for nearly half a century. Crowley, however, made no secret of the fact that he was seeking fame, or that he believed he deserved it.

In climbing, fame meant breaking new ground, and in his second summer on rock, Crowley found his venue. Vacationing with a cousin and his tutor on the south coast of Britain, Crowley became obsessed with the idea of climbing the 500-foot white chalk cliffs of nearby

Beachy Head. The source of the obsession certainly was not aesthetic, as the "rock" of the cliff is little more than compressed, dusty mud that is miserable and dangerous to climb. Instead, Crowley was drawn to the crag primarily because it had repelled attempts by many of the best climbers of the previous fifty years, and was obviously a place to stake his claim. Beachy had been declared unclimbable "except by a madman"; Crowley accepted that warning as an invitation.

Over the course of two weeks, Crowley pushed three new routes on the wall which truly were of an unprecedented caliber of difficulty and risk. Often unable to get any form of protection, Crowley effectively free-soloed, at a technical standard that would not be matched for years. Brian Wyvill, a British climber who made the second ascent of one of Crowley's chalk routes, described the climb as "terrifying," even with modern skills and tools. Nearly ninety years after Crowley, Wyvill and his partners had ice axes, crampons, and ice screws to forge their way up the continuously shedding cliff; Crowley had used nothing but his fingers and toes, occasionally resorting to scraping out a hole for his chin so he could manage to give his arms a rest. Crowley blithely described his technique for ascending chalk: "One does not climb the cliffs. One hardly even crawls. Trickles or oozes would perhaps be the ideal verbs."

The hardest of Crowley's routes would eventually be given a modern grade of 5.10, astounding for 1893; but if Crowley thought he was going to earn a name for climbing so close to the edge, he was mistaken. Crowley was dismissed as a braggart by climbers, and the local papers called the climbs "insensate folly." As always, Crowley shot back, swearing that the critics were fools themselves. Besides, Crowley pointed out (channeling his acquaintance Oscar Wilde), a bad reputation was better than no reputation at all.

That summer at Eastbourne, Crowley also took his first steps to pursuing sex with as much commitment as climbing. Contracting the first of many bouts of venereal disease, he treated the "clap from a Glasgow prostitute" with as little concern as he had viewed any of his risks.

Crowley's campaign for fame and his hunt for dramatic experiences played out in other arenas as well. He began writing and publishing poetry that pushed limits, just as he did in climbing. His poetry, seen by some as a breakthrough and by more as simply offensive, was as openly erotic as anything seen in public at the time. Crowley was as modest about his writing as he was about his climbing; in his autobiography, he noted that the county of his birth, Warwickshire, had produced the two greatest poets in the English language: Shakespeare and, well, Crowley.

Sex, climbing, poetry: They were all simply interesting turns on the journey of experimentation that Crowley was starting to map out for himself. Crowley's directions for the journey were as simple as the climbing on Beachy Head: fear nothing. The goal of life, he wrote, "was simply to escape from the oppressors and enjoy the world without interference of spiritual life of any sort." If his goal was a problem for anyone, he added, the blame for his lusty pursuits lay not with him but with his "oppressors," as they were the ones who had passed him "bound and blindfolded to the outraged majesty of nature."

He intended, he explained, to endulge that majesty "without limits."

By the time Crowley entered Cambridge University, his world was dramatically different. He was no longer an awkward teen, but had morphed into a handsome, athletic man. Reaching majority, he had inherited a fortune from his father's estate worth about $20 million today, and this wealth opened a thousand new doors. No longer under the thumb of his mother, uncles, and tutors, Crowley was free to choose from a hundred tempting options—or, as he sometimes elected, to choose them all.

As a student at Cambridge, he found himself in a stimulating intellectual world where his ideas and actions were accepted as daring and novel instead of being dismissed as foolish or obscene. Crowley celebrated the change by rechristening himself again—this time as "Aleister," a Gaelic name he felt suited his literary stature better—and he started barging through the free-swinging doors of his new world.

During his university summers Crowley uncovered the Alps, going first to the Tyrol in 1895, where he performed well, then the following summer to the Bernese Oberland. There he made impressively fast ascents of the famous kings of the region, the Eiger, the Mönch, and the Jungfrau, and completed first ascents, some of them solo, on several lesser peaks. Even climbers who had initially been repelled by his arrogance—notably Britain's Alpine heroes Norman Collie and A.F. Mummery—began trumpeting Crowley's talents.

Although Crowley's writing betrays a hint of pride about receiving this recognition, he was soon up to his old tricks, pompously challenging anyone's right to gauge his accomplishments, given that his skills were "so far superior." He ridiculed the guides that his British peers most often relied on, complaining with imperious condescension that the guides he met were "superstitious and ignorant peasants" who were "often drunk" and incompetent. He sneered at the prestigious Alpine Club, which promptly banned him for life. No bother, Crowley concluded; he was better off alone anyway. "I found," he wrote, "that I could go pretty well anywhere without the least danger or difficulty, whereas all the people I met were constantly on the brink of disaster."

Other developments in Crowley's life at Cambridge were more complex and less predictable. Hovering in the margins of university life ("I was not interested in the average man; I cultivated the freak," he wrote), and refusing to "lower" himself by pursuing a degree, Crowley grew increasingly engrossed in expanding his sensual experiences. "Hunting new sins," he dabbled in drugs, socialized in the world of alternative art and literature, and began exploring Eastern mysticism, always promoting his activities as avant-garde "challenges to the mediocrity."

If Crowley's acts of self-important rebellion and his challenges to the prevailing climbing standards had been the limit of his "excesses," he would have been in good company in risk sports. The films, literature, and fireside legends of adventure are filled with larger-than-life characters who push back against the status quo, walk along a finer edge of risk than the generation before them, and act as though their talents should be recognized as a revelation.

But even within the risk community, there is little question that there are people whose behaviors cross a line and seem pointless, disturbed, or even dangerous—so much so that their achievements are tainted. Crowley is an interesting example. There is little question that he was talented and made noteworthy contributions to contemporary adventure (more so than many of the characters in this book), but his "oddities," to describe them gently, almost completely shroud his accomplishments.

No matter how fine a climber Crowley was, his inner turmoils were always more the story. Crowley may have set climbing standards that stood for several generations, but he also evolved into an abrasive, drug-addicted, and sexually exploitative man who helped to ruin the lives of many people who brushed up against him.

In late 1896, when he was twenty-one, Crowley faced an aspect of himself that would endure as one of his most resilient struggles. Previously voraciously and adamantly heterosexual, Crowley started an extended relationship with a man whom his biographer Richard Kaczynski calls "the first intimate friend in [his] sheltered life."

It was a difficult, conflicted step. While Crowley openly acknowledged the relationship with the actor Herbert Pollitt as one of the most blissful and true of his life, at the same time he always claimed that this and all of his many subsequent homosexual experiences were motivated purely by a pursuit of the enlightenment that this "most shameful" desire could impel, while never acknowledging that he actually had the desire himself.

The depth of Crowley's conflict could be partly explained by the times—the authorities of Victorian England rabidly condemned "nonproductive" sexual acts such as masturbation and homosexuality as the most grievous sins. But Crowley's ambivalence about his fundamentalist roots made his battle against the hypocrisies of the time a far more complex and personal issue than it was for others fighting homophobia. Many artists opened the door to erotic expression, and several suggested that sexuality held a mysterious, magical power, but Crowley took both paths to their furthest extremes.

Clearly struggling against the rules of his Brethren past, Crowley sculpted a complex rationalization to explain his attraction to men: Facing—and overindulging—what "most disgusted" him would be a path to knowledge. "It was an experience of horror and pain," Crowley explained, " . . . yet at the same time, it was the key to the purest and holiest spiritual ecstasy that exists."

The "revelation" that he experienced with Pollitt, and his circuitous rationalization of it, pushed Crowley into the world that became the focus of the rest of his life: the pursuit of spiritual revolution through the practice of "sex magick" (spelled this way by Crowley to highlight the alleged profundity of his system). It wasn't an original approach; in looking to sex to free the soul, Crowley joined a centuries-old occult tradition that ran through Hinduism, Tantric yoga, Gnosticism, Rosicrucianism, and Freemasonry, and was enjoying a renaissance in Europe when he stumbled upon it at the turn of the twentieth century. But with the same modesty he brought to mountaineering, Crowley crowned himself the master of the art not long after he began his studies in 1896.

Crowley leapt into the arcane and opaque rituals and literature of dark magic and was soon initiated into one of the most prominent mystical associations. The Golden Dawn was an ancient order that included a number of British intellectuals, including the poet W.B. Yeats. Crowley raced up through the ranks of the Dawn through the last years of the century. Crowley liked to claim that his quick climb was attributable to his unparalleled powers, but according to contemporary mystics, his rank was unjustly awarded by orders more than glad to accept his money.

In either case, Crowley soon began to rewrite his own history to fit his growing reputation in the occult community. Everything about his life, Crowley insisted—from the symbols of his birth to the successes of his climbing—pointed directly to his unique magical faculties. But Crowley began to make so many claims of profound mystical experiences that he was soon as unpopular in magical circles as he was in mountaineering. He handled this condemnation just as he did in climbing: He eventually split from the Dawn in 1906, and charted his own path in which he was the sole master, and, in his words, the "herald of a new era of mankind."

Crowley's new esoteric society, the Argentium Astrum, (referred to more commonly by its enigmatic symbol, A.·.A.·.), involved a fantastically exaggerated version of the rituals of the ancient orders, complete with psychotropic drugs, bestiality, homosexuality, blood-letting, and even rumors of sacrifices—which Crowley both angrily denied and happily fueled in equal measures throughout his life. Crowley ostentatiously claimed to have channeled the founding spirits of the Golden Dawn and summoned demons to do his bidding, and also to have achieved levels of power never conceived of by previous masters. These claims infuriated competing magicians, including Yeats, whom Crowley insisted was attempting to kill him telepathically. (Crowley absurdly insisted, however, that Yeats's fight against him was motivated by Yeats's jealousy of his talents as a *poet,* not as a magician.)

———————

Through all of these turns, Crowley also continued to climb, though he now insisted that climbing, like sex, was a test of his magical, rather than his physical, power. In 1898, Crowley found a partner with as grand ambitions in the mountains, though perhaps more grounded motives. Oscar Eckenstein was a powerful climber with a strong résumé in the Alps, and nearly as poor a reputation as Crowley's in the climbing community. Vocal and condescending to anyone whom he judged less competent than himself, Eckenstein had alienated the Alpine Club and most other British climbers, despite his genius at developing technique and equipment, including the modern crampon. (Eckenstein so angered the leading British climber Martin Conway that Conway essentially excised him from the record of the first expedition to the Karakorum Himalaya in 1892. Conway later claimed that Eckenstein had attempted to poison him on the expedition.)

Although they were an odd pair off the mountain—the arch sensualist Crowley chasing orgasms with prostitutes and virgins to master corporeal transcendence, while the ultra-rational Eckenstein struggled to corral Crowley's excesses—they got along like fire and brimstone in the hills, setting records in the Alps and boasting their superiority to anyone who would listen.

In 1900, Eckenstein proposed a radical plan: The pair would climb K2, the fiercest of the 8000-meter Himalayan giants. Eckenstein had fallen under the spell of the great mountain on Conway's expedition, and understood that an ascent would be a mammoth achievement. To Crowley, climbing a mountain as large as K2 would be proof of his magical prowess; to the scientist Eckenstein, it would offer a very different challenge—to examine and overcome the problems of high altitude. The difference in the men's approaches was highlighted during a training expedition to the high volcanoes near Mexico City: Eckenstein came prepared to rigorously test his hypotheses about acclimatization; Crowley spent weeks in an opium stupor surrounded by a harem of Mexican prostitutes to harness his sexual magic. Each man later claimed that the success they enjoyed on the volcanoes, including several first ascents, was due to his own unique training regimen.

It took two years to assemble the K2 team and get permission to travel on the Baltoro Glacier. In that time, Crowley descended deeper into the underworld of magic. Living in a new base at Boleskine Castle on the shores of Loch Ness, Crowley was dangerously pushing the limits of his drug exploration, and was involved in increasingly perverse rituals with his many sexual partners. He continued to publish his poetry, most of which was execrable and poorly received, and he was spending more time creating books on his magic, many of which never sold a copy. Crowley escaped increasing local outrage about his rumored activities at the castle only when he started his long journey to the Himalaya in 1901. On the trip, Crowley alternated between indulging his opium addiction and sexual excesses, and committing to genuine, ascetic study of yoga and Buddhism.

By the time Crowley reached the mountain, he was exhausted, suffering from a number of illnesses, and battling almost all his teammates, even Eckenstein. Partly as a result of Crowley's insisting on hauling an enormous library to base camp (which he believed was his privilege, because he was funding the trip) the expedition had ballooned to nearly 250 men, which made it painfully slow to mobilize.

Crowley was histrionically dramatic in his outbursts, beating porters and hectoring the team, the members of which he described as nothing more than "a nuisance." In the most notorious conflict on the expedition, Crowley pulled a gun on Guy Knowles, the only English climber he and Eckenstein could seduce to join them on K2. In the descriptions of the episode written into adventure history, Crowley exploded into inexplicable anger and threatened to kill Knowles if he did not agree to follow him up the mountain after a dangerous storm. Crowley's occult biographers have been kinder, apologizing for him by saying that he was delirious with malarial fever at the time. Crowley himself never wrote about the matter.

Despite all its troubles, the expedition actually succeeded in reaching above 22,000 feet on the mountain, the highest altitude yet reached on any mountain at that time—and the achievement was almost exclusively due to Crowley's skills and drive. In spite of his illness, Crowley was by far the strongest member of the team, in the end pushing alone to the high camp. The expedition failed when one of the "completely intolerable" Austrian members came down with pulmonary edema and had to be evacuated.

To the anger of the other team members, Crowley dubiously claimed that he could have reached the summit if the others had not held him back. After the long road out, Eckenstein and the rest of the team had little more to do with Crowley. Just as Conway had excised Eckenstein from his K2 trip, the Crowley expedition's achievements disappeared from most contemporary histories as well.

Returning to Britain, Crowley acknowledged that he was feeling lost and in need of another of his "transformations." It came, this time, in the form of a woman whom Crowley described as the "most beautiful and fascinating being" he had ever seen. Rose Kelly was the sister of an occult acquaintance, and she was every bit as dramatic and impulsive as Crowley himself. Crowley proposed marriage the afternoon they met, and though she was already engaged, Rose accepted, marrying Crowley the following day in August, 1903.

It was a tragic decision: Her life with Crowley became a misery of sexual exploitation (which Crowley argued was mutual), and of drug abuse and alcoholism. Crowley initially held Rose up as an oracle whom he worshipped in awe—especially when she claimed to have channeled an ancient Egyptian god with a message about Crowley's divine purpose as the prophet of a new age—but their relationship was always turbulent. Their marriage lasted six years and ended with the devastating death of their only child, the gaudily named Nuit Ma Ahathoor Hecate Sappho Jezebel Lilith Crowley. The two-year-old succumbed to typhoid fever contracted in Asia, where Rose had dragged the child in pursuit of Crowley on one of his eclectic pilgrimages. Rather than accepting any responsibility himself, Crowley publicly blamed Nuit's death on Rose's weakness as a mother. Buckling under the weight of abuse from Crowley, the shame of her daughter's death, and her drug use during her time in Crowley's hands, Rose permanently checked herself into a mental institution not long after the divorce. She was the first of several of Crowley's women driven either to suicide or madness.

While his marriage was spiraling downward, in 1905 Crowley committed to another Himalayan expedition: an attempt on the third highest mountain in the world, the massive 28,207-foot Kangchenjunga. The leader of the trip was a Swiss doctor, Jacot Guillarmod, whom Crowley flatly dismissed as an "inexplicable imbecile."

The expedition was an unqualified disaster, scarred by four deaths, with as many controversies and episodes of bad behavior on Crowley's part as there had been on K2. Early in the expedition, Crowley had inserted himself into a role as climbing leader and made a number of absurdly dangerous decisions, but took no responsibility for the consequences— especially the deaths. In Crowley's view, he had once again been the only strength on the expedition, and felt that his contributions outweighed any obligation to feel "sympathy" for the losses, given that most members of the team had been rebelling against his leadership.

But Crowley's claim of only being "unsympathetic" grossly minimizes his behavior on the mountain. As even his most flattering biographies admit, when the second fatal accident happened—an avalanche just below his tent at Camp V—Crowley refused to budge from his sleeping bag, sipping tea while survivors screamed for help. For the next three days, while the others on the team dug out mutilated bodies, Crowley refused to join in.

The situation only worsened when the team came home without four members and without having come anywhere close to the summit. As he had done after K2, Crowley suggested that he would have been able to reach the top of the mountain had he not been saddled with a weak team. It was only when the fractured expedition returned to Europe, and other members publicly challenged his self-glorifying accounts, that Crowley paid the price for his arrogance. What little reputation Crowley still had for the technical merit of his climbing disappeared in the fallout from the tragedy, and his name was stricken from most climbing records of the era.

It is tempting to give Crowley some degree of sympathy for the burden he carried after Kangchenjunga, and to see the proof of his turmoil in the fact that he never climbed again after that 1905 expedition; in many ways, he never really moved forward again in other areas of his life either. But sympathizing with Crowley disregards all the troubles that were building well before his trials in the Himalaya. Kangchenjunga was the result, not the cause, of Crowley's actions; it simply marked the point where the angle of the downhill slide steepened.

Within a couple of years of Crowley's return to Britain, his daughter had died, his marriage had ended, and Crowley's "spiritual" journey detoured into darker and darker practices. By the beginning of World War I, Crowley's sexual magic was fueled by an astonishing mix of drugs taken daily: opium, ether, cocaine, laudanum, hashish, mescaline, and alcohol. Crowley wrote volumes about his carefully controlled, ritualized use of these "magical" agents to achieve transcendence, but his own ritual seems to have been no more profound than "take everything, every day."

In the last decades of his life, Crowley progressively distilled his magical philosophy until it amounted to little more than his signature phrase: "Do what thou wilt shall be the whole of the law." His occult biographers insist that this mantra, which Crowley called "Thelema" (from the Greek for "will"), was not permission for hedonistic self-indulgence, but instead involved a complex mission to discover and do the will of the universe. There is little evidence, however, that in Crowley's hands it led to anything other than unbridled debauchery.

Within a decade of Kangchenjunga, Crowley was a self-drawn caricature, courting any media attention he could get, outraging people whenever he could, acting, dressing, and writing more and more bizarrely. He bulldozed his way through the lives of a number of partners, male and female, several of whom were left broken by the degradation they suffered at Crowley's hands. He conceived three other children with the eleven magical concubines he called his "Scarlet Women," but, painfully for Crowley, he had virtually no contact with two of the children, who were secreted away by their mothers. Crowley was devastated when Poupée, the only child who had been kept a part of his life, died in infancy, just as his first daughter Nuit had died fifteen years earlier.

Wherever Crowley went, he found himself embroiled in controversy, surrounded by rumors of deaths, sacrifices, and depravities in his various homes, to the point that he was chased by authorities from one country to the next. In the 1920s, having squandered virtually all of his inherited funds, Crowley hid in the Abbey of Thelema, a commune of his followers on the island of Cefalù off the coast of Sicily.

For three years, Crowley subjected its residents to acting out his conviction that experiencing the "depths of Hell" and "worst of sins" would give them "permanent mastery of their minds." The outcome seemed quite different in reality: There were suicides in the aftermath of some of the degrading rituals, and multiple deaths from disease (not surprising when Crowley had people eating each other's feces as a ritual of purification). Finally, in 1923 Crowley was deported by Mussolini.

The last years of Crowley's life played out as a mess of self-constructed contradictions. He claimed to have reached the highest plane of awareness and physical strength, but he was obviously deteriorating. Photographs show him bloated, drawn, and suffering his various illnesses as well as the ravages of his addictions. Crowley alternately denied and exaggerated the rumors of excess in his "religion," writing books and poems that graphically described the rituals (such as the lurid *Diary of a Drug Fiend* and *A Ballad of Passive Pæderasty*). Then he turned on his heels and sued critics for libel because they dared suggest that he was practicing black magic. (Crowley himself acknowledged that the suits were frantic money grabs, as he was now bankrupt.) Crowley railed against any efforts to dismiss his magic as showmanship, but then ridiculed those "fools" who took him seriously at other times. The tabloid newspapers in Britain and America ate up his antics, labeling him "The Wickedest Man in the World," and Crowley reveled in the notoriety. To the moment of his death, people never quite knew what to make of Crowley.

Despite all the accusations of evil, despite the man's contradictions and bluster and transparent failings, when Crowley finally died, penniless and homeless, in 1947, he enjoyed as much renown as he ever had in his life—and things have only gotten better since. By the 1970s, his "do what thou wilt" was arguably a mantra for an entire generation, and various twists of his creed had been adopted as the core truths for any number of libertine and occult sects. Recognizing Crowley's influence, in 1969 *The Times of London* included Crowley in its list of the "1000 Makers of the 20th Century." In the 1990s, Crowley's name was added to Britain's august *Dictionary of National Biography*.

Crowley's rehabilitation in climbing circles has been as dramatic as it has been anywhere. The extent of his talents has been much easier to measure in hindsight. Also, by the late 1960s, the vanguard of climbing in both Europe and the United States was made up of characters who lived, at least some of the time, as though they were following Crowley's "do what thou wilt" law. The elegant and proper mountaineering carried out by the gentlemen Crowley despised was upstaged by dangerous climbs done by people fueled by beer in Britain and hallucinogens in America. Instead of retiring to their country estates and writing eloquent, poetic accounts of their ascents as their fathers had done, the new climbers danced like pagans on the edges of society, pissing on those who did not get their special message: Living like theirs was the best, the *only,* way to live, pushing the boundaries further than ever, with drugs, alcohol, rock and roll, or whatever made the new world possible. The change suddenly made Crowley seem, just as he had claimed all along, like a visionary of a radically different future, instead of simply a madman.

part 3: the lost

For several of the characters in this book—and thousands more outside these pages—adventure is a balm that can fill the holes in a life, or soothe its rough edges. The self-affirming thrills of risk and the grand scale of adventure can offer a promise of greater purpose, a connection to a more heroic history, or even simply be an escape from discontent with the everyday world.

But it is a very different matter when the hope for a cure for personal pain is the core reason for adventure.

When that kind of hope is the seed, there are just as many stories of disappointments, disintegrations and even deaths as there are of cures. There are pilgrims whose romantic notions about mountains are shattered by the brutish realities of high places; innocents who walk into wild deserts looking for redemption but find starvation; damaged souls like Claudine Juedel who set sail because they have lost their way, and end up losing their lives.

Still, there is an understandable attraction to the innocent dreams in the four stories that follow. To face the wilds—both of the self and of the world—equipped with faith and little else, is one of the great human journeys: a theme that runs throughout history, literature, and myth.

The characters in this section are the most difficult to measure and judge, both because their stories are more complex, and because they are the most clearly troubled souls described in this book. They have all had the label of "madness" applied to them more insistently than the explorers appearing in the previous chapters; but their stories also raise some of the most intriguing questions about the nature of that judgment.

And yet in many ways, these people are also arguably the most innocent, forgivable characters here. Their stories invite more ready understanding and compassion than those whose tales were solely about hubris or fame. All of the people in this section consequently have champions who hold them up as noble characters whose stories needed to be resurrected or redeemed of unfair criticisms by history—even when the redemption was a stretch. A perfect example is Dennis Roberts's view of Maurice Wilson. Roberts, a journalist in Britain in the 1950s, became fascinated by the story of Wilson's 1933 journey to Mount Everest when he accidentally stumbled upon it in old newspaper pieces about the "mad Yorkshireman."

Roberts brought Wilson's tale back from the dead, filling in an enormous number of blanks about the man, and trying to reestablish his place in the history of the great mountain. However, to make Wilson's story sound like a great adventurer's tale rather than the sad story of a lost soul, Roberts had to selectively choose what to include about him in his book *I'll Climb Mount Everest Alone*—and what to leave out.

Ironically, though Roberts ultimately wanted to make sure Wilson was admired by climbers and readers, he failed to some degree because his version of the story excluded much of Wilson's darker side, and this left Wilson looking even more naive and foolhardy than people already believed. Roberts was well-intentioned he simply wanted Wilson to be given a fair shake—but I think each of these people is better served if their tales are told fully. If Wilson was "crazy" and innocent in equal measures, to tell both sides of that story ultimately respects Wilson more.

The same is true for all of the characters here. Each has been both harshly judged, and viewed with compassion. Claudio Corti, who was involved in a terrible tragedy on the Eiger in 1957, was selected because his story is one of the most compelling examples of the problems raised by the adventure advocate's belief in the right of *every* person—even troubled people—to challenge themselves in risky places. Wilson's story is one of the best studies of a search for redemption in the wild. And Earl Denman's Everest story is a classic tale of emptiness and despair being not solved, but rather confirmed, by adventure. The final story in this book, of the American climber Johnny Waterman, his father, Guy, and his brother, Bill, is a rich example of the risks of adventure as both a cure—and a cause—of madness.

Claudio Corti, holding a picture of Stefano Longhi (Collection of the International Commission for Alpine Rescue).

CHAPTER 8

CLAUDIO CORTI

Only a Madman Would Try Such a Thing

THE DRAMA THAT HAD BEEN UNFOLDING over the long week had thousands of people enthralled. High up on the most notorious mountain face in the world, a team of four men had slowed to a crawl. Then, as storm clouds rolled over the top of the face and pulled a veil of winter over the mountain, they stopped moving altogether.

Rumors started to percolate among the captivated watchers at the base of the mountain, and in the minds of hundreds more devouring the daily press reports, that one man was dead, or two were, or that all four had perished.

The elite climbers of Europe started to gather in the village below the hill, offering their services to salvage any hope in what was obviously turning into a tragedy. There was no shortage of opinions among the climbers as they glimpsed hints of the drama on the wall through breaks in the clouds: Why had these men continued *up* when retreat was clearly the only sensible decision? How could anyone move so slowly and yet still believe they could climb such a face? Were they amateurs? It certainly appeared so from their routefinding choices. How much longer could they possibly survive in the worsening weather?

The media was filled with less informed, but far more vitriolic opinions. Climbers, not for the first time, were proving themselves to be fools. Enough was enough. They should be banned from this wall for their own good. No sensible man would think of setting foot on such a dark, obviously deadly, piece of stone; these thrill-seekers could obviously not be trusted with their own lives.

Arcing through it all, even for the climbers who completely understood the attraction of the great wall, was the thought that there was something terribly wrong with these people stuck high on the notorious *Eigerwand*. The opinion that the world was watching fools or madmen would magnify tenfold when the story became clear a tragic few days later—and all the judgments would fall onto the shoulders of one man.

So many people's understanding of mountaineering—and perhaps all risk sport—has been shaped by their exposure to Jon Krakauer's spellbinding account of the deadly 1996 season on Mount Everest. *Into Thin Air* was not only the best-selling adventure book of all time, it was also a scathing indictment of outdoor adventure at the turn of the twentieth century. Everest, the mountain that once was the ambition of every climber, had, in Krakauer's and many climbers' opinions, been reduced by the mid-1990s to little more than a carnival of narcissistically misguided characters stumbling over conflicted ambitions.

Of the many criticisms Krakauer leveled about the situation, the one that he and many other adventurers were particularly concerned about was the presence of several very inexperienced people on the mountain. To them it seemed ludicrous that anyone would have the arrogance to attempt to climb the highest mountain in the world without being tempered by years of preparation. Yet there was a waiting list of novices ready to invest enormous sums of money to be shepherded up the mountain by rapaciously competitive guiding companies. Equally troubling was that these same people appeared to have very little sense that the mountain was far out of their league; instead, they seemed to feel that they had as much right as any of the great climbers who had preceded them to be on Everest, and this illusion deeply influenced many of their actions. It seemed self-evident to many experts—well before the tragedy that killed thirteen people in May, 1996—that Everest was a disaster just waiting to explode.

While it is tempting to view the situation on Everest as a uniquely modern crisis—a culmination of the mix of commercialism, self-absorption, feelings of entitlement, and a demand for immediate gratification that plagues our culture—it is important to understand that the psychology that drove relative novices to Everest in 1996 is not unprecedented. The same pattern has happened—and continues to happen—in other eras and in other adventure sports. People who apparently have no place on a mountain or in the middle of the ocean *will* go if they can, and adventurers have always debated their rights to do so.

In the end, freedom usually wins out in the adventure community. We all, adventurers argue, must have the liberty to take chances. A decision to limit anyone's risk-taking is potentially a decision to limit everyone's. However, the freedom to risk is a liberty that comes packaged with the possibility of harsh judgment. To head into the wild with few skills, or to grossly overestimate the skills you have is not only an invitation to harm; it is also an invitation to be ridiculed, or even to be judged mad.

This was certainly the case when Claudio Corti stepped up to the base of the demon of the Alps, the Eiger, in 1957.

If *Into Thin Air* has a parent, it is Jack Olsen's *The Climb Up to Hell*. Olsen's 1962 book about Corti's tragic ascent of the Swiss mountain has the same tone of insight, criticism, and compassion as does *Into Thin Air*, all the more remarkable in Olsen's case because he did not have the insider's privilege that made Krakauer's book so rich. Olsen was an American journalist, with little experience of climbing, who became fascinated with the Eiger story after the fact, but dove into the characters and culture of alpinism with as much depth and rigor as Krakauer used to plumb the Himalayan scene.

The protagonist of Olsen's account was a twenty-nine-year-old Italian villager from Olginate, a small market factory town in the foothills of the Italian Alps. By all accounts, Claudio Corti was a simple man who came to climbing not as the result of any grand dream, but as the easy extension of childhood scrambles up the limestone crags around his town.

Corti had a hill peasant's build—short, lean and muscular—but his impressive strength did not always serve his climbing well. He could get up modest climbs through brute force, and occasionally managed even harder lines where strength was the key, but he never really developed the nuances needed for more demanding routes: a dancer's sense of balance and a chess-player's ability to calculate moves far out in advance. Corti's partners told Olsen that the Italian would attack climbs as though he were wrestling rather than seducing them.

What Corti had in spades were ambition and fearlessness, both of which allowed him to climb well above the level that his competency should have permitted. Several times, he got himself into trouble, though with consequences far more serious for his partners. On the jagged spire of the Piz Badile in the Italian Alps, Corti saw the first of several rope-mates perish; another died less than two years later, tied to him on a crag closer to home. In the Alps two years later, Corti and another partner came within an angel's breath of death when they both fell off the Petit Dru in the Mont Blanc range.

It took Corti nearly six months to recover from his injuries, but he handled the setback exactly as he had the deaths and other close calls: He saw them as signs to climb harder. When his partners died, Corti took his own survival as a signal of providential blessing; when he survived his own fall, he believed that he was obliged to respect that blessing with a climb that would do it justice. There was only one that would: the Eiger.

———————

The 13,025-foot Eiger is a brooding cathedral of brittle, shattered limestone rearing up out of the idyllic pastoral meadows of Switzerland's Bernese Oberland. It is rimmed by picturesque Alpine villages, but the peak is appropriately named: Eiger is German for "ogre" and there is no question that this is a beast of a mountain. The north face of the peak—the expert climber's side, the *Eigerwand*—is an enormous black scoop of rock, almost perpetually in shade, riven with towers of teetering stone, waterfalls, ice runnels, and a web of rock-scarred snowfields that climbers negotiate to ascend the 6000-foot face.

The Eiger carries a history as dark as its rock. The early climbers of the Alps echoed the opinions of the Franciscan brothers who named the wall: This was an evil place, where deadly missiles of rock fell almost constantly, terrible storms seemed to boil up conspiratorially right above the great face without the slightest warning, and the whole gloomy wall glazed with ice at the slightest fall in temperature. It was felt for generations that it would be madness to attempt to climb the *Eigerwand*.

Of course, its hazards, its technical difficulties, and the opinions of the elders all made the *Eigerwand* the most natural target of climbers interested in proving themselves. The wall's fierce reputation made it a perfect anvil on which not only individuals, but nations, could forge claims of strength. Just as the British said about their quests for the Poles, a nation with sons strong enough to face the Eiger was surely a heroic land.

The thought had particular resonance for one nation with a desperate need to prove its steel. In the aftermath of Germany's defeat in World War I, its politicians and media started watching the exploits of a new breed of young German climbers with interest. Hardened by poverty, embarrassed by defeat, and faced with little hope for the future, a string of young men who seemed utterly fearless and willing to take on any challenge emerged out of Germany in the 1920s and '30s. They propelled a dramatic leap in climbing standards, especially on dangerous faces, and the swelling National Socialist movement was more than happy to hold their bravery up as proof of the indomitable German spirit.

Through the early 1930s, the Nazis started spinning Alpine advances by Germans as victories for the Fatherland. They pulled young climbers under the umbrella of the Nazi party—climbers who often had little interest or knowledge of politics, but had ready allegiance to funding for their climbs—and the media wove their exploits into a myth of Wagnerian sacrifice. These climbers were portrayed as doing battle for Germany, with the deaths of a few as the price of heroic victory. The fallen climbers were spun as martyrs to the national glory, and this of course kept the line of aspiring German Eiger climbers growing.

The mountain responded to the bombast as any ogre would, slapping away each successive wave of aspirants. The very first try at the face, in 1934, ended in a rescue when the climbers fell and were left hanging by their ropes. (The rescue was possible only because of another oddity of the *Eigerwand*: Behind the face, a small tourist railway runs through a long tunnel to the summit of a nearby mountain, and there is a window that opens onto the *Eigerwand* about a third of the way up the wall. Rescuers were able to perch in the window and lower ropes to the stranded climbers.)

The second attempt, in 1935, ended more tragically when two very experienced climbers perished in a storm on their fifth day on the mountain. Their bodies hung frozen in place for years, but this macabre totem only seemed to inflame the conviction that the face had to be conquered.

In 1936, the *Eigerwand* was the stage for one of the great tragic moments in Alpine history, when two Austrian and two German climbers joined forces on the wall in mid-July. They moved well, and managed to solve one of the most difficult puzzles of the climb, the infamous Hinterstoisser Traverse, before a rockfall injury obliged a retreat. Over the course of two agonizing days, as horrified tourists watched through telescopes below, the conditions worsened and the team started perishing, one by one. One climber fell, one died of exposure as the temperature plummeted, one was caught in a confused tangle of ropes and strangled. At the end, only one man, Toni Kurz, was left, spinning in space at the end of his rappel rope, just short of the railway window. For several frozen hours, Kurz worked to rig himself a rescue line, and finally lowered himself down to within whispering distance of guides who could almost touch the soles of his spinning boots; then Kurz jammed up against a knot. He turned his head to the side, simply said, "Ich kann nicht mehr" ("I can go no further"), and died.

Kurz's death only cemented the iconic place of the wall in the minds of climbers. But it appalled both the international media (except for the German press, which glorified it) and the local Swiss government, which attempted briefly to prohibit climbing of the face, then settled for announcing that rescues would no longer be mounted for anyone foolish enough to test the wall. The increased risk stopped no one; the wall was finally climbed for the first time in 1938 by a very strong party that included Heinrich Harrer, of *Seven Years in Tibet* fame.

The acclaim the ascentionists received (and the awareness that the wall was, indeed, *possible*) opened floodgates, bringing climbers from several nations to wait for their opportunity on the meadows below the face. By the late 1950s, the mountain had become an icon of personal rather than national obsession, and it consequently continued to take a shocking toll. By the end of the decade, eighteen people had lost their lives and the Eiger's reputation as a badge of strength had grown well beyond the tight circles of the climbing community. As was the case with Everest in the 1990s, this renown drew the best, and worst, suitors.

In 1957 the great wall had never been climbed by an Italian, but certainly not for a lack of talent. Italians like Riccardo Cassin and Walter Bonatti were the finest Alpine climbers in the world, but they, along with other top climbers of the era, were growing disenchanted with the worship of the Eiger. In fact, there were several other harder, more significant climbs in the range. The *Eigerwand*, which had now seen thirteen ascents, was increasingly, though perhaps unjustly, disdained as the target of less-talented, less-imaginative climbers looking to establish their credentials while the best climbers went elsewhere.

It is doubtful that Claudio Corti understood these subtle distinctions. To him, climbing was a way to prove fearlessness and strength. It made no sense to consider looking elsewhere for a challenge when the fiercest enemy was so evidently the big black monster in the photograph he kept in his wallet. Corti's bigger problem was that he could not find a partner with a similar mind. Better climbers either shunned Corti due to his reputation for accidents, or shunned the mountain itself; and lesser climbers would quite sensibly never consider attempting the Eiger.

The situation was in many ways similar to that faced by many of the Everest climbers castigated by Krakauer in *Into Thin Air*. Corti had an ambition that was probably well out of his reach, and he was unable to interest anyone in the climbing community in the folly of an attempt. Just as Corti could not easily find a partner, it seems highly unlikely that many of the Everest climbers, some of whom Krakauer described as not even knowing how to put on their crampons, would have ever been able to find a place on a legitimate Everest expedition. The difference on Everest was that guides were willing to step in and offer someone like Corti a place on that mountain, where none would do so on the Eiger.

Much to everyone's surprise, Corti did manage to find a last-minute partner, though he seemed a dubious candidate for the mountain. Stefano Longhi was an overweight, 200-pound-plus, middle-aged man with little more than weekend climbing under his belt. Longhi had climbed nothing but rock, but somehow felt that it was irrelevant that the Eiger would involve demanding snow and ice that would be challenging even for an experienced alpinist. The sole factor in both Corti and Longhi's decision to have Longhi on the climb was that he was keen.

The pair's unpreparedness for the wall could not have been clearer when they arrived at the Eiger's base on August 2, 1957. They were forced to walk blindly back and forth beneath broken cliff bands, looking for the start of the route, because though there were numerous route descriptions and maps available, neither had bothered to purchase one. Both men had assured themselves that their enthusiasm for the climb would be more than enough to show them the way.

It was another eerie similarity to the attitudes on Everest in 1996: There you had climbers with considerable physical fitness but few technical skills, who treated Everest as if it were hardly more than a 29,000-foot high Stairmaster—just a big, hard cardiovascular workout during which someone else would take care of safety. On Everest, the fatal flaw was blindly leaving that caretaking to guides and porters; on the Eiger, the situation was even more perilous. Corti and Longhi trusted their survival to fate.

Corti and Longhi began their first day on the mountain quite lost. Instead of discovering the start of the easier, original route taken by the first ascent team, the pair accidentally started up the far more difficult and dangerous "Eiger Direct." They were understandably slow, and spent their first night on the mountain well below the stance that a fit and experienced party would expect to reach. The second day's climbing saw them manage to get back onto the original route, not thanks to skill, but because the 1938 route zigzagged across the face connecting all the obvious weaknesses of the wall, and many routes intersect it at some point. By the second night, they were barely at the point where most parties would have been placing their first bivouac.

If the pair needed an illustration of the snail's pace they had been setting, it came the third morning. While Corti and Longhi sorted out their confused routefinding, they looked below and caught sight of two climbers firing up the wall. Though it was barely breakfast, the new pair had already climbed the entire distance that had taken the Italians two and a half days. The second team were both twenty-two-year-old Germans. The more experienced was the very technically proficient Günther Nothdurft, a well-respected climber who had not only already been high on the

Eigerwand two years before, but had climbed up there *alone*. His second was Franz Meyer, newer to climbing but full of promise.

Both men were the polar opposites of Corti: calm, reasoned, very meticulous in their planning, aware of the moods of mountains, and clear on the risks of misinterpreting those moods. Although Nothdurft and Meyer made their decision to go to the Eiger at the last minute when they saw the weather improving, they were far better prepared than the Italians, who had spent months ruminating about the wall. The Germans knew the route, had the equipment the wall demanded (whereas the Italians definitely did not), and completely understood the dangers. They were conscious enough of the rockfall, for example, to understand that it would probably be fatal for one team to be above the other, so they elected to offer to join forces with the Italians instead of staying behind in their gun sights. It was not a complex conversation, for the foursome had no language in common, but the Germans got the message across. They shook hands and set off together.

Whenever climbers were spotted on the wall, curious onlookers flocked to the telescopes at the inns of Alpiglen, the tourist resort at the base of the Eiger. This time, it was clear to expert climbers in the crowd, and to the self-anointed experts derisively called the "Eigerbirds," that something was very wrong with the men on the face. By August 7, the Italians had been up on the wall for five days, the Germans two; and though the conditions were apparently perfect, all the men were moving very slowly and the top was still a long way above. Worse, the weather was not likely to stay perfect for long: Clouds were building down-valley, and—invisible to the climbers, but disturbingly clear to the people below—massive thunderheads were roiling up behind the summit. It should have been an obvious time for retreat, but the ropes kept crawling upwards, and opinions started flying about the possible fate of the men.

The true experts on the ground—proficient amateurs, experienced guides, and rescue team members—understood the seriousness, and also the wrongness, of the situation. The premier French alpinist Lionel Terray had joined the gathering group of potential rescuers, and this was his acrid assessment: "What was going on before my eyes was a hundred times more stupid than the normal run of heroic follies which the nature of the sport sometimes entails. . . . Only a monstrous vainglory stronger than instinct could lead them on like this to certain death."

Word of the situation on the Eiger quickly spread well beyond the telescopes at Alpiglen. By the end of Corti's first week on the wall, reporters from around Europe were filing stories, and soon the *New York Times* and *Life* magazine were on the scene as well. By the sixth day, the climbers neared the lower arms of the White Spider, the tendrilled snowfield two-thirds of the way up the face. The Spider was a deadly place to be moving slowly, as it was a funnel for all the ice and rock debris that daytime warming loosened from the upper reaches of the wall. Stay long on the steep flatiron of ice and snow, and you were bound to get hit by the missiles that screamed down the face with terrifying regularity.

The watchers were distressed to see that the foursome was moving as slowly as any who had ever climbed to this height. The group's pace was a puzzle, especially because the ground crew knew that the talented Nothdurft and Meyer were on the wall, and they should never have been so slow. The first thought from the observers was to blame the other pair, who remained unknown. (Corti and Longhi had told no one they were aiming for the Eiger that week, so that Corti's young wife, who rightly feared her husband's climbing, would not worry through their time on the wall.)

It would be days before anyone would figure out who the Italians were, but the men on the ground correctly guessed that the lead climber in the red jacket who kept on making routefinding errors was not one of the Germans. This man repeatedly made decisions that baffled the observers and forced tedious retreats that ate up valuable time, and yet the others seemed to be faring worse. All three were moving slowly, especially the man in the rear, who was often slumping in his tracks. There was little question that the party was injured, near exhaustion, or both, and with the ever-gathering storm, either a rescue would have to be mounted or the climbers would be left to die. Either way, the climbers' arrogance had placed many people at risk.

———————

The climbing roles that might have been expected on the mountain had been jumbled not long after the two ropes joined forces. Sometime during their first night together on the wall, Nothdurft had accidentally dropped the German food bag down the face, leaving them with no reserves for the rest of the climb. With hand signals, he managed to explain to the Italians that he and Meyer were now planning to double their pace and race for the top without food. Other teams had made the climb in a single day's climb from that point, and Nothdurft felt confident they could too. Corti accepted the decision, but first passed Nothdurft some coffee and bread slathered with honey from the hives of his village. The Germans flew off impressively, while the Italians, particularly Longhi, struggled through the early morning.

Corti was very surprised to catch up to the German rope after only a short time and find Nothdurft bent over in excruciating pain. He was seized with abdominal cramps and barely able to move, but the Italian offered a cure. He gave the German some pain tablets, and Nothdurft soon felt well enough to listen to Corti's suggestion that they push on for at least another night instead of retreating. The foursome moved reasonably well over the easy terrain of the day, but spent an absolutely dreadful night, with all four men forced to stand on a tiny ledge, drenched by a constant spray of water from high up on the face.

In the morning, Nothdurft was feeling even worse, but Corti was not going to see his Eiger dream forsaken to get the German off the wall. Despite the clouds now blanketing the valley, Corti was adamant that the best course was to continue up, with him in the lead. He explained to the other three that he had a great deal of experience in the mountains, and that they could rely on him to lead to the top. As the day wore on, there were moments when Nothdurft seemed better, and it looked as though heading up had been a valid choice. But when the men were forced to suffer through another drenched, upright bivouac that night, with Nothdurft in spasms and Longhi almost delirious with exhaustion, Corti's push to ascend seemed remarkably self-centered.

The following day—the seventh on the wall for the Italians—began poorly. Nothdurft was now feverish, still cramping severely, and the men discovered that the dropping temperatures had incapacitated Longhi. The Italian's hands had been frostbitten during the night, and he was virtually unable to function in his role as the last man on the rope. They slowed down even more, taking hours to complete single rope lengths. Their only inspiration of the day came when a small plane flew close to the face, and they were able to signal some of their situation to the pilot. The thought of someone being aware of their predicament helped, until one of them reminded the others that rescues from the Eiger were no longer supported.

There was, of course, no shortage of information in the valley about the men's plight—some of it actually true. By that seventh day, every hotel room in the area was booked by vulturish tourists drawn by the grisly developments, and radio stations were posting regular bulletins about the deteriorating situation.

Several of the world's best climbers had arrived, including Lionel Terray, the great French climber of Annapurna fame, Riccardo Cassin, the Italian master of the Alps, and an entire team of Poles training for the Himalaya. So had international leaders in technical rescue, including Ludwig Gramminger, the charismatic German chief of the Munich Mountain Guard, his likable protégé Alfred Hellepart, Robert Seiler from the Bernese rescue team, and the Swiss Erich Freidli. Both the climbers and the rescue technicians had converged on Grindelwald after they had heard the local rescue leader flatly state, on the fourth day of the climb, "There is no hope for the men." The locals would not be forced into danger by the stupidity of the climbers on the wall; they had seen it all too many times before.

This stern denial of responsibility did not surprise the rescuers, but they were shocked to receive no welcome at all in the village. The valley inns were so busy with Eigerbirds that the climbers who came to help were forced to stay in barns and dormitories; the local guides offered no support or information; and, most troubling, the railway staff refused to let rescuers hire a train to carry them up the Eiger tunnel to stage a rescue from the summit of the nearby Jungfrau.

Still, the rescuers' goodwill won out over the petty politics. By Saturday August 10—Day 8 for the climbers—the polyglot crew were assembled at the high rail station with hundreds of pounds of Gramminger's high-tech rescue pulleys and cables, and began threading the corniced ridge to the Eiger, to position themselves on the sharp summit of the wall. There, they would have to guess where the climbers might be, then descend into the storm to try and find them.

The situation on the wall, down in the clouds, had deteriorated as badly as any of the rescuers could have imagined. Early on Friday morning, as Corti and the Germans brought Longhi the last few feet across an ice-glazed traverse into the White Spider, the exhausted Italian slipped as he was removing a piton and flew down and through the air, screaming as he dropped more than ninety feet. There Longhi was left spinning, unable to touch the wall, with 5000 feet of space below him.

Corti's hands were shredded by the whipping rope, but after desperate minutes he finally managed to lower his partner to the safety of a ledge, and Longhi was able to get his weight off the line. But this hardly solved the problem: There was not enough rope to get down to Longhi, the men could never hope to pull him up, and Longhi had no strength to climb back up himself. Corti and the Germans lowered the sobbing Longhi a bag of food, and left him where he stood, shouting down, "Courage! Courage!"

Responding to Longhi's accident put the other three men onto the shooting gallery of the White Spider at the very worst time of the day, and in terrible weather. Waves of rain washed over them as they dodged a cannonade of stones and ice, aiming blindly for the Exit Cracks that would lead them finally to the top of the wall. Getting this high had been a colossal feat, but all three men were nearing the bitter limits of their strength as they began slithering their way up the cracks' black ice chimneys.

By mid-afternoon they had made only a few rope-lengths' progress, and were losing all hope of the summit, when a rock pinballed down the alley they were in and struck Corti square in the head. He pitched over backward and fell sixty feet down the long seam in the rock, his head bleeding profusely. When Corti regained his senses, it was clear that it was now up to the Germans to go for help. Corti tied himself into the wall, and Meyer and Nothdurft climbed into the clouds.

The rescue on the Eiger was every bit as dramatic, complex, and ultimately rife with conflict as the one forty years later on Everest. The Italian rescue team, led by Riccardo Cassin, went to the edge of the face while another group began the intricate process of rigging winches on the summit. When they called into the mist, the Italians were stunned to discover that it was Stefano Longhi who answered back. They knew the man as a marginal member of their climbing circle, and they had to ask each other: who in the world would have brought Longhi onto the Eiger? There was no way that he could have managed such a climb.

Cassin scrambled to figure out a way of getting down to Longhi. Meanwhile, the team on top had begun to lower their first man down a different section of the face, where he saw, but could not reach, a small red tent set onto a ledge. There was no answer from the tent, but it appeared that at least two people, Longhi and the resident of the tent, might still be alive. The Italians boosted their efforts, but it was soon clear that the rescuers would be spending the night, only marginally better equipped than the survivors below.

Just after dawn the next morning, the maze of cables, pulleys, and winches was finally untangled, and Alfred Hellepart was slowly lowered down the long snowslopes, then over the edge of the terrifying abyss of the north wall. The descent took almost an hour, until Hellepart finally heard a muffled voice carried on the wind. It was Corti, sitting beside the red tent. Hellepart could not speak to the Italian, and had to get Cassin on the other end of his walkie-talkie to calm Corti down and get him up on Hellepart's back.

It took most of the morning to raise the two men. Hellepart had to manhandle Corti, without the help of the cable, the final 250 feet to the summit. When Corti was finally lowered from the exhausted rescuer's shoulders, he turned to his countryman Cassin and announced that he was the "first Italian to climb the North Wall." Olsen quotes a friend of Nothdurft saying it "was like taking a fist in the face" to hear that absurd claim, but it was perhaps the most telling insight into Corti's blind belief in his right to be on the mountain.

Dramatically worsening weather ensured that Corti was the only member of the foursome to survive the wall. It was two years before the Germans' bodies were discovered on one of the lower ice fields on the face; it appeared that they had fallen to their deaths during their last try for the summit.

Stefano Longhi perished sometime during the long night of Corti's rescue. Longhi could not be reached in the storm that fell. For years the Eigerbirds could see his corpse frozen to the wall, still hanging on the fraying ropes.

In many ways it was the bitter aftermath of the 1957 Eiger disaster that most resembled Everest '96. There was mutual blame amongst the various parties, lawsuits were threatened, and the media had a field day with the climbers, rescuers, guides, and politicians condemning each other for their roles in the tragedy. Books and magazine articles followed that alternately lionized and castigated many of the players, especially Claudio Corti. He was called dangerous, "not very intelligent," and "childlike." Several people went as far as suggesting that Corti might have played an active hand in eliminating the others, in order to ensure his own survival. Many critics called Corti "a lunatic." The suggestion seemed to revolve around two issues that are intriguing both here and in the case of Everest. First was Corti's decision to contemplate the wall at all. To everyone but Corti himself, it seemed like an absurd presumption. He had marginal talent, was poorly equipped and, in interviews after the tragedy, showed remarkably poor understanding of both the route and the risks involved.

But does choosing to climb in the face of these limitations make him mentally troubled? It is a difficult question. Answering "yes" might require a similar judgment of all adventurers, because most try something in their careers that takes them to the very edges of their capacities. Walking that edge is, after all, part of the joy and spirit of adventure. But the naïveté with which Corti attacked the climb, and the way he treated the climb as an angry vendetta rather than a reasoned challenge, made the motives for his ascent seem far more pathological than most peoples'.

The second issue is more complex. In many people's eyes, Corti showed a complete disregard for the lives of others in pushing his desire to climb. He dragged Longhi into a climb that the older man clearly could not manage. He pushed Nothdurft and Meyer to continue up when it seemed to many that they would have voted to go down if it had not been for Corti's misrepresentations. He also dragged a number of rescuers into the mix.

All of these arguments have ready counterpoints, the same ones that are brought up in the aftermath of every adventure tragedy. Corti really believed he could complete the climb, and Longhi went along of his own free will. Longhi could have said "no," just as all of Corti's other prospective partners did. Corti really believed the Germans *would* be better off if they continued up, and they *could* have descended if they had wanted. He had not forced anyone anywhere. The rescuers obviously made their own choices to come and get him, and he had not *expected* a rescue.

In the end, history has been gentle in its judgment of Corti—perhaps out of compassion for a man who, until his death, never really understood that his actions might have led to the tragedy. Riccardo Cassin, who actually befriended Corti after the accident, was as forgiving as anyone. Corti was not a bad man, Cassin believed, just a simple, unintelligent man who did not understand himself or the mountains well enough to make sensible decisions about training, preparation or routefinding, let alone complex moral ones.

In the end, Jack Olsen was just as compassionate. After traveling to see Corti in his home village several years after the accident, Olsen wrote, "So we had found not a lunatic, nor a braggart or a liar, and certainly not a criminal, but only a driven, befuddled child in the body of a man." It was a verdict not unlike that applied forty years later on Everest.

*Maurice Wilson, with Ever-Wrest, and Leonard and Enid Evans behind
(Courtesy The Alpine Club, London).*

outskirts of the town of Meteren, near one of the only remaining woods in the area. Wilson began this first true battle of his war as one element of a forward line; but when the Germans intensified their attack on the second day of the battle, the other units pulled back, leaving Wilson and his men alone, exposed to a heavy mortar and machine-gun assault. The cost was enormous: Every single man in Wilson's unit was either killed or wounded. But Wilson himself was miraculously spared. Without a scratch on him, he managed to hold the position long enough for British and Australian troops to rally again and hold the Salient for another few weeks.

Wilson was awarded the Military Cross for his "conspicuous gallantry" that day, but his magical luck did not hold. Only a few months later, as the tide on the Salient swung once more in the favor of the Germans, Wilson was back in Meteren, this time as a captain. He was leading another counter-offensive when he was felled by machine-gun fire. Wilson had near-fatal wounds in the chest and left arm. As soon as it was possible, he was moved to France and then back to England to recover. Wilson's impressive strength allowed him to survive, and even to serve with his unit for the rest of the war in a diminished capacity, but he never regained full use of his arm. He was left with disabling physical pain and, the subsequent years suggest, even more crippling emotional scars.

Like so many men of his "lost generation," Wilson was haunted after the war, unsettled, apparently unable to see value in the life he had been planning before he enlisted. For a variety of reasons, we have come to believe that the emotional scars of battle are something uniquely attached to recent wars—especially American wars such as Vietnam and the Gulf Wars—and that the public approval of the World Wars meant that veterans of those wars survived the horrors better.

The numbers do not support this verdict at all. British army records for the First World War show that nine percent of the medical discharges from the British forces in World War I were for "mental illness," a rate actually higher than for American forces in Vietnam. Maurice Wilson was left shattered by the war, as were thousands of others who served with him. What makes his story unique is where his emotional scars eventually took him.

There is nothing in Wilson's pre-war life to predict that the Yorkshireman would find himself at the foot of Mount Everest a decade and a

CHAPTER 9

MAURICE WILSON

An Elaborate Suicide

THE LARGE, MUSCULAR YORKSHIREMAN found a spot in his camp sheltered from the dusty Tibetan winds, and sat down to write in his small green diary about the day's journey. On April 10, 1934, as always, Maurice Wilson offered the diary little. He had been traveling for twenty days now, through some of the most majestic and varied terrain on the planet—the tea hills of Darjeeling, the great hardwood gorges of Sikkim, and now through the rugged desolation of the Tibetan foothills in the shadow of Mount Everest—but his diary gives no hint that Wilson was moved at all by the grand geography around him. There is no mention of the arduous trek over the many high passes, no glimpse of the stark beauty of the plateau, nothing said of his Sherpa companions.

Instead, Wilson's terse journal entry, penciled in his spidery hand, was all about home. He mentions a book on "Courage" that a friend gave him as a birthday present before Wilson left for Everest nearly a year before ("[The friend] Always seems to send the right thing at the right time"). He laments his dwindling food supply ("No more tea, no more honey, so shall box on without them"). He seems nostalgic to be back with the other friend he was writing the diary for, instead of being deep in the loneliness of traveling with people he could barely share a word with. "Wonder what you are thinking about at home," he asks, "now that you're well aware I'm on the job?"

A few days later in the diary, Wilson would start to forecast that he was finally coming to the end of his long Everest adventure, but on April 10, he was thinking back to the very distant beginning of his journey to the mountain. Wilson started the entry for the day by noting that he was marking an anniversary of sorts. Sitting beside his primitive canvas tent pitched in the moonscape of the high Tibetan hills, Maurice Wilson wrote that it had been, "Sixteen years since I went into [the] line in France."

There are few places on Earth that seem less likely to seed a great mountain adventure dream than the Flemish lowlands. Straddling the Franco-Belgian border, hard by the North Sea, Flanders is about as far from the vertical world as one can get. The land is almost continuously flat, and dangerously close to sea level in places. The only relief breaking the horizon is a gentle swell of connected ridges, like veins under the marshy skin of the land.

At the dawn of the twentieth century, the region's daily life was scarcely more uplifting than its geography, but everything would change in a very short time. It took only a few months of the First World War for Flanders to lose its simple innocence, to move from invisibility into infamy. That brief span changed millions of lives. When the German army pushed its way into the Netherlands and France, it ground to a halt at the Allied trenches in the Flemish mud. For the next four years, both sides ferried hundreds of thousands of men into Flanders to fight over the wasteland called the Western Front.

The Front was the worst face of the war: Here trench warfare began, chemical weapons were used for the first time in history, and nearly two million soldiers were killed while the front lines moved barely twenty kilometers in four years. The toll on both sides was horrific. The blood-filled trenches of Flanders seem likelier to inspire nightmares rather than grand alpine dreams, but there is little question that one of Mount Everest's oddest stories began there: Maurice Wilson's tangled path to the great peak.

Born in 1898 in Bradford, England, in the heart of industrial Yorkshire, Maurice Wilson was one of four sons of a comfortably middle-class family. In a time of widespread poverty, Wilson's childhood was content, and his future relatively assured, especially when his father became a director of one of the larger local weaving mills. Wilson attended a good school, performed well, and appeared ready to happily follow his father and his brothers into the family business—until the war began.

There was no question that Wilson would follow his brothers and friends into the Army. It was a duty and Wilson was a responsible boy. A day after his eighteenth birthday in 1916—the earliest he could enlist—Wilson signed on with the 5th Battalion of the West Yorkshire Regiment, a unit with a proud, tough, working-class history.

It took little time for the Army to recognize potential in the sturdy, well-muscled Yorkshire boy. Wilson was likeable, with a spry wit and a contagious one-of-the-lads enthusiasm. He bumped up quickly through the ranks, becoming a corporal during exercises, and a lieutenant by the time his unit was finally sent to France. But Wilson was impatient with all the work involved in becoming an officer; he spent more than a year waiting in Britain, "aching," he later wrote with his trademark enthusiasm, "to give Jerry a good talking to."

When Wilson finally got his chance, in early November, 1917, he and his men were thrown into one of the worst hell storms of the war. He joined the 146th Infantry Brigade at the front line of the Ypres Salient, the bubble in the trenches on the Belgian border that had claimed nearly 600,000 lives, repeatedly changing hands from the beginning days of the war. Wilson's unit stepped right into the Fourth Battle of Ypres, just hours after an especially brutal gas and artillery assault by the Germans.

Photographs from Fourth Ypres show everything that was so horrific about this war: Charred bodies stuck in knee-deep mud; soldiers huddling together against bitterly cold rains, the worst in Flanders' history; faces futilely wrapped against the terrible burns of the phosgene and mustard gases. From the air, Flanders was a treeless moonscape of water-filled trenches, pocked with mortar shell-holes, the bucolic villages of the region reduced to burned, empty skeletons.

Wilson's unit was sent in to counter a German breakthrough on the Salient near Hazebrouck, France. They set up a machine-gun post on the

half after he returned from battle. There is no record of his having a connection to nature, to the aesthetics or the history of mountaineering, or to adventures of any kind. He was a fit man, but not particularly athletic, and though Wilson was born on the edge of one of the birthing grounds of rock climbing—the gritstone edges of the Peak District in Britain—he knew nothing of the sport. Wilson's convoluted path to Everest seems more like a series of accidental stumbles in the dark than it does a dedicated mountain pilgrimage.

When he was demobilized in 1919, Wilson returned to his father's mill in Bradford. He lasted barely a year before beginning to drift, searching for his place in the world. Through the 1920s, he was chronically dissatisfied and developed an edge that he had not had before the war, a pushy, loud façade that either enchanted people in a "hail-fellow-well-met" kind of way, or drove them away shaking their heads at the boorish lout. Wilson's thick Yorkshire accent and his endless supply of great schemes to make his fortune in the world completed an almost cartoonish image.

Wilson drifted around, first to London, where life suited his expansive ambitions better. But even there he soon strayed, first to New York, then to San Francisco, then across the Pacific to New Zealand. He stayed longer, and even prospered there, but still raced through a dizzying array of jobs: traveling salesman, farmer, owner of a dress shop, and— perhaps most oddly—shiller of snake oil: a tincture of opium and alcohol that Wilson bottled himself and hustled out of his car.

Nothing that Wilson did, and no place where he lived, settled him. He was modestly successful at everything he tried, but he remained anchorless. He had done nothing in his twenties that he could imagine doing for the rest of his life: he had certainly struggled to find a partner to share his world; he married briefly in Britain, divorced, married a Maori woman in New Zealand, and divorced again. At thirty, he packed his bags yet again and booked passage on a slow mail boat headed back to Britain, ready to try yet another change.

The long journey was clearly the next pivotal moment in Wilson's life. He shared the boat with the full breadth of society, mingled with everyone from the posh to the poor, and found himself struggling to get a sense where he fit in best. Nothing in life had ever fulfilled him the way so many things seemed to have satisfied others on the ship. He was surrounded by people who had identity and purpose, families and futures, even if they did not have the perfect lives that Wilson himself was casting about for.

The most puzzling, and most unsettling, of the passengers came aboard in Bombay. They were a troupe of Hindu *sadhu*, sages on their way to convert London. Wilson wrote to friends that he was drawn to them, fascinated by their asceticism and mystical ability to withstand hardship.

Typical of Wilson's resilient self-regard, though, he also described the yogis as fascinated with *him*. He reported that he engaged the group in many spirited conversations during the voyage through the Suez, and finally, back home to Britain for the first time in years. By the time he reached London, Wilson believed that he *was* home and was finally ready to be there. He considered settling down, hoping to find the peace that he had seen in so many others on the boat. He moved into London, returned to visit his family, and began to look for a job. But his peace was short-lived.

Wilson's experience with the yogis had not been just an intellectual exercise; instead, sadhus had challenged Wilson to look more closely at himself, especially at his perpetual dissatisfactions. Wilson was left haunted, and it was not long before he fell into what, at the time, was vaguely called a "nervous breakdown." Wilson was sick; he was losing weight and coughing, and had lost the energy that was so familiar to him. But instead of seeking physical remedies, Wilson became enthralled with a mystic who offered a very different sort of cure.

Wilson never clarified who the mysterious man was, (and some writers have doubted that the man actually existed) but it seems Wilson was powerfully affected by him. The mystic told Wilson that he himself had been diagnosed seventeen years before with a fatal illness, but had survived through a simple, yet profound plan: He fasted for a month, drank only sips of water, and prayed. After the power of the experience with the yogis, Wilson was ready to try anything. He followed the man's cryptic advice, disappeared, then within a few months surfaced again—apparently a completely new man.

The dramatic change was witnessed by a young couple who had befriended Wilson soon after he arrived in England. Wilson had met Leonard and Enid Evans by happenstance, but they were to play a key role in the man's future. They had watched with concern when their new friend had started to deteriorate physically and mentally not long after they first met, and their concerns doubled when Wilson simply stopped coming around to see them.

But when Wilson returned, he looked energized, and claimed to be completely healthy. The cough was gone, his strength was back, and Wilson had a message to share with the world. Every ill—physical, moral, spiritual—could be cured via the path of fasting and prayer that the mystic had encouraged him to follow.

Wilson was exuberant and completely resolute. "I believe that if a man has sufficient faith he can accomplish *anything*," he told the Evanses when he took them out to dinner to celebrate. "I haven't gone mad and I haven't got religious mania," he insisted. "But I've got a theory to prove and I intend to prove it. I'll show the world what faith can do! I'll perform some task so hard and so exacting that it could only be carried out by someone aided with Divine help." Wilson stood and very earnestly announced that he had the perfect stage on which to act out his missionary scheme: "I'll climb Mount Everest alone," he told the stunned couple.

Everest was very much in the public eye in 1932. It was not so long since the grand expeditions of the 1920s had mesmerized a British public aching for heroes in the aftermath of the horrors of World War I. The stories of those mythic trips—especially the deaths of George Mallory and Sandy Irvine in 1924—had only managed to whet the British appetite for Everest, and even more strongly convince them of the nation's destiny on the peak. There was simply no more visible place for Wilson to perform what he called his "superhuman feat," and no more dramatic way to do it, than to hop on the bandwagon of the *newest* way of attacking the mountain.

In 1933, for the first time since Mallory and Irvine's fatal trip, Britain was sending a climbing team to Everest, but it was also concurrently mounting a very different kind of expedition. In 1932, a team of high-profile pilots, including the Marquess of Douglas and Clydesdale, announced a plan to *fly* around the 29,035-foot summit. Their scheme—a perfect blend of exploration and science—received huge press, and the salesman in Maurice Wilson knew an opportunity when he saw one.

He wrote to the flight team, suggesting, absurdly, that he be given the opportunity to get a "wing-lift" high up the slopes on Everest: He would parachute onto the mountain. He explained that, with the advantage offered by his fasting, with his instant position high on the mountain, and without the "encumbrance" of a large team, he would just race to the top. He had *read* about mountaineering, he wrote, and knew just what it would take to speed to the summit: "All you need to climb a mountain," he suggested to the team, "is a tent, a sleeping bag, warm clothing, food and faith."

Wilson was understandably turned down, but the rejection only sharpened his resolve; he would simply have to fly to the mountain himself, and then climb it alone. All he had to do was learn how to do both.

The reasonable question to ask about Wilson's scheme is whether it was the plan of a madman. On the surface, Wilson's naïve grandiosity, his expansive mood, his unwillingness to listen to those who were trying to talk him out of his plans, his commitment of a huge amount of time and money to his "expedition," his theatrical self-promotions to the media, his disregard for ridicule by others, and his dramatic bursts of activity all have the discordant texture of mania.

People who met Wilson during his rush to leave for Everest described the man as difficult: obsessed, overbearing, blustering and arrogant—all parts of the social presentation of mania. Wilson also had a history of melancholy and despair, supporting the possibility that he suffered both horns of a manic-depressive or bipolar affective disorder (or at the very least the disease's milder cousin, hypomania).

The manic phase of the illness, especially when it follows a depressive episode (as might have been the nature of Wilson's mysterious illness that was cured by the mystic), often inspires explosively exuberant behavior in the sufferer as he rebounds out of the darkness.

In Wilson's case, he certainly came out of his "nervous breakdown" with unbottled energy. He was an utterly larger-than-life character, flamboyantly parading around London in what he seemed to think was the proper dress for a mountaineering pilot: leather jacket, fawn riding breeches, and an oversized pair of hobnail boots. His outfit and his bravado invited disbelieving stares, but these did not seem to faze him at all; they became simply a way of drawing attention to his mission. Wilson even took to calling himself "the flying nut" as a means of opening doors.

At the same time, however, a number of factors weigh against a diagnosis of either depression or mania in Wilson. Most prominently, the extended span of Wilson's Everest pilgrimage was far longer than the typical course of these illnesses. As well, the disruption caused by a true, or full, episode of mania—or depression, for that matter—is usually severe enough that the sufferer would have a very hard time functioning as successfully as Wilson did.

It seems most likely that if Wilson had a clinically diagnosable disorder, he would be best described as hypomanic (a less-severe, minimally disruptive mania) or cyclothymic (a low-grade cycling of depressed and manic moods). Both conditions would be weighty, unsettling burdens, leaving the man alternately energized and exhausted, optimistic and then suddenly despairing, doubting the validity and reason behind any of his grand plans. There is ample cause for such a disorder in Wilson's war experience, and much in his later history to suggest that his wanderings may have been efforts to escape, or cure, his volatile moods.

Certainly, in both his own time and since, Wilson has been called mad, especially by mountaineers. While Wilson did have—and still has—a few champions who "admire[d] his pluck," on the eve of his departure a British newspaper, to Wilson's fury, called his plan "an elaborate suicide." Other papers simply ignored him. Most Everest historians handily dismiss his journey as an absurd, and ultimately pointless, misadventure.

But at the same time, Wilson's story is a perfect illustration of how so many aspects of any risky adventure start to look abnormal when judged through the narrow perspective of "normal," safety-conscious lives. Wilson spoke in inflated terms about his plans, but so do many adventurers who are either thrilled with their ambitions, or are trying to sell themselves; his mood was expansive, but so are the moods of many climbers about to head to Everest on the greatest adventure of their lives. Wilson threw money away as though he would never need it again, but many Antarctic explorers have had to sell everything they owned to raise plane fare. Wilson could seem like a bluff, bombastic, monomaniacal character, but so do many of the explorers who have invested years of their lives convincing themselves and others of the importance of their journey. It was not common sense for Wilson to go to Everest, but the same could be said for the sailors who signed up to go to the South Pole with Scott.

There is no question that Wilson was poorly prepared to go to Everest, but this too is not so uncommon in adventure; many great adventure stories have arisen out of marginal preparation. Besides, Wilson believed that he had a spiritual power behind him. As Dennis Roberts wrote, "He knew his belief was indeed pure and absolute. And he realized what he *must* do." Wilson said that Everest was "the job I've been *given* to do." People might laugh, ridicule him, and try to stop him, but no matter: He *was* going, and his steps on the summit of Everest would prove that his faith was warranted.

Wilson jumped into his plans at a fever pitch, especially when he saw the accelerating plans for the 1933 climbing expedition led by Hugh Ruttledge. Wilson felt that he needed not just to climb the mountain but to be the *first* to the summit to prove his point, so he had to get at his plan if he wanted to beat Ruttledge's team to Tibet. By day, Wilson began his pilot's training; by night, he started digging up everything about Everest he could get his hands on—studying maps, memorizing expedition accounts, and sensibly planning out how to attack the mountain's various key features in stages.

What was incredibly less sensible was Wilson's almost complete lack of concern for technical mountaineering gear and skills. Before heading to Everest, Wilson purchased no climbing equipment, and the only skills training he did consisted of walking several hundred miles from London to Bradford, where his family still lived. There he spent barely a month in the gentle local hills, where he did little more than scrambling and hill walking.

Several writers have pointed out that Wilson's understanding of the mountain may have suffered as a result of the arch understatement that was typical of British mountaineering literature of the time, which disingenuously reduced significant technical difficulties to mere "bothers." But surely even the most naïve look at a picture of Everest would convince a potential climber that he might need to learn how to climb snow. Wilson did nothing of the sort.

His flying preparation was little better. His first step, before taking even one lesson, was to buy a plane. Wilson purchased a Gipsy Moth, and signed up to learn to fly at the Stag Lane aerodrome.

He must have presented a staggering image: arriving at the flight school in his "pilot's outfit," with the name "*Ever-Wrest*" hand-painted on the engine cowling of his newly purchased Gypsy Moth; and announcing that he needed lessons so he could fly to India, intentionally crash on the lower slopes of the world's highest mountain, then stroll to the top.

Understandably, Wilson was met with ridicule and scorn—which only increased when his eccentricities mounted, such as "training" by marching around the airfield in his hobnails. Wilson refused to socialize with the other pilots, turning down invitations for drinks because he was "an apple and nuts man," and this didn't win him many supporters, either.

Wilson's place as a risible outsider was only amplified when he began to fly. His violent, rodeo-style handling of the Moth terrified his instructor so badly that it took Wilson nearly twice as long as an average pilot to earn his license. Even when he finally did, his teacher advised him that he would never make it to India, a flight that would have seriously challenged even the most capable pilots of the day. Wilson ominously replied that he *would* get to Everest, "or die in the attempt."

Wilson spent far more of his time immersed in his image than he did in any other part of his plan. As the deadline for the flight approached, he had Leonard Evans working for him as a press agent, securing him a modest degree of coverage in the papers in Britain, even if only as something of an oddity. There were daily news reports on the front pages about Lady Houston's team's ultimately successful flights around the mountain and occasionally, buried in the back pages, there were also human-interest columns about the "plucky war hero."

Wilson also had Evans scrambling to arrange permission to fly *Ever-Wrest* to the mountain—a scramble that was, finally, fruitless. An increasingly angry Wilson wrote again and again to the Air Ministry to get clearance to fly over Nepal to the north side of Everest, but there was no way the bureaucrats were going to condone such an inexperienced amateur's flight. Wilson responded by simply ignoring their "blindness" to the merits of his scheme.

Within a remarkably short time—it was really only a matter of months since he had announced his plan to the Evanses—Wilson proclaimed himself ready to go. He told the newspapers that he would make one last trip to see his mother in Bradford—this time piloting *Ever-Wrest*, in his longest flight to date—and, watched by a curious and skeptical press who gathered to see him off a few days later, proceeded to stall the plane and cartwheel it down a country road.

Wilson himself was unharmed, but *Ever-Wrest* was trashed. The damage would require about a month's work to repair, and it was obvious that Wilson would never make it to Tibet to "race" Ruttledge's team to the summit. Instead, he did the sporting thing: he committed to getting to

Tibet for the post-monsoon season instead, and he "crossed [his] fingers" that Ruttledge would fail.

By the time Wilson finally took off a month later, it already looked as though his childish wish had come true: Ruttledge's team had been beaten by the mountain and were on their way home. Wilson, characteristically immodest, announced that their defeat was only fair, as he was the more legitimate suitor of Everest.

On May 21, 1933, Wilson gathered the press once again at Stag Lane—this time adding the flourish of dramatically tearing up the Air Ministry's refusal of permission in front of the reporters, barking, "The gloves are off. . . . Stop me? They haven't got a chance."

Enid and Leonard Evans were there, supporters to the end, as was Wilson's mother, who praised her "very brave" son with the "left arm [that] is practically useless." The pilots from Stag Lane also gathered for Wilson's takeoff, though more than likely out of morbid curiosity rather than support, and for a moment it looked as though the morbid were about to be satisfied. Wilson made the most basic of piloting errors and launched into the wind the wrong way, clearing the trees at the end of the field by only inches. But he was on his way.

If Maurice Wilson's ambition had been "to fly to India alone!" as evidence of the amazing powers of fast and prayer, we might have a different appreciation of the man's remarkable resolve, and offer him a more honorable place in history. For not only did Wilson make it to India, he ended up doing so with only nineteen hours' flying experience, in a style and at a pace that would have been competent for any pilot of the day—let alone a novice blocked at every stage of his flight by authorities.

Wilson was blessed with good weather for the first four days of his trip, but that was partly due to a good decision on his part to avoid roughening skies over the Alps. He landed in Italy to the acclaim of local pilots ("With great pomp and many toasts to his success," Dennis Roberts tells us), then kept churning east, roaring one day on the back of a tailwind that pushed him along at a near-record 100 miles per hour. "So far," he wrote the Evanses, "the trip is a piece of cake."

It did not stay that way, though arguably not through any fault of Wilson's. He managed a blind flight through clouds nearing the North African coast, only to begin a string of difficulties getting fuel. He first landed at Tunis, couldn't find anyone who seemed to understand what he wanted, then headed north to Bizerte, where he was promptly arrested. No one ever explained why; Wilson was simply driven back to the airport in silence and told to leave. Back in Tunis, he filled his tanks himself, which proved to be a grave mistake. He lasted barely a dozen miles before his engine started to stall; he managed a last-ditch landing at a small airport near the Libyan border, where he was told that his entire fuel line would have to be drained—Wilson had inadvertently mixed water in with the fuel.

The human glitches continued in Cairo, where Wilson had wrongly expected to get a permit from the British Legation to cross Persia. Furious, he was bumped from one bureaucrat to the next, getting stonewalled every time he tried to make his case. He eventually convinced himself that the British Air Ministry had sent word to stop him in Africa. Wilson dodged the authorities, planned an alternate route to Baghdad, and cast his luck to the winds. Flying only by his primitive compass over the featureless Arabian sands, he managed more than 1000 miles in a single day, coasting into Baghdad just in time to start looking for maps to take him on a new course round the south coast of the Persian Gulf.

Wilson soon discovered there weren't any maps in Persia—at least not the highly detailed ones he would need for safe flying. Unruffled as always, he managed to scrounge a child's school atlas, which showed barely more than the coastlines of the region. The following day, he flew completely by that—and by luck—to Bahrain. There, he was stalled by bureaucracy yet again, when it was pointed out that there were no options within the Moth's range that would not land him in Persia, where Wilson was convinced he'd be immediately arrested. But Wilson refused, he later wrote, to let "them" "do the dirty on me."

He surreptitiously traced the roughest details off a map in the Bahrain airport, stuffed one extra fuel drum in the front of the Moth, and took off for the faraway Indian town of Gwadar, which sat at the very limits of his fuel. Nine and a half hours later—cramped, broiled by the fierce sun, and terribly tired—Wilson coasted the gasping Moth over mangroves on the hem of the Arabian Sea, and landed in India.

Wilson's success in getting to India brought him back into the news. The "flying nut" was now a flying hero, having taken just under two weeks to get to India. The British press stringers were now more than happy to give the louder-than-ever Wilson the opportunity to spell out his "daring plan."

Wilson was now an "expert airman and rock-climber," who still planned to crash *Ever-Wrest* at 14,000 feet, then climb to the top "with enough rice and dates to last fifty days." He promised that he would "succeed where a large group [Ruttledge's now finished expedition] have failed." He elaborated on his "careful training" of special foods and fasts that would, he rather ridiculously insisted, "enable me to breathe deep down in my stomach, taking in a vastly increased supply of oxygen."

In another interview, Wilson more baldly claimed, "People do not realize that I am an experienced climber, that I have starved myself and have locked myself up in an airtight container to learn the effects of low oxygen levels." He was confident enough that he even challenged Mahatma Gandhi to a fast. But he made sure that reporters understood, "There is no stunt about it. Mine is a carefully planned expedition."

Unfortunately for Wilson, the authorities did not agree. When he finally arrived in eastern India, after several weeks parading for the press, his airborne plans ground to a halt that even he had to acknowledge. *Ever-Wrest* was impounded to prevent Wilson from crossing into Tibet, and the monsoon season settled in. To pay for his mounting expenses, Wilson finally had to sell the plane.

But these setbacks proved to be nothing more than another hurdle in the path of Wilson's "divinely given" mission; within a few days of losing his plane, he committed himself to traveling overland, heading for the great climbing center of the day, Darjeeling.

If there is one perfect place from which to fathom the scale of the Himalaya, it is the northern edge of Darjeeling, the Indian hill station that was once the crown jewel of the Raj. There is perhaps nowhere else on Earth with such a jaw-dropping insistence of *big;* but where another would-be climber might blanch at the stunning enormity of the endless wall of peaks, Wilson "was delighted." He decided that he had enough money to spend the winter training and fasting, while he figured out how to trick his way past the Indian authorities, who were unwaveringly refusing permission to pass through Sikkim.

Wilson had not settled too far into the routine of the tea plantation life in Darjeeling when he was introduced to Karma Paul, the Tibetan who had become the self-appointed general factotum of all the initial Everest exhibitions. Karma Paul convinced Wilson that he would be an invaluable resource, but Wilson was soon butting egos with the equally flamboyant Tibetan. Wilson decided to end their relationship, and found three experienced Sherpas himself. These men would accompany him on what was evolving into a clandestine run through Sikkim and on to the north side of Everest.

There was no way Wilson was going to get official permission, and so he started making plans to dress as a Tibetan monk. He sorted out his complex route—much of which would have to be run at night—and went for training walks in the forests around Darjeeling. He spent the long, cold winter fasting for up to three weeks at a time, waiting for the weather to finally break so he could bring the last chapter of his epic adventure to a close in the spring.

On March 21, 1934, Maurice Wilson snuck out of Darjeeling with his partners, Rinzing, Tewang, and Tsering Sherpa. It was nearly a year and a half before the world heard of him again.

———————————

Virtually everything we know of the last few months of Maurice Wilson's life, from the moment he snuck out of Darjeeling in early spring, 1934 until his last days on Everest, come from the brief scrawls in Wilson's pocketbook diary. Where Wilson had once been speaking opinionated volumes to anyone who would listen, from the day he passed out of sight of Darjeeling there were no more letters to the Evanses, no more newsflashes, and no great proclamations of his mission. Instead of the flamboyant, exuberant man of the planning phase, Wilson seems almost mute during the approach march. Slowly, but irrevocably, he seems to descend into despondency, disconnecting from the world around him.

Wilson's diary offers only the leanest details of the journey, with brief, flat descriptions of views that have brought other travelers to their knees. He made few observations about the unique places he saw, complained about the locals ("[the] people are filthy"), and about his loneliness. More and more, his thoughts were of food and the life at home.

A prominent facet of Wilson's diary that has had surprisingly little attention from other writers is the fact that the entire diary is constructed as a quite personal letter to Enid Evans. There are several winking asides to "you" sprinkled throughout, and in the April 18 entry Wilson clarifies who the "you" is: "Of course," he explains, "I'm writing all this to Enid; she's been the golden rod from the start." Perhaps in addition to his fasting mission, Wilson was also motivated by one of the most easily confused forces of all: an unrequited love.

The days on the trail were hard work, and Wilson's plan to subsist on the barest rations to "train" for the mountain fell aside. He was soon "going off the rails with a pot of tea." The high point for Wilson seemed to be the Sherpas, writing that he "couldn't have wished for better" companions.

The overland journey to Everest in 1934, following the route of the early climbers, was a very different trip from either of the modern approaches to the mountain. When Wilson and the three Sherpas started winding their way north through the dense jungles of Sikkim, they traveled hundreds of miles through some of the most varied terrain on the planet, beginning in the luxuriant valleys near Darjeeling, then climbing sharply over pass after pass across the lay of the land before cresting onto the windswept high plateau of Tibet.

The journey was arduous for all the early Everesters, but it was doubly so for Wilson, with little knowledge of the route, almost no experience in trekking, minimal ability to communicate with the locals, and a dire fear of being stopped by the police. Wilson was forced to disguise himself as a traveling monk, bound in a Tibetan *chuba* and a girdle of "about four yards of bright red silk." He described himself as looking like a "cross between the Prince of Wales and Santa Claus." He wore dark glasses to hide his blue eyes, and had the Sherpas explain to anyone who came close that their friend was deaf and mute—a restriction that proved an agony for the gregarious Wilson.

Despite the precautions, it was only a matter of hours before the team crossed paths with their first policeman and then another. The first time, Wilson crouched under an umbrella to hide his six-foot-plus height while the Sherpas greeted the official. The second encounter drove Wilson into a ditch filled with stinging nettles. Those close calls were enough of a lesson to force Wilson to start traveling at night.

After only a week, the team reached the 15,600-foot Kongra La pass into Tibet, where Wilson said, "Now in forbidden Thibet feel like sending government a wire: 'Told you so!'" But Wilson's impatience with the journey, and his belief that he could prove something by setting a speed record, endangered the men. Wilson crowed that he was bettering the times of previous expeditions, dubiously insinuating the great early climbers like Mallory, Somerville, and Norton were not his equals, when in fact their more gentle approaches were sensibly planned to prevent altitude sickness. As a direct result of Wilson's rapid climb, he and the Sherpas were suffering from headaches and weakness, seriously threatening their future performance. The obvious problems did not, however, stop Wilson from proclaiming that he was "halfway up the mountain already" when he had reached the pass. It was vintage Wilson: literally true, as he had reached half of Everest's 29,035-foot altitude; but a self-deceiving absurdity, given the complete lack of technical challenge he faced getting there.

Once in Tibet, Wilson dropped his disguise, gave up any pretense at hiding, and began to race even more feverishly toward the mountain. Some days on the dusty moonscape of the plain, the team pushed thirty miles or more, leaving them exhausted and burdened with more pronounced symptoms of altitude sickness, which were made insufferably worse by plummeting temperatures and cutting winds.

Wilson's diary entries were as bleak as the landscape, filled with blinding sandstorms, terrible winds, searing sun, and a longing for a return to greenery. The only, brief, break in the monotony came after three weeks on the trail, when Wilson finally saw Everest on April 12. It "looked magnificent," he wrote. "One half in snow plume."

But he followed this claim of excitement with a darker line missing from Roberts's account: "Don't get the slightest kick out of the whole adventure as already planning the future after the event. I *must* win."

Wilson was so fixated on his escalating plans for the future after his victory over the mountain—ambitiously forecasting, "Maybe in less than five weeks the world will be on fire"—and was so often caught up in his dreams of getting home to tea with the Evanses, that for many days of the walk, the mountain itself is invisible in his diary, as though it was just an irritating hurdle on the way.

By the time Wilson strolled into the Rongbuk monastery, the re-nowned Buddhist retreat at the foot of Everest where climbers came to receive blessings for their ascents, his plan for the climb included little else than fasting for two days, and aiming for the summit on his birthday, April 21. Wilson insisted the scheme "couldn't go far wrong," as his sign, Taurus, would be ascendant at the end of the month. (In the diary, Wilson erroneously writes that his sign is "Zodiac," suggesting a lack of knowl-edge of astrology which might indicate he perhaps should have had less faith in the omen!) Zodiac or not, Wilson was convinced he was nearing victory. After all, it was "only another thirteen thousand feet to go!"

Wilson's plan added up to only five days to climb between base camp at 16,500 feet and the summit at 29,035, but he suggested this would be adequate, as he would not be burdened down by all the "crowds" that he believed had complicated previous expeditions. Wilson packed his poorly-considered provisions (no crampons, nothing more to eat than bread and oatmeal), then set off alone the following day, insisting that he no longer needed the Sherpas.

The beginning of the first day, on the rough path following the gentle rise of the Rongbuk Glacier, went well. Wilson was fit from the walk in, and, even though he was carrying a fairly large load at forty-five pounds (though not, as he fatuously boasted, a "terrific load, greater, I should imagine, than any Sherpa was allowed to carry"), the terrain was straightforward.

He made good distance and gained reasonable altitude by the time he stopped for the night, but it should have been immediately obvious that, even at this pace, he was not going to make the summit in five days. Obvious, at least, to anyone but Wilson. That night he wrote, "19,200 feet up—only another 10,000 feet to go—sounds easy," but he was wrong on both counts: He was actually still well below 19,000 feet, and the coming days proved far from easy.

Wilson had been gone from the monastery for nine days when he stum-bled, exhausted, bruised, and nearly starving, back into the arms of his Sherpa friends. He gorged on a meal, then collapsed and slept for thirty-five hours.

When he finally woke, he told a harrowing story of inexperience and misjudgment. When he had turned onto the East Rongbuk, the arterial glacier that leads to the North Col and the northeast summit ridge, Wilson was finally faced with his first serious mountain challenge. The glacier tumbled down in a frozen cascade of crevasses, rock debris, and precarious towers of ice. Wilson, who had naïvely expected to find a marked path, was soon helplessly lost. Without crampons, and with little understanding of how to navigate the labyrinth of hazards, he slipped and fell repeatedly, "floundering about doing 50 times more work than necessary." He was puzzled by his altitude-induced lassitude, but refused to rest, and did nothing to quench his relentless thirst but eat snow and ice, and drink rare cups of tepid tea.

It took Wilson three brutal days just to reach Camp II, where he had prayed he'd find food; he cursed when he only turned up a pair of crampons. Though these were actually the most useful thing he could possibly have found, Wilson tossed them aside with disgust, and pushed on.

Above Camp II, the going was even worse. The glacier was increasingly broken by jigsaws of crevasses. Wilson continued to choose the least efficient route, heading straight up the glacier rather than following the safer moraines. Pinned down for a day by a violent blizzard, he started complaining unrealistically about his predicament, insisting, "If I had the service of coolies like exp[editions], I would be at Camp V by now." Finally, exhausted and despondent on his birthday—the day he had grandiosely planned to summit—Wilson gave up and turned back toward the monastery. The descent was a nightmare of hunger, falls, "hellish cold," snowblindness, excruciating pain in his war-wounded arm, and a badly twisted ankle. Wilson was also caught up in delirious reveries of home, especially of his mother, of whom he wrote: " . . . the only true romance I've ever had in life." Wilson collapsed when he saw the Sherpa camp, and did not set foot on the mountain for another three weeks.

It is tempting to say—many writers have—that when Wilson staggered back into the monastery, common sense should have impelled him to forget Everest, feel pride in what he had already accomplished, and save himself from likely tragedy. But, of course, Wilson was not the typical adventurer, and his decision to head back up the mountain is not a simple matter to decipher.

The moments of doubt that most adventurers describe as they waver between retreat or commitment have a very different feel than what Maurice Wilson was going through during his long weeks of recovery in the monastery. It is this period that seems most crucial in appreciating Wilson's story. Dennis Roberts and other writers have suggested that there were "no hints of giving up," but this claim is not supported by the diary. Yes, Wilson needed time to regain his strength, but there are more threads of apathy, withdrawal, and a wish to be somewhere else in his words than there are signs of commitment to climbing the mountain. Wilson sleeps through most days, writes nothing of the peak except when he expresses his hope to "get it over with," and beyond taking food and climbing gear from the Ruttledge cache at the monastery, makes few alterations to his plan.

The crux of Wilson's tale lies in whether his return to the mountain was truly a dedicated last shot at the summit, or more honestly a sad resignation to fate—as though he simply ended the journey by going up rather than down. His critics, no matter how much they admired his "pluck" and endurance, have always questioned whether Wilson's steps toward the North Col beginning on May 12 were a form of suicide, even if not explicitly expressed.

There was so much riding on his success, so many grandiose claims to live up to, that it does not seem unfair to wonder if Wilson felt little choice but to go back to the mountain, with success or death as the only solutions to his predicament. What could he say if he came back empty-handed after all his brash pronouncements? What would he do if his "mission" failed? Wilson's actions hint at his state of mind: Sitting in the Rongbuk, he drew up a will and wrote a note that freed the Sherpas of responsibility for his death. He left instructions to give the diary to Enid Evans while not really bothering to organize his plans and gear. With all these steps, Wilson seems to have been preparing himself more for failing and dying than for success.

And yet Wilson supporters, such as Dennis Roberts and Thomas Noy, bristle at the suggestion of suicide when it is broached. It angered Roberts enough that he cut off our conversation, saying he was tired of seeing Wilson criticized when "he should be seen as a hero."

Both men insist that the key to Wilson's behavior was his faith. In their eyes, Wilson believed that he had a mission, one that was ordained by a God who had blessed his efforts. If he was passive in those last days, it was because he believed his inspiration to climb the mountain would come when he needed it and could not be forced. They pointed out that Wilson wrote that he felt all the obstacles had been put in his path for a higher purpose: to make his mission all the more real. He could not turn back, because doing so would betray a lack of faith in the mission, and "faith is not faith that wavers when its prayers remain unanswered." However dangerous or pointless it might be, when the time came, Maurice Wilson had to climb.

But Wilson, by his own admission, was clearly not ready to go when he started out again. Though he made good speed to Camp III this time, (only three days, thanks to the fact that he took Rinzing and Tewang with him, who made far better routefinding decisions), Wilson wrote that he was weak and despondent, and plagued with altitude sickness throughout the journey. He was frustrated when he arrived in Camp II to discover that he could not find the crampons he had thrown away earlier, finally understanding that his poor planning would make progress higher on the mountain nearly impossible.

When he did arrive in Camp III, Wilson stayed in his tent without moving for days, bent over by his headaches, and openly admitting a lack of will. Even when he stumbled on the food cache left the previous year by Ruttledge's party, and ate "everything about the place," "wallowing in . . . a one pound box of King George chocolates," he revived only for a brief moment before slipping back into apathy—perhaps partly because he had to admit that his grand scheme to show the world the power of fasting fell apart when he gave in to his hunger.

Wilson's last days on Everest saw a sad string of futile attempts punctuating long, inactive spells in his tent. After a week lolling at Camp III, Rinzing guided Wilson to the foot of the moderate slopes leading up to the North Col and pointed out the standard route through the maze of seracs and snow ramps. Even though a year had passed, Wilson naïvely expected to find fixed ropes or steps cut in the ice by Ruttledge's team, and was thumped by the work it took to chop his own. Rinzing finally left him in the afternoon, after which Wilson exhausted himself with his inefficient technique, complaining that "whoever selected this route ought to be poleaxed." Two days later, after bashing himself again and again on the first moderately steep piece of ice he encountered well below the 23,000-foot North Col, and then falling head over heels down the slope above Camp III,

Wilson stumbled back into camp and collapsed in his tent, refusing to speak to the Sherpas for three days.

The men pleaded with Wilson to return to the monastery, but he insisted that he was ready to continue. "I feel successful," he wrote. On May 29, Wilson sent the Sherpas off with orders to leave if he was not back to the monastery within ten days. Then he packed a small pack, and started back up the hill. He got barely a few hundred yards from the camp before pitching his tent again. On the 30th, he stayed in bed all day, on the 31st he scratched out his last spidery words, "Off again, gorgeous day."

On July 9, 1935, under a searing morning sun, the members of Eric Shipton's Everest reconnaissance team moved laboriously up the broken, crevassed terrain of the high end of the East Rongbuk Glacier. Just a few hundred yards above the traditional Camp III, on a last flat before the arch of the slopes below the North Col, the team doctor Charles Warren saw a boot in the snow. As Warren called the others over, he saw that the boot led to a wind-shredded tent ten yards away, then to a desiccated corpse curled in the fetal position. The body was lightly clothed and sockless as though the man had died in his sleep, and one hand reached out, grasping a rock to which the tent was anchored. A few weathered belongings were scattered in the snow.

Warren knew immediately who this must be; he called back to Shipton, "I say, it's this fellow Wilson." The team gathered quietly round the body, taking stock of the situation. Wilson appeared to have died of starvation or exposure. The team picked through the gear, discovering a bare minimum of equipment and virtually no food, though Wilson's camp was an easy flat walk from the large cache of thirty to forty boxes of Ruttledge's supplies that he had raided before. Wrapped in the tatters of the tent was the small Union Jack that Wilson called his "friendship flag," signed by Len and Enid Evans just before his departure from Stag Lane more than two years before. In Wilson's small backpack, the climbers found his spartan diary and, nearby, a few rolls of film.

The diary and the film, the Union Jack, Wilson's gold pen, and an elephant-hair ring were the only things the climbers carried away from the mountain. After a few moments of thoughtful quiet, the team wrapped Wilson in the remains of his green tent, carried him to a nearby crevasse and, in the most painful and poignant ritual of mountaineering, gave the troubled soul to the mountain.

Earl Denman in Tibet, photo taken by Tenzing Norgay (Courtesy Graham Denman).

CHAPTER 10

EARL DENMAN

The Romantic Heart

MAY 29, 1953, 11:30 AM. In an unusually light wind, Tenzing Norgay Bhotia began unrolling four small flags wrapped around his ice ax. As the colors of Britain, India, Nepal, and the United Nations began to snap in the breeze, Tenzing set his right foot in the steep snow, cocked his left leg onto the top of the world, and raised his ax in triumph. Finally, after seven trips to the mountain, Tenzing stood atop Everest. He tilted his head slightly to the left, and his partner Ed Hillary snapped one of the best known photographs in history, the only image of the first climb to the top of the world.

No one deserved the honor more. Tenzing had been born in the Kharta Valley of Tibet, truly at the foot of the mountain. He had spent far more time on the peak than had any man, going first with the great British climber Eric Shipton in 1935 on the expedition that discovered Maurice Wilson's body. Then he went back, again and again, with the British, then the Swiss, and then the British finally in 1953. Tenzing grew in stature with each expedition, starting as a simple high-altitude porter, moving into privileged ranks with the Swiss, and then at last into position as the natural summit candidate with John Hunt's Brits and

New Zealanders. Each successive expedition was larger, more complex, and increasingly more certain to force the peak into submission. Every time, that is, except for one.

There was one journey that stood out as completely different from the others on Tenzing's résumé, the one he called his "craziest trip" to the mountain. Six years before the 1953 expedition, with its crew of more than 200, he had joined a team of three that stole through Tibet without permission, and without, Tenzing always said, much hope of ever getting up the mountain. Tenzing gave up other opportunities on other mountains for that odd little trip, because he just couldn't resist a chance of going to Everest; nor could his partner, the thirty-three-year-old Canadian whom Tenzing called "a strange man"—Earl Denman.

Earl Denman's story is as rich and romantic as that of any innocent who has looked to wild nature for self-purification. And from the beginning, it's a story of sadness, the journey of a flawed man.

He starts his book, *Alone to Everest,* explaining that his obsession with mountains began when an unsettled childhood made him a lonely dreamer, a characteristic that would follow him the rest of his life.

When quite young, Denman was displaced from his home and then effectively orphaned. Illness first forced his family to leave their home in Canada and return to Britain, and then killed Denman's father "seven painful years" later. Denman writes that his mother struggled "valiantly," but laments that she and her three boys could still "not escape the harsh, grinding realities and sacrifices which each had to bear at a time when schooling and games should have been their only concerns." Denman deifies his mother's selflessness and "determination never to forsake her children," but his family told me that this acknowledgment was more for-giveness than fact. In truth, when his father died, Denman's mother was incapacitated permanently by exhaustion and grief, and Denman and his brothers were separated and sent off to live with strangers.

Denman's nephew Graham filled in the early details that his uncle's book left bare: Denman's father was a British engineer who first came to Canada to work on the construction of the White Pass Railway in the Yukon. Then he moved south to Vancouver Island and was involved in the construction of the renowned Butchart Gardens. Earl Denman was born outside Victoria in 1917, where he and his family were still living when his father fell ill with a crippling strain of rheumatoid arthritis just a few years later. The family moved back to Britain, seeking treatment, and spent the last years of the father's life near Nottingham. After his death in 1926, the family fragmented, and Earl Denman, already a lonely child, was left with distant relatives and pulled further into his shell, turning, eventually to an unusual fixation.

Denman's description of his obsession with mountains is one of the strangest laments in alpine literature: "I grew up with an ambition and a determination," Denman writes, "without which I would have been a great deal happier." Mountains, he suggests, were not so much a noble goal as an "overpowering distraction" that pulled him against his will and better judgment.

Denman anchors his thoughts of mountains to memories of seeing the Canadian Rockies as a child, but his nephew Graham clarified that this perception might be more imagination than fact, as Earl was barely three when his family was forced to move to Britain. Denman's mountain dreams, in any case, were not of the Rockies, or any of the great ranges that fuel most young imaginations. The quiet, sad boy dreamed of the mountains of Africa, because his heroes were the giants of African exploration, such as Stanley and Burton.

Though it took him years, it was Africa's Mountains of the Moon, the Ruwenzori, that Earl Denman first saw. During World War II, Denman—like his father, an engineer—was posted to the Sudan. At the first chance he took a furlough to the mountains he had been dreaming of since he was a child. Though he acknowledged that he had "neither time nor equipment to do . . . any real climbing," on seeing his first high peaks he felt that he had found the "purpose for which I had been searching within myself." Sitting at snowline after a day's hike, Denman looked south from the Ruwenzori to the tropical cones of the Virunga Mountains, and devised a remarkably audacious (and, some have suggested, ludicrous) plan: If he could manage the first ascent of all eight summits of the Virungas, he would climb Mount Everest. Though Denman's scheme of leaping from the Virungas to the Himalaya would be the mountaineering equivalent of going from a first boxing lesson directly into a title fight with Muhammad Ali, Denman was strangely adamant. He guessed that, at the heart of things, climbing the Virungas and Everest required the resource that had already gotten him through so much in his life—"tenacity and little else."

And then Denman added a note that would prove telling through the rest of his adventure to Everest: The mountain would give him "a chance to get to grips with myself and the problems with which I battled." It is one of the more honest admissions of conflicted motives in the history of mountaineering.

Though they were snowless scrambles barely 15,000 feet high, the Virungas still involved major hurdles—but these just happened to be logistical rather than technical. Denman had read almost nothing about mountaineering, had no partners to teach him how to climb, and had little sense of the challenges he might face, or the equipment and techniques required. He was in Central Africa, and was unlikely to find the equipment even if he knew what to look for. He had no permission to climb the peaks. He had no money. But Denman was blindly committed.

In the words of Everest historian Walt Unsworth, "His training was more unorthodox than any climber's before or since." He would learn to climb by climbing. If he couldn't get equipment, he would learn to do without ("I dispensed with footwear altogether and climbed barefoot. . . . To travel light became so much of a habit with me that any really non-essential article of equipment I looked upon as an encumbrance."). If he could not get permission, he would sneak into the Virungas because "Mountains should be a place above the laws of man." If he couldn't find partners, "I would go with none but the black men who lived in the vicinity." And if he had no money, he would live on nothing more than rice and bread.

However unorthodox, Denman's Virunga scheme worked; "I was successful in that undertaking, even beyond my wildest dreams," he wrote. Between April and August of 1946, Denman and his porters hacked their way through jungles and slithered over mossy slabs to the mist-shrouded summits of all the Virungas. Denman was pleased with himself, but he understood that the accomplishment really had little to do with Everest: The hazards he had encountered in the Virungas were no more serious than rain, mud, bugs, and mild vertigo. The mountains' long approaches had gently acclimated him to the altitude, and there were no technical difficulties to challenge his skills or his commitment. Denman had enjoyed the expedition—especially his time with the local people—but not the climbing, which he dismissed as unpleasant "scrambling."

Most of all, though, Denman's disappointment lay in the fact that he experienced none of the changes in himself that he hoped the mountains might catalyze. There are several hints in his book that Denman wished that the Virungas alone would provide the answer he had been seeking, but he ended the trip concluding that they "were not sufficient in themselves for the real truth, the ultimate peace, the greater wisdom." A less romantic man might have sensed that no mountain would offer those answers, but for Denman there was only one path to follow: "Everest it had to be."

At first read, it can be frustratingly difficult to get a clear picture of Denman from *Alone to Everest*. Infuriatingly inconsistent, he can be cynical and bleak one minute, then almost childlike in his innocence the next. Unabashedly, nakedly open about himself on one page, he turns head-shakingly blind to his faults on the next; warm and gracious to one local man, then arrogantly racist to another; self-effacing one moment, then bombastically grating the next. Most of all, he is grandly, extravagantly idealistic one day, then shattered, betrayed and pessimistic the next, by completely predictable events. He insists he knows nothing about a subject (mountaineering being the most obvious example), but then pontificates at length about it.

Running unsettled at the core of the book is the question of why Denman felt so impelled to go to Everest. His need seems so much more complicated than the challenges or the romantic dreams invoked by many other climbers. There are hints all the way through *Alone to Everest* that Denman knew he was embarking on a futile quest, but every time he bumped into this likelihood, he insisted that he had *no choice* but to go. He writes that "the power of past problems robbed me of all ability to think clearly," though he never clarifies what "the problems" are. He acknowledges that he would have seen Everest to be "insuperable if I had stopped just once to weigh up the possibilities of success or failure in an atmosphere of calm reasoning," but he insists that he had "no freedom to stop and reason" the journey through. To not go, he writes, would have been to forsake an opportunity to "lessen [his] burdens."

Denman took Everest on, it seems, as a Goliath that had to be faced and defeated. The initial burden of the obsession with Everest might have been psychological, but the challenge was soon fully practical: Even the naïve Denman understood that he was going to have to be better prepared for the Himalaya than he was for the African jungle volcanoes (he had, after all, "read that it would be cold"). In a masterstroke of understatement, he later pointed out that "Africa proved a most unsuitable continent in which to gather together equipment for high altitude mountaineering in the Himalaya."

He scoured back-alley shops in Nairobi for boots (clearly regretting that he would "likely not be able to get very high on Everest in the bare feet which I preferred"), fashioned a homemade tent from a scavenged barrage balloon, and dug up a heavy canvas-and-fleece sleeping bag. Most remarkably, he contracted two Italian internment camp inmates to forge an ice ax and crampons, and hand-braid a cotton climbing rope. Denman had only £250 to cover the expenses of the entire expedition, and he was well aware that the previous pre-war expeditions had cost as much as 300 times that amount. But he would not be stopped: He begged his way onto a freighter bound for India, hopped a third-class train to Darjeeling, and finally stood on the balcony of the Himalaya on March 13, 1947, only months after hatching his plan.

It is tempting to cast Denman as kin to Maurice Wilson—as the same kind of tragically misguided soul who should never have gone to Everest, or perhaps to any mountain. There certainly were similarities between the two: Both had blind ambition, naïveté, inexperience, and a need to go alone. For both men, Everest served as a proving ground, reached by a long and gruelling approach across Tibet without permission. By coincidence, both men even bumped into Karma Paul within hours of arriving in Darjeeling. But it's intriguing to hear Denman's own take on their differences. He had never heard of Wilson before meeting Karma Paul, and he was shocked to hear the details of his story; but he rejected Karma Paul's suggestion that his mission was as troubled, or as risky, as Wilson's.

"He seems to have been a very determined but totally inexperienced man, and something of a fanatic," Denman wrote. "I was, unlike

Maurice Wilson, an experienced mountaineer of very sane outlook who could be relied upon to take care of myself and others."

Denman's claim is an interesting illustration of how readily a person can rationalize his own behavior and condemn another's, despite facts that seem obvious to an outsider. He goes as far as labeling Wilson's plan "suicidal," and his fasting scheme "incredulous." Then, overruling his earlier convictions that his own "tenacity" could be enough to conquer Everest, Denman argues that Wilson's greatest flaw was that he had not "developed the skills" that Denman believed he himself had forged in the Virungas.

But what skills were Denman's, exactly? He had never strapped on crampons, touched a glacier, or chopped a step in ice, yet he was heading to the highest mountain in the world. He had no maps, and his only description of the route was an outline of the mountain from one of the early Everest books, penciled by Denman onto tracing paper.

If there was one hopeful difference between Wilson and Denman, it was that Denman at least had the good sense to be stunned by the size of the Himalaya. Where Wilson had described the rearing bulk of Kangchenjunga as looking "easy" from Darjeeling, Denman wrote, "I found myself gaping with astonishment, almost unable to believe my eyes."

Karma Paul made it clear that he did not want to have anything to do with Denman, as his association with Wilson had already brought him some trouble twelve years earlier, but he did say he would introduce him to someone who might be able to help. Denman could not possibly have had better luck, as the man Karma Paul had in mind was Tenzing Norgay. The "wiry and vigorous Bhotia" that Denman met over afternoon tea had a climbing résumé that was stunning.

In 1947, Tenzing was the most experienced Himalayan climber in history, having not only attempted Everest three times, but also Nanda Devi, Kamet, Nanga Parbat, and other very difficult peaks, with some of the world's finest climbers. Tenzing also brought his compatriot Ang Dawa Sherpa to the meeting. Ang Dawa was only slightly less experienced than his friend, with two trips to Everest under his belt. It was a perfect team to accompany Denman, if only he could convince the men that the plan was not absurd.

The relationship between Tenzing and Denman has been a subject of criticism by some historians, who have suggested that Denman took advantage of Tenzing by dragging him into his madcap exploit,

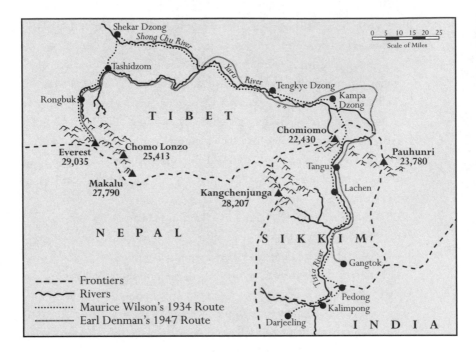

but several people who knew Tenzing well—and Tenzing himself, for that matter—argued that this simply was not the case. George Lowe, who became a lifelong friend of Tenzing's during the 1953 ascent, as well as Tenzing's grandson Tashi Tenzing and Ed Douglas, Tenzing's recent biographer, all told me that the man knew exactly what he was doing with Denman.

Ed Douglas pointed out that Tenzing was always a shrewdly pragmatic man, an expert at getting what he needed out of his business dealings. He discovered that Denman's willingness to pay for the trip into Tibet—even if the pay was pitiful—gave Tenzing the first chance in years to visit his family home. Tenzing wrote that a "real expedition" would never have permitted the detour that he surreptitiously arranged on the march with Denman. (Intriguingly, Denman never knew that the "kind family" with whom he, Tenzing, and Ang Dawa stayed for a few days in Tibet were Tenzing's kin.)

Lowe and Tashi echoed what Tenzing himself said was most important in his decision: He simply could not pass up an opportunity to go back to Everest. Tenzing was as obsessed with Everest as Denman was, and would prefer to go there over any other mountain if there was even the faintest hope of success. Although Tenzing obviously had a much more legitimate claim on the mountain, he sensed a kindred spirit in Denman. He is quoted in his biography *Tiger of the Snows* as saying that, while he generally believed there was little chance of getting up the mountain with Denman, the man did seem unstoppable. Tenzing and Ang Dawa committed to the journey on a strict schedule to minimize the investment of time. Barely a week after arriving in Darjeeling, without permits to enter either Sikkim or Tibet, the three men snuck out under the blanket of darkness and started their long march to Everest.

Though Denman was insistent that the reasons for his journey were completely different from Wilson's, their walks to the mountain were remarkably similar. They followed an almost identical route off the main path. To get through Sikkim, Denman had to disguise himself or travel at night. The men had to avoid villages wherever possible. Several times they came very close to getting caught, which would have been a huge threat to Tenzing and Ang Dawa's livelihood. True to form, Denman began the trek barefooted, but the terrain soon proved much harder than he had experienced in Africa, and he was soon back in boots.

Just as it was for Wilson, the trip to the mountain was a severe trial for Denman. He complained about the group's "irritating slowness" (though they were actually traveling just as dangerously fast as Wilson had); the jungles were "inhospitable" and "dead" compared to his beloved Africa; the villages, and villagers, were "dirty" and "ill-mannered"; the trails were "poor"; the food was a "tasteless misery" served by "indescribably dirty hands." Even the great mountains were "not really beautiful in the sense that the African mountains are beautiful." Although Denman had moments of joy, more often than not he despaired. "I had little enthusiasm for anything," he said later.

To be fair to Denman, though, even Tenzing acknowledged the hardships of this trip. With such a skeletal budget, there were none of the comforts of a typical "real" expedition. Tenzing later explained, "We simply lived from day-to-day and hoped for the best, never knowing what the next would bring" but "almost every day, something went wrong." There was "never enough food," and almost daily there were troubles with the animals carrying the team's equipment or run-ins with villagers. Before even reaching the Tibetan border, Denman realized his money would not last, but Tenzing suggested that they continue on regardless (though perhaps only to see his family, now only a few days' walk away).

By the time he was halfway through Tibet, Denman was thoroughly miserable. His feet were blistered almost to the point of incapacitating him, he suffered piercing altitude headaches, and he was growing lonelier by the day, and ever more fearful of being caught. Several times, Denman had confrontations with village dogs. At the lower elevations, Denman had filled his journal with complaints about leeches; in Tibet, he grew increasingly obsessed with the "vicious" hounds, filling pages with his efforts to thwart the dogs' "fearsome designs." Denman was plagued with thoughts that the trip might prove fatal, but he hung onto the belief that he must continue to the mountain.

Consoling him in his struggle was Denman's faith that he was sharing a deep bond with his companions. Justifiably or not, he described himself as woven from the same fabric as the Sherpas, and in doing so gave us one of the more sharply focused snapshots of his vision of himself: "We were the poor who have no pride; fending for ourselves. . . . We were idealists too. Tenzing in his own quiet way, and Ang Dawa none the less, and I, perhaps more than either. People like us are adrift from our age, and at times this gives us pride, but always, in the process of our pride, we are being hurt."

Reading Denman's account of the trip, it is easy to believe that the team's approach was one of the longest in Himalayan history; but just as in Wilson's case, quite the opposite was true. The team had reached the Rongbuk monastery in only seventeen days, a month less than it had taken the average pre-war expedition, and four days fewer than it had taken Wilson. But also like Wilson, Denman was physically and emotionally at the end of his rope when he arrived.

––––––––––––––

By the time Denman and the Sherpas left the Rongbuk monastery for the mountain on April 10, his struggles were completely manifest. Although he had been "strong, resolute and daring" on the approach, according to Tenzing, his commitment and faith in himself quickly eroded during the long slog up the East Rongbuk in bitterly cold winds, and he grew dramatically despondent.

It was very clear to Denman, and to Tenzing, that he was not up to the climb at all. In his inadequate sleeping bag the first night in the tent, Denman found the cold unbearable, and Tenzing saw the man starting to visibly unravel, sobbing and shaking. Denman understood the likely outcome—"I was too numbed in mind and body to realize the truth, but this first night was really the beginning of the end"—but his sad hope to "see at least one major dream through to completion" impelled one final push. "With only the three of us," said Tenzing, "the work was backbreaking. The wind and the cold were terrible. In fact they seemed to me the worst I had ever known on the mountain, until I realized it was not so much they themselves as that we were so badly equipped."

They suffered through another cold night, and then moved up to the foot of the North Col at just over 21,000 feet. "Now we faced the wind in all its fury," wrote Denman. They struggled to erect and weigh down their tent. Once inside, Denman—who by now was barely eating—realized that if the wind would not die down, the expedition was doomed. That night, he prayed: "God help me. . . . Do not rob me of the chance to go forward, but give me strength to go back if I must." But at the same time, his obsession was almost overwhelming. "My whole life was Everest. I did not want to live if we failed. I was not concerned about death." That was *not* the view of the Sherpas. Tenzing simply wrote, "This was the end of it." The next morning, they took down the tent, and they turned around. Denman sadly wrote, "We had played our hand."

Common sense would call it a good decision, but Denman was shattered, taking his "failure" right to the heart of himself and his feelings about life. "To some mountaineers," he wrote, "Everest is no more than a glorious adventure. To me however . . . the physical adventure counted for very little in relation to the underlying motives. I thought I saw in the vision of success a wonderful meaning to life. . . . With failure I saw a *world* which was not the world as I wanted it to be." Denman hurried away, calling the retreat "a humiliation," and left the mountain "trying to hate what I really loved. Seeking to convince myself that life meant nothing and would end in nothingness."

The entire trip had taken only five weeks. "It was as quick as that," wrote Tenzing. "As strange and mad as that. In another few days . . . it almost seemed to me that I had not been to Everest at all, but only dreamed about it."

Although Denman hinted at a return to Everest in subsequent years, and even made an abortive try to encourage Tenzing to return in 1953, mountains effectively disappeared from his life when he turned his back on Everest in 1947—though he was far from finished with his adventures. He continued his geographic, moral, and psychological explorations for the rest of his life, all of which echoed the good and bad of the Everest pilgrimage.

Stuck in India after Everest, with no money and no way home, Denman found work as a reporter with an English-language newspaper. He stayed in Delhi nearly two years before finally heading back to Africa, where he earned a position as the editor of *African Wildlife* magazine in South Africa.

While living in Cape Town, Denman continued to take solitary journeys from time to time. He became the first man to ride a motorcycle from Cairo to Cape Town, and crossing the Sahara by camel, but also taking on far more complex challenges. At the helm of *African Wildlife*, he fought against poaching and other dangers to animals, writing his second book, *Animal Africa*, in 1957. Through the 1960s and '70s, Denman was also an angry and consistent voice in the anti-apartheid movement, regularly writing to local newspapers, decrying the treatment of Steven Biko and others. He eventually wrote a bitter attack on racism in a book called *The Fiercest Fight*. He married an Afrikaner woman, and lived in the relative luxury afforded to whites. But just as he angrily and idealistically condemned the "moral outrages" of modern mountaineering from the edge of adventure, he lamented the injustices against blacks in Africa from the edge of their circle.

Denman was finally ordered to leave South Africa, though in his unpublished memoirs the reasons for this "exile" were somewhat unclear. Denman insists that he was never given a specific justification for his deportation—the government simply told him that his "sojourn in the Republic should be terminated"—but Denman was certain that it was his writing that had gotten him in trouble.

Denman was understandably bitter when his wife took many months to follow him to Ireland, and then left him shortly after. His wife, it seems from the memoirs, believed that Denman had brought his fate upon himself by facilitating his anger at injustice, and she was furious with him. "She did not say 'I told you so,'" Denman wrote, "but the words could be read into her stunned silence." They never spoke again.

For the rest of his life, Denman drifted from continent to continent, through a series of jobs that he despised. He finally reconnected with his brothers, who had had little to do with him for years; but they clearly found him eccentric and difficult, while Denman found them shallow and rigid. Denman's nephew, Graham, however, thought his uncle was a wonderful man: fantastic to Graham's children, filled with interesting stories.

After a brief, unpleasant stay with family in Britain in the 1980s, Denman went on a long and difficult trip back to India, traveling overland on a "hippie bus." He ended up in an ashram in Northern India, where, once again, he felt bitterly disillusioned—this time, by the morals and standards of the ashram's teachers. He left in anger, and from there went to first Australia, then back to Britain, and then finally to New Zealand.

———————

In 1990, a middle-aged New Zealand couple, driving a small country road on the North Island, saw a tall elderly gentleman get knocked off his bicycle by a speeding car. The car took off; the couple stopped and helped get the man to the hospital, where it was discovered that he had broken his hip and a leg. He had no family, nor any friends, it seemed, so John and Vivian McLintock stayed with him for a time in the hospital. Over the next four years of his difficult convalescence, they adopted him into their family.

He seemed such a lonely man, this Earl. But the McLintock children adored him, and he did have some interesting stories to tell: He'd had a brief career as a professional boxer; written two books about Africa; befriended Desmond Tutu; and petitioned the South African government for the release of Nelson Mandela. It took the McLintocks three years to find out that Earl had once been married, and that he had brothers still alive.

The McLintocks thought Earl could use a forum to express his strong opinions, and got him started writing a column—a rant, really—in the local newspaper. It was vintage Denman: railing against apartheid, the devolution of the sport of rugby, the lack of support for the monarchy, and a hundred other injustices.

In 1994, a check-up on Earl's healing legs revealed that he had developed bone cancer. It was only then at the end, and at the prompting of the McLintocks, that he reached out and made some efforts to contact his brothers. Two days short of his eightieth birthday in 1997, Denman was gone, as quickly as he had come into their lives.

Vivian McLintock took it upon herself to go through Earl's house after his death, and sort his things out. She told me that she was "stunned" to find a copy of a book called *Alone to Everest* with Earl's name on the spine. He had never said a word about Everest in five years, not even on his deathbed. She had heard him talk several times about his other books, but never about *Alone*. There was not a single photograph, nor a prayer flag, not even a stone—not a hint of Everest in the entire home. But there was this remarkable book; and stuck inside the back cover, she found several kind letters from Tenzing Norgay, and another from a fellow named Heinrich Harrer, who had written to Earl thanking him for a sleeping bag. Tenzing had sold Harrer the bag—the same bag Denham had sewn for Everest—to take to Nanda Devi in 1954. Harrer hoped that Denman would be happy to hear that the strange bag found its way onto another of the Himalayan giants.

Another bit of Denman gear also has a place in mountain history. In that famous photograph of the first ascent of Everest, Tenzing stands with one foot proudly high on the summit. His hood covers the right side of his face, and his oxygen mask hides more. But if you look closely, you'll see the corner of a red balaclava. Earl Denman found that balaclava in some back-alley shop in Kenya, and gave it to Tenzing at the end of their grand adventure. Tenzing had worn it in 1953, in memory of his friend. So, as Tenzing wrote, "at least a little part of him has reached his goal."

from left: Don Black, Johnny Waterman, Dean Rau and Dave Carman on route to Mount Hunter, 1973 (Photo: Dean Rau).

CHAPTER 11

GUY WATERMAN, JOHNNY WATERMAN, BILL WATERMAN

Walking into Darkness

THURSDAY, JUNE 15, 1978. *The Southeast Spur, Mount Hunter, Alaska. Day 83.* It was personal from the beginning. He called the climb a "vendetta," but he approached the battle with a samurai's rules of honor: Fight with everything you have, but fight virtuously.

That was how he had been taught to climb: to meet a mountain on its own terms rather than subjugating it with force. He was filled with respect and awe for his opponent. He was terrified, but committed to stay through the fight; and he understood that the storms and frostbite, and falls and misery, were just part of the rules of engagement. Climb the mountain by forging a hard new route. Climb the *entire* mountain, up one side, down the other, hitting the main and satellite summits on the way. Climb alone.

It was the only way, he believed, to measure himself and to get the true measure of the mountain.

Instead of just rushing in for a brief race to the top, he knew he wanted to see the mountain on its own schedule: see it change through seasons, watch it breathe and shed its winter skin, learn how to climb through any condition. The sheer work of it was unparalleled. Hauling everything, every step of the way, being on the climb for so long, meant going up and down every foot of the route again and again, ferrying huge loads between his precarious camps on the ridge.

After a time, it was little surprise that he started to anthropomorphize the mountain. It is written into our nature to see faces in clouds and hear voices in the wind, but he saw darker forces in the mists around him. The gargoyles of rock and ice that drifted in and out of view for weeks became his "Judges." They assessed him, they questioned his right to be there, they threw things at him and judged how he handled the fear.

In time, the storms became the breath of mountain demons that had already taken so many of his friends. They tore at his tent, kept him awake for days, threatened to simply whisk him off the mountain, but he couldn't just lie down in his tent and wait for them to pass. He had to fight. He'd saddle another load and walk out into the teeth of the gale, shrieking back at the top of his lungs: "Take *me* then!"

He was nearly ninety days into the torturous odyssey, exhausted, doubting his fate, almost completely out of food, with no sense that he still had another sixty-two days left before he would touch flat ground again: It was enough to break anyone, but it was exactly the test Johnny Waterman had been searching for.

So many of the stories in this book have turned out to be family stories: tales of lost parents, lost dreams of earlier generations, grieved siblings, and absent love. This is nowhere truer, or with sadder consequences, than in the story of Guy Waterman and his sons Johnny and Bill. In this story, everything twists around family. The threads of strength and weakness, faith and despair, ran from father to son as clearly and painfully as they could in any family. The paths from joy to sadness to despairing self-reproach and, finally, to suicide ran not once but three times in the Watermans.

And yet the striking thing in the family's story is not the predictable line between father and son, but rather how circular the threads became in the end: How a father's story became one son's, then another's, which in turn became the father's story again. You can't know one without the other, but to first catch the thread, begin with the father.

Guy Waterman was an excellent climber, a superb wilderness writer and advocate, and a hero of the back-to-the-land movement; an iconoclastic, modern Thoreau. He came to wilderness the way most children do, in idyllic backyard forests—in his case, the broad ten-acre woods surrounding his family's farm near New Haven, Connecticut in the 1930s. In his unpublished reminiscences, Guy anchored much of his journey in those woods, wondering if he hadn't been struggling throughout his life to regain the promise of simple serenity from that time.

Guy came from privilege, the youngest child of a family of the intellectual aristocracy of America. His physicist father was the director of the National Science Foundation; his mother was a brilliant woman herself, Phi Beta Kappa, scion of the Mallon family, with deep roots in New England society. Her father was close friends with presidents; her brother Neil gave George H. W. Bush his start in oil.

The Waterman home was a paradise of mental and physical stimulation, with the parents leading the children through eclectic dinnertime debates, classical music evenings, and sporting events on the property. The children were surrounded by cousins and friends, and shared adventures in the woods. But in his deeply self-searching memoirs, Guy also acknowledged how isolated and alone he felt from a young age.

As the youngest child, it often seemed that he was an only child despite the full house. In a way that would haunt him through adulthood, he always felt that he was *different*. He believed that he did not have many talents for getting close to people, and could not easily form friendships in the way that others seemed to be able to. He often pointed to his parents in searching for the roots of his early despair, wondering if they had not somehow expended all their love on his older siblings. He always believed that everyone else, inside and outside his own family seemed to have a connection that was denied him.

Perhaps he had just missed the perfect moment. By the time Guy was ready to enjoy it, the best days of the family's life seemed to be gone; the fabled Waterman canoe expeditions that his brothers spoke of so fondly had stopped, the eldest children had moved away from home, and worst of all, his parents had moved Guy away from the family farm to live in the city. In his memoirs, Guy betrays a feeling of disappointment, an aching longing for something: perhaps for the farm, where he recalled spending hours blissfully lost in his imagination; perhaps for his father, whose distance—in Guy's eyes at least—colored the boy's faith in himself and in all his later relationships.

Not surprisingly, adolescence was nothing short of "misery" for the despairing boy. Shy and awkward, small like his father (and his son Johnny), Guy was resentful and angry. He found relief in music and rebellion and alcohol. He drank to smooth his tense edges, and lessen the swelling arcs of his moods; he rebelled to roughen himself back up and prove *he* was in control. Both choices cost Guy, but also emboldened him.

He saw himself as a "flaming radical" with his "smoking and drinking and necking," who would never be one of the prep-school boys his parents sent him to school with. Instead, he insisted he had more in common with the underdogs of America—the blacks, the poor. He said that he wanted to be with them, where he felt at ease, not in some elite private school where he was alone and miserable. Guy had impressive musical talents, which took him into very different worlds from the one he was raised in. He was adopted by older musicians, drinking and playing piano in late-night jazz clubs when he was still only a sophomore in high school. His parents saw little but trouble in his music and the places it took him.

Guy's willingness to push limits also nudged along a forbidden relationship with the girl who would eventually become his wife. Emily Morrison, a year older than Guy, came from a similar elite background and was fighting her own demons. She was resisting her own parents just as forcefully as Guy was rebelling against his, but the Morrisons did not respond as harshly to their troubled teen as the Watermans. While Guy acknowledged as an adult that he "must have been a pretty unpleasant 17-year-old," he was stunned when his parents had him committed to a locked "psycho ward in George Washington Hospital" for several weeks after running away with Emily.

In his memoirs, he forgives his parents in retrospect: "I am at a loss" he writes, "to suggest what they could have done otherwise." But it is difficult not to see the struggles that followed as connected to the moment of their "betrayal." If he seemed better after coming out of the hospital, perhaps it was only because the experience made him less visible, both to the world and, more sadly, to himself.

For the rest of his life, Guy fought to maintain his identity against the pull of contrary forces. It was really nothing more than the task of passage from adolescence, learning how to carve out his unique identity in the world, but Guy's early history seems to have weighed this struggle with a psychic gravitas that made it exceptionally hard for him to resolve. Everything seemed to have a greater, more serious meaning for him.

For quite some time after coming out of the hospital—years, really—it did appear that Guy had chosen the path of conformity: he married, he went to college, he began a family. But in his memoirs, Guy wondered whether marrying Emily at eighteen and taking on the weight of children and university at the same time was not maturity, but in fact, one last rebellion, a "last swipe" at the adult world: marrying not for love but to prove himself free from his parents' control, and having children to prove himself an adult.

For a time, though, on the surface at least, conformity seemed to work. Guy did spectacularly well at college. He and Emily had their sons Bill and Johnny in quick succession in 1951 and '52, and then their youngest, Jim, in 1955. Guy established a side career as a jazz pianist of some note, while he also found prestigious work in the corridors of power after he graduated, first with the United States Chamber of Commerce, then with various senators, then as a speech writer for Gerald Ford and Richard Nixon during the latter's run for President in 1960, and finally with General Electric.

But below the successful surface, the other, opposing forces that played such a role in the life of the Watermans was wreaking havoc. Guy suffered, in his own words, a "self-destructive streak" that "has tended to surface and destroy whatever good things come my way." Such a streak, according to a cousin of Guy's son Johnny, appeared in several others on both sides of the family tree and it ran through the Waterman blood: from Guy to his two older sons. By his late teens, Johnny was already writing to friends about his own "darkness that ruins everything"; Bill had demons that were less well understood by his father, but no less ruinous. Only Jim seems to have been free of the curse.

Guy was prey to volcanic mood swings, alternating between bursts of euphoria and moods Guy described as "very, very, very low." Like many who are tormented by their moods, Guy self-medicated (in his case, with alcohol) to take the pain and the volatility out of the swings. To deal with his growing dissatisfactions with work and his marriage,

Guy amped up his dependence on alcohol, to the point that it caused problems in all aspects of his life. (Later, Bill and Johnny turned to the drugs of their own generation, hallucinogens and pot, with even more tragic results.) His marriage began to unravel; he alienated his coworkers with his growing bitterness, and was fired from one job and then another. He walked away from his music and his friendships there; he spent less and less time with his sons, inexorably becoming the distant father that he had vowed never to be. He woke up one morning in jail. And for the first time in his life, walked to the rail of a bridge one night and considered suicide.

But no matter that his self-destructive demons pushed him in ways that puzzled even him, Guy was a fiercely moral man who would ultimately, despite the stumbles along the way, do the right thing. Shamed into action by the thought of suicide, Guy caught himself in the middle of his downfall, plainly saw where he was heading and grabbed a lifeline.

The lifeline came, ironically, in the shape of Jack Olsen's original *Sports Illustrated* articles on the rescue of Claudio Corti from the Eiger. In these stories, Waterman did not see any of the conflicts and selfishness that troubled other readers; instead, he believed he had finally found the higher purpose—the heroic, pure morality and kinship—that he'd been looking for all his life.

"I was swept off my feet," he wrote in his autobiography. "Mountains and climbing dawned on my drunken, shamed, lonely life like a beacon of hope. Here was a whole new world of aspiration and effort, contrasting with the nightmare my life had become." He was thinking not only of his life, but also of his failure to be a father to his boys.

Once again showing his remarkable willpower, and his capacity for reinvention, after a brief, fierce, battle Waterman cast off alcohol for the rest of his life, and became a climber.

A man who has seen the light of adventure is just as evangelical as any born-again believer; and a new climber who is also newly sober can be twice the zealot. Waterman dove in with an unbridled passion; reading, talking, living climbing. He forged a plan for the *right* way to climb: a moral code of practicing the highest standards and commitment. No dependence on gear. Climb hard, and climb fully engaged. Be brave, but completely self-aware and safe.

Guy began walking everywhere, working with weights, building his finger strength. He started developing ambitious plans for hikes and climbs, especially in his beloved Shawangunks north of New York City, where he first tasted rock climbing. As soon as Bill and Johnny were old enough, he started bringing them along. The family was soon a happy fixture in the small local climbing scene; many climbers still fondly remember the hyperenergetic threesome who came every weekend and climbed from dawn to dusk.

Of the three, Johnny was the natural. Bill Waterman drifted in and out of climbing, Guy worked exceptionally hard at the game, but Johnny was a force. Like his father, he was shy and awkward, withdrawn and eccentric as a child, disappearing into complex board games and Civil War history while other boys played, but he leapt when he was given a rope. First alongside his father, and then far surpassing him, Johnny had both skills and attitude which quickly won the attention of the men who were pushing the technical standards at the 'Gunks.

I spent an afternoon following Johnny around the boulders of the 'Gunks in the summer of 1975, my first year of climbing. He was in his twenties by that time, and some of the shades of black that later ruled him were already beginning to show, but the passion and the squealing enthusiasm that he was famous for were still very much there. He transparently adored climbing, and showed off his favorite climbs with the enthusiasm of a child pulling out his Christmas presents.

He wasn't the most stylish climber—at barely five-foot-three, and with muscles like steel cables, his strength got him through without the need for balance and grace that other climbers depend on—but he was fast, incredibly focused, and remarkably bold. I don't think I had ever been around someone so unabashedly joyous. Johnny's unrestrained exuberance could bring out the best in people, and that was true with me that afternoon, as it was for many other climbers who came into contact with the lightning bolt that was Johnny. Winters on ice, summers on rock, Johnny trained obsessively, letting nothing get in the way.

It had been similar for Guy; soon after he began climbing in 1963, his work and his marriage clearly came second to the mountains. He had found his place, and had entered one of the happiest and most stable periods of his life, but Emily was completely uninterested and unsupportive, treating climbing as little more than a foolish thing for a grown man to be doing. After nineteen long years of hidden bitterness and occasionally open rage, Guy and Emily fell into a series of separations, then finally ended their marriage in 1969.

Divorce was a relief for Guy, who capitalized on his freedom by climbing, and climbing more still. Life couldn't have been fuller, and then he met Laura Johnson. Laura was a younger woman who shared many of Guy's passions—for music, for literature, for simple living in nature, for climbing. In Laura, Guy found the soulmate he had always dreamed of. They quickly became inseparable, pursuing a number of great adventures, traveling to Alaska and the West to climb. They co-wrote books on wilderness practice, history, and advocacy that brought them quite a bit of fame; and in 1971, they committed to living the kind of life in the wild that both had thought about for years.

It was this step into self-reliant living that was perhaps Guy's biggest rebellion of all. He finally removed himself from the parts of the world that had disenchanted him for years. He and Laura quit their jobs, built a rustic homestead in Vermont they called "Barra," and lived as fully off the land as they could for the rest of Guy's life. They had no electricity, no plumbing, no road access; they grew all their own food, played music together in the woods, read to each other after dinner, hiked voraciously, and still climbed.

It is interesting to ask whether Guy's move to Barra was the product of the best or the worst in him. Was his turn to the wilderness a way of embracing the greater purpose that he had been looking for all his life, or was it a run from the parts of society that he found hard to handle? Equally, did it really bring out the best in him? Was he happier, healthier, less depressed and vulnerable to mood swings than he had been in the past? Or did his new life simply allow Guy's troubles to be less disruptive?

Guy Waterman embodied the complexities of any withdrawal from society. In his public writings he was both eloquent and evangelical about the joys of his life at Barra, but he was also more open than most about what he called his "negative points"—his reasons for escape.

"One side of me," he wrote in his memoirs, "has always had trouble dealing with people, especially when I'm in a bad mood." In his case, this meant profound depressions, not just irritability. "By living in relative isolation, the only person I have to face is Laura."

As for many back-to-the-landers, both the beauty and the relief of the lifestyle is the distance it requires from the petty concerns of the self. For Guy Waterman, all aspects of the wilderness—living, playing, and working there—were a way of getting past himself, accepting himself more, being free of the unpleasant mirror that people put in front of him. But even insulated from the world in his perfect retreat, safe with his love and his daily order, the fates and the stories carried in his blood could still track him down.

It is remarkable how family patterns repeat themselves. Despite every best effort, and every promise, deep family history and even deeper biology have a gravity that can curve any story back toward the way things have always gone. The sons of drinkers drink when it is the last thing they thought they would ever do; abused children abuse as though they were possessed; the daughters of depressives find themselves suicidal even when everything seems ideal.

It can be a dismaying blow to your sense of free-will, and an especially distressing thing for a parent, to watch history re-create itself in a child you tried so hard to protect from the past. It is worse when you realize that you may have played a hand in the repetition.

The realization of the power of blood was a terrible weight on Guy Waterman. While his own life swung upward, toward Laura, toward Barra and his life as a writer, he watched with despair as echoes of his own erratic moods started to show themselves in his oldest children. It was also difficult for Guy, who continued to mourn the distance from his own father, to witness a growing separation from his boys despite all he had shared with them in their mid-teens.

The boys—especially Johnny—struggled with their parents' separation, and with Guy's new relationship with Laura. Johnny, whom Guy thought he might have insulated with the remarkable bond they shared through climbing, seemed stuck in a silent darkness at the prospect of having to choose sides with one parent or the other.

Bill's darkness was more tangible and more easily attributable to factors outside the family—and therefore less filled with self-recrimination for Guy. There were drugs: Bill took serious chemicals in serious quantities all through adolescence and beyond. There was Bill's drift away from the balm of climbing: by his twenties he was only dabbling and rarely joined up with either his father or his brothers. And then there was the accident: In the summer of 1969—the summer his parents were splitting—he headed west on a grand adventure. But in a freight yard in Canada, he was caught under the wheels of a train he was trying to hop, and his leg was nearly severed.

He changed then. As Guy wrote of Bill, "His prospects dimmed." He became darker in a way that must have been familiar to his father. Once a National Merit Scholar, Bill now drifted, managing only one semester of college before dropping out and heading north to Alaska. On the surface it might have looked as though Bill was following Guy's own lead, turning to the wilderness, and away from civilization; but it really was not the same path at all. Guy's life at Barra was so structured, so intentional, while Bill's seemed more a slow, aimless disintegration.

Bill stayed for a time with his mother's brother's family in Fairbanks, and was joined for a time by Johnny. Both boys were a mystery to the Morrisons; their cousin Alice told me that she was always puzzled by how dirty and poverty-stricken both Bill and Johnny appeared to be. Her father, she explained, was more certain about the roots of the problem: Peter Morrison angrily insisted that Guy's self-centered focus on his own new life simply displaced the children as his primary focus.

But Alice Morrison herself disagreed: "I really thought that Guy always loved his kids. It wasn't like he didn't want to be a father anymore." She added, "Bill and Johnny were grown up then. It wasn't like he had kicked them out of the house." Whether the boys themselves understood this might have been a different matter. The many writers who have told the Watermans' story insist that both boys (and Jim too, for that matter) were hurt by Guy's withdrawal into his new world, and his inaccessibility now that he was living at Barra. In an ironic twist on Guy's conscious intent to offer the boys a deep connection during their teenage years, his absence now seemed all the more pronounced.

Bill tried to stay connected for a time; there were occasional visits in the early '70s, and letters of decreasing frequency, but then, after a brief, ambiguous note in May, 1973, nothing. Bill vanished off the map.

It remains unclear what happened, except that there were never any signs of him again. Romantic stories float around that Bill took the Waterman attraction to the purity of wilderness to another level, insisting that he disappeared into the bush of Alaska or Canada. But more people have suggested that Bill was the first sacrifice to the family's troubled blood. Alice Morrison believes what her mother said when Bill first disappeared: "Bill is dead. He walked off into the woods and killed himself."

Guy's journey to acceptance about his eldest son's disappearance was agonizing. It took years for him to openly acknowledge that Bill was not coming home, years more to believe that he was dead. Guy's reasoning was perfectly self-protective rationalization: "People have asked me why I never made a serious effort to try and locate Bill or any evidence of his fate. I try to tell people that I don't know whether I'd rather assume that he's dead, or find out that he is alive but has chosen not to contact his father for 20 years."

As difficult and painful as Bill's story was, Johnny's was even more tortured.

In Johnny's own words, there was always "John the climber" and "John the rest of the time." The two were never in sync. The success, the fame, and the joy that Johnny got from climbing, he never found in the rest of his life. Climbing was the balm to the loneliness, awkwardness, and agonizing alienation Johnny felt in the world. But he understood perfectly well that climbing wasn't everything, and did not solve all his problems. And, of course, the two were never independent. The pain in the rest of his life affected Johnny's climbing, pushing him harder and harder to find answers to his problems in his climbs, and Johnny's climbing colored the other parts of his life in less-than-positive ways. Johnny's singular focus drew him even further away from "normal" life, so much that Guy despaired of his son ever having a normal adolescence. Instead of hanging around with kids his own age, instead of meeting the girls that he could never attract, Johnny was always off on some expedition.

Worse still, Johnny was deeply, dangerously changed by the hardest truth of climbing. By the time Johnny was twenty, nine of the people who had been mentors to him—among them the man who tied him into his first rope, the one who took him on his first Alaskan expedition, and the man who first brought him into the brethren of harder climbers—had all been killed in climbing accidents. Death is a reality that most risk-sports participants will have to deal with at some point, but

Johnny's sensitivity, and the sheer numbers he was exposed to so young, gave it a much more crippling weight in his case. Johnny was always one to anthropomorphize the struggle against the mountains, and this habit served him poorly when he saw the mountains kill his friends. The line of deaths turned the peaks into evil spirits for Johnny, rather than the noble foes others were able to imagine.

After a short but intense apprenticeship with his father, Johnny began to be obsessed with some of the fiercest mountain spirits, the great peaks of Alaska. At only sixteen, the same year when his parents split and Bill lost his leg, Johnny went with a much older group of climbers to Denali. There he performed very well, becoming the youngest climber in the history of the mountain to reach the summit.

Before arriving home, he already had far more ambitious plans to return to Alaska. The following year, he returned to try the South Ridge of the infinitely more serious Mount Hunter, the mountain that Johnny would come to call his nemesis. The mountain smacked the team with terrible weather and left them unsuccessful in their bid, but Johnny was hooked. Although he was once again the youngest member of the team, he had done almost all of the lead climbing. By the end of the trip, he felt he had a special talent for enduring suffering that the others just didn't seem to have. He would be back.

Johnny's third trip to Alaska was a dramatic one. He and a strong, small team made the first ascent of the East Ridge of Mount Huntington, a dangerous and difficult line up a peak with a formidable reputation. Once again, Johnny led the pack to the top, but he also unnerved his partners with his incautious speed and immoderate drive. Johnny's unrelenting push showed itself again and again that summer in climbs across the continent, earning him his first renown, but also starting to leave some partners shaking their heads and wondering about his stability.

This pattern only solidified the following year when Johnny returned for a second go at Mount Hunter. He was fiercely strong now—perhaps the best alpine climber in the United States—but also more clearly showing the strain of such severe climbing. He would explode into rages about the smallest things, could be suddenly euphoric at one moment and uncomfortably odd at another, and he seemed to have little of the social reserve that most people have. Johnny would go into explicit detail about his love life (or lack thereof) and be embarrassingly open, disclosing his darkest thoughts and his self-condemned weaknesses.

Johnny was the force that got the team up Hunter this time, but his behavior on the mountain caused considerable friction in the team. It was perhaps this conflict (and the shattering discovery that the team had probably only made it to a false summit 300 feet below the top, and not the true summit) that propelled Johnny into the adventure that elevated him into the alpine pantheon: his marathon return to Hunter, alone.

Spring 1978. For several years, Johnny had known that something was wrong. He was plagued by his mood swings (which tellingly began at sixteen, the same age as his father's had, but had become much more pronounced in his twenties than Guy's ever had). He was painfully aware of the trouble he had fitting in with others. He struggled with a desperate longing for a woman in his life. His relationship with Guy seemed to have soured, and he was more and more concerned about the role that climbing was playing in his life.

He was also having grimmer and grimmer thoughts as he approached his climbs. "I'm afraid," he wrote in a letter to a friend, "if I continue to climb at such a high degree of intensity, I won't live a year more. I'll either fall or 'flip out,' either of which will result in the removal of myself from this earth (death)." Johnny described climbing as "a deeply tragic affair." Understanding that "there might be something wrong with me mentally," at eighteen he began to see a psychiatrist; he was just a year older than Guy had been when he was sent to the "psycho ward."

But however Johnny tried to find balance and moderate his undercurrents, he remained obsessed with Hunter, and still seemed to believe that the mountain could offer him the answers that no amount of therapy or sex or school could ever provide. At the very least, he was clear that he had to be free of the obsession with his "vendetta," to move on in his life.

He did settle for a time, moving to Alaska, enrolling in the university in Fairbanks. For nearly three years his life was uninterrupted by expeditions, but he was far from "normal" or happy. If he was not going on expeditions, it was only because there was only one mountain plan that captured his attention: Hunter. Alone.

Through 1977 and into '78, Johnny trained obsessively—and bizarrely—for his secret project. He jogged in big boots and crampons, immersed himself in bathtubs of ice cubes to accustom his mind to hypothermia, slogged through town with enormous loads on his back. He also continued to use drugs heavily, and the combination of hallucinogens with his natural personality quirks gained him a reputation for bizarre acts around town.

In letters, Johnny referred to the drugs he was doing as a "pretty bad idea," but he did not temper his self-destructive urges any better than his father or his brother had. The drugs, and the walks out to the edge with his climbing, all started to have the same feel: a growing fascination with finding relief from himself.

Johnny also began to have clearer thoughts that death might be the only way to get the relief he was seeking. When he was finally ready to face his nemesis in March 1978, and flew in to the base of the route with thousands of pounds of gear, he told the pilot, "I won't be seeing you again."

———————————

Hunter was the perfect climb for Johnny to measure his place in the world. It was just him and the great soaring knife-edge of the ridge. Almost continuously steep and difficult, the route offered almost no places for Johnny to relax or let down his guard. The nature of the climb and of his solitary plan meant that he would be up and down every inch of the ridge dozens of times, as he was forced to run out a rope, tie it in place, rappel back down, then haul his huge gear bags up the wall.

He carried a radio that allowed brief two-way contact with the world, but he was otherwise completely alone. He suffered huge falls, several times, held only by marginal protection and pure luck. He contracted body lice so bad that he had to radio for a drop of lice powder. He sobbed with anguish at his frostbitten fingers, and he wept with frustration at the work of it all. He even composed a ditty in his head entitled "Arbeit Macht Frei," a chilling reference to the slogan of the Auschwitz death camp—"Work sets you free." Auschwitz, Johnny wrote bleakly, was "another place" where "inevitable death ensues."

It took him 124 days to get to the first of the mountain's three summits, and another twenty-three days to climb the others and descend. It must have been tempting, so many times, to give up, either by bailing off the climb, calling out to get picked off the summit plateau, or by simply sitting down in the snow and letting the mountain take him. But at some point, despite his bitterly morbid predictions, Johnny decided to push on and live.

Whether living was Johnny's truly preferred choice is still a matter of debate. In many ways it seems that he felt he had betrayed the mountain by actually living, as though he had lessened the spirit of the great route by succeeding. Perhaps because he expected to die, he finished the climb crying, he wrote, "at the thought of living." In the eyes of some of his friends, Johnny felt profoundly guilty that he had survived such a difficult mountain when so many of his friends had perished on lesser peaks. In some twisted sense, it seemed that he had decided to live not as a statement of joy, but to punish himself—as though dying would have been the nobler path.

The self-destructive streak that ran so forcefully through the Watermans seemed to find its strongest course of all in Johnny. It was little surprise that the experience on Hunter seemed to break him into fragments. After the mountain, Johnny was more unsettled than ever, saying the whole effort had been a spectacular failure. He became increasingly bizarre and openly acknowledged that he was in the grip of a "Mount Hunter psychosis." There were times when he was able to keep it together and seem relatively stable emotionally, but these were increasingly rare.

Occasionally, Johnny's positive moments happened in front of the climbing world, and added to his legend. He gave rare but apparently electrifying slide shows that were equal parts theater and very public, very manic, therapy. He published an account of the ascent of Hunter in the 1978 *American Alpine Journal* that was an odd mixture of banal facts and insightful self-disclosure and still receives praise as a piece of writing.

But most of the time, Johnny was more clearly in a dark place. He became one of Fairbanks's oddball characters, people who live on the fringes and might be judged mentally ill anywhere else, but in the North are gently called the "colorful five percent." He took to wearing capes around town, playing his guitar (badly) and singing off-key on street corners. He announced that he was going to run for the local school board on a platform of free sex and even freer marijuana for students and then, when he lost, said he would run for President of the United States. His platform—his new all-encompassing obsession—was feeding the poor.

According to Johnny's friends, until his political "campaign," he had no clear climbing ambitions in the wind. But when he announced his candidacy, such as it was, he said that he would complete a difficult new route on Denali, in winter, with nothing but the most basic food, to draw attention to his campaign.

On December 20, 1980, in near twenty-four-hour darkness, Johnny was flown to the base of the mountain with a huge mound of gear, ready to repeat the style of Hunter. But only ten days later, he was flown out again, perilously distraught, feeling that he was teetering on the brink of a terrifying madness.

Things came to a head just a few weeks later, when Johnny's primitive cabin in Talkeetna, Alaska accidentally burned to the ground while he was away. It was as though Johnny himself had gone up in flames. Like his father, Johnny had kept extensive detailed records of every aspect of his life in journals, clippings, songs, and poetry, and it was all lost to the fire. Two days later, Johnny checked himself into the Alaska Psychiatric Institute.

Johnny was diagnosed at the API with schizoaffective disorder, an illness that combines profoundly unstable moods with psychotic ideation and bizarre behavior. It seems an entirely fitting label, much more reasonable than other suggestions, such as that he suffered from schizophrenia. (Schizoaffective illness has a far more variable course than schizophrenia, explaining how Johnny could move in and out of apparently psychotic episodes. The course of schizophrenia is far more consistent, and the depth of dysfunction of that disease would have made it almost impossible for Johnny to function on a mountain.)

The help that Johnny might have received at the API was lost when he discharged himself after only two weeks, convinced, his friends say, that agents of the government were trying to gain control of his mind. Because his had been a voluntary admission, there was little anyone could do to force him to stay.

The last months of Johnny's life saw him slipping further away, becoming more chaotic and more despairing. His interactions with friends and family were pressured and fragmentary, and he seemed obsessed with sex and death—so much that Guy Waterman refused to let anyone see Johnny's letters. In February, 1981, much to the dismay of people who knew him in Alaska, Johnny set out to walk back into Denali, where he planned, again, to complete his winter ascent.

A few days later he was back in Fairbanks, ostensibly because a minor piece of gear had failed him, but he started making plans immediately to return to the mountain. In March, he started walking again, this time to try the mountain's unclimbed, exceptionally dangerous east ridge. Various people encountered Johnny around the base of the mountain, and all were concerned: He was unroped in heavily crevassed terrain, he was poorly equipped, and he seemed very disoriented—but no one could stop him.

Johnny Waterman was last seen on April 1, 1981, threading his way through a lair of crevasses high up on the Ruth Glacier, skiing into a torment of ice that no sane man would enter.

Johnny's death, however tragic, was far from the end of the Waterman saga. In the end, it all circled back to the father.

In mid-April 1981, Guy Waterman walked into town from Barra to return a phone message from the Denali Park rangers. The park staff told him that his son was missing—his second missing son. This time, there was little room for romantic hopes that Johnny would still show up at Barra one day, as Guy sometimes dreamed Bill would.

Although Johnny's disappearance would be officially classified as a climbing accident rather than a suicide, Guy knew what had happened. In his memoirs, he wrote, "Suffice it to say that Johnny sought this death in the mountains."

The suicidal demon that chased Bill, and then Johnny, stalked Guy Waterman's own final years ferociously. As the psychiatrist Kay Redfield Jamison points out in her book, *Night Falls Fast*, "suicide is a death like no other." It is followed by a thousand questions, by guilt, blame, and a relentless demand to know "*Why?*"—a question that is never so insistent in other deaths.

Guy Waterman clearly had to answer that question more than anyone ever should. For nearly twenty-seven years, he asked it about the lives of two sons, and then of his own, again and again. He had considered whether his boys were now at peace, and he ruminated about how he might end his own pain, thinking of ledges he might suddenly "slip" from, but he was unable to bring himself to take the step.

Then on February 6, 2000, he had breakfast at the table at Barra, kissed his wife Laura, got dressed, and joked that this time he "wouldn't be coming home to tell the tale" as he had always done after his walks. He said he would not even be able to "send a postcard." He told her to bake bread that day, said he would "always be with [her]," and told her to "be brave."

Then Guy walked to the summit of Mount Lafayette in the White

Mountains of New Hampshire, and sat down to die. His frozen body was carried back down the hill five days later by a group of friends who knew exactly what they would find.

For years, Guy had been pushing on valiantly, so much so that others who knew him and understood all he had been through thought he was a marvel of strength, that his peaceful life at Barra had given him the resolve to deal with perhaps the most terrible tragedy of all—the suicide of a child. Of two children.

Guy himself placed the credit for any strength he had had squarely on Laura's shoulders. She was, he said, what Johnny never had; a gentle force that balanced out his darker side. But there was, Guy felt, so much weight from that other side, especially as he got older and found less and less energy to do the things that had always given him joy and identity: climbing, hiking, writing, baseball, wilderness advocacy.

Guy said that aging "appalled" him. Yes, there were beautiful moments of profound connection to Laura and to the land that he loved, but there was always the pull of the self-destructive urges that he had endured in silence for so long, hidden with his "protective covering of smiles and talk," but still feeling "alienated from [his] fellow humanity and dwell[ing] in a private world of storm and darkness."

There were many times in the nineteen years after Johnny's death that Laura found Guy simply paralyzed by his sadness. But it was not until near the very end that she understood how resolutely suicide was chasing him. At some point, he had given up (far earlier than she thought; after Guy's death, she discovered carefully considered suicide notes dating back to 1992) but Guy had been so closed about so many things that it was so hard to know what was really passing through his "private world."

In the end, Guy gave himself over to the mountains with the planning that he had invested in all things. He and Laura negotiated his right, his need, to end his pain, so that "soon the voices will be still." Still, Laura was as distraught and confused as any outsider to suicidal thinking would be. How could she possibly support what he was asking? How could she simply let her husband walk away and freeze to death, alone?

And yet Laura knew Guy's persistent will better than anyone else in the world. It was only a matter of when. There was no uncertainty, however, about *how* Guy Waterman would die. He would walk into the wilderness, just as his sons had.

epilogue

THE ANSWER TO THE PERPETUAL QUESTION of adventure—Why?—is as elusive in this book's stories as it is anywhere, but there were clearer signposts that seemed to guide the path of most of the adventures here: A fragile, unsettled ego. A vague sadness that evolved into chronic despair and dissatisfaction. A desperate hunt to remedy the pain through adventure, even at great personal risk and sometimes despite only minimal experience in the arena of the adventure. And finally, too often, an apparent willingness to sacrifice to that adventure, to a degree that most "healthy" adventurers find chilling.

In a striking number of these cases, the troubled path seemed to begin with the loss of a parent—in most cases a father. Lewis, Andrée, Franklin, Corti, Wilson, Scott, Denman, Crowhurst, Batten, and Juedel all lost fathers when they were quite young, either through death, abandonment, or estrangement. The frequency of the loss of a father—in these cases, most often a beloved, *model* father, rather than the abusive or distant male who haunts so much psychological literature—simply seems too high to be passed off as chance.

Looking at perpetrators of expedition hoaxes, the writer David Roberts found very much the same pattern. Although Roberts worries that it might be "facile psychologizing" to link his difficult stories to parental absence, I don't think it is too much of a stretch to wonder if the characters here were not searching for the lost male presence in their lives when they dreamed up their dramatically male schemes, filled with risk, calling for bravery. All these people followed the mythic masculine journey found in cultures around the world.

Neither is it a stretch to trace the threads of the loss of a parent through to the troubled self-image, chronic depression, and search for constant external validation of self-worth that plague the adventurers in all these stories. The impact of such a loss can be profound, and even permanently disabling.

Still, instead of being seen only as pathological oddities of adventure history, I'd suggest that these stories might also give us some of the best insights into the components of the healthiest adventure. Often the best way to understand how the mind and the body work is to observe illness or dysfunction; the stories of what went *wrong* here might offer clues to what goes right in the best cases.

Instead of being pursued as an answer to an unsatisfying life, adventure can be an ecstatic affirmation of a rich and positive existence. Although many laypeople—and psychological theorists—sometimes lump the kinds of stories that appear in this book with the best adventures and call them all foolhardy, or even say they have "indirect suicidal intent," a more informed look readily shows just how different most of the risk-taking in this book is from the real thing.

Instead of being perilous walks by novices with questionable motives along a very uncertain edge, the best adventures are carried out by devoted athletes who are experts at measuring and controlling risk. Although the chances they take might understandably *appear* uncontrollable and even fatal to the uninitiated, the experts of the dangerous edges can be perfectly at home, experiencing moments of joy and completion where others would feel nothing but terror.

The best adventurers are also aware of their place and time, thrilled by the beauty around them, appreciating where their journey fits into history and respecting what has come before. This was sadly not the case for most of the adventurers in this book. Many of the characters here had little sense of the arena they played in, or how and where their stories fit into the histories of the mountains they intended to climb, or the seas they planned to cross. Instead of having experiences sculpted by the world around them, most of these stories seemed to have been so driven from within that the mountains, poles, and oceans were little more than an incidental stage for a troubled psychodrama—and that is never what true adventure is about.

notes on sources

THE SUBTITLE OF EACH CHAPTER WAS A description of the protagonist by contemporaries or historians.

CHAPTER 1
MERIWETHER LEWIS

"Our Melancholy Hero" was written in a letter to Lewis's family by Thomas Jefferson.

Readers interested in the traditional, heroic view of Lewis can turn to Gary Moulton and T. W. Dunlay's *The Journals of the Lewis and Clark Expedition* (Lincoln: University of Nebraska Press, 1987) and D. Jackson's *Letters of the Lewis and Clark Expedition* (Urbana: University of Illinois Press, 1978).

Examples of works seeking to "protect Lewis's reputation from the 'taint of suicide'" can be found in Vardis Fisher's *Suicide or Murder: The Strange Death of Governor Meriwether Lewis* (Chicago: Sage Books, 1962); and E.G. Chuinard's "How Did Meriwether Lewis Die? It Was Murder," in *We Proceeded On* (Lewis and Clark Heritage Trails Foundation: Great Falls, MT) 17 and 18 (1991).

More comprehensive and critical—but still humane—views of Lewis can be found in a range of books, the best of them being Thomas P. Slaughter's *Exploring Lewis and Clark* (New York: Vintage, 2003); Stephen Ambrose's *Undaunted Courage: Meriwether Lewis, Thomas Jefferson and the Opening of the American West* (New York: Simon & Schuster, 1996);

James Ronda's *Finding the West: Explorations with Lewis and Clark* (Albuquerque: University of New Mexico Press, 2001); and Kay Redfield Jamison's excellent *Night Falls Fast: Understanding Suicide* (New York: Knopf, 1999).

CHAPTER 2
ROBERT FALCON SCOTT

"A Struggle for Existence" was biographer Elspeth Huxley's characterization of Scott's endurance of his black moods.

Scott's own version of his story is told in *Scott's Last Expedition* (London: Smith, Elder & Co., 1913). A more complete sense of the man, however, can be gained from Elspeth Huxley's *Scott of the Antarctic* (London: Weidenfeld and Nicholson, 1977).

Accounts that help place Scott in deeper context included Roland Huntford's *Scott and Amundsen* (New York: G. Putnam's Sons, 1980); John Maxtone-Graham's *Safe Return Doubtful: The Heroic Age of Polar Exploration* (New York: Charles Scribner & Sons, 1988); and David Thomson's *Scott, Shackleton and Amundsen: Ambition and Tragedy in the Antarctic* (London: Allen Lane, 1977).

CHAPTER 3
SOLOMON ANDRÉE

"We Cannot Fail" was Andrée's ambitious prediction of the *Eagle's* promise, made to the Swedish Academy of the Sciences.

The heroic version of the tragedy of the *Eagle* can be found in *Andrée's Story: The Complete Record of His Flight 1897*, compiled by the Swedish Society for Anthropology and Geography (New York: Viking, 1930).

Per Olaf Sundman's *The Flight of the Eagle* (New York: Pantheon, 1970), and the feature film of the same name directed by Jan Troell, are gripping, though highly fictionalized, accounts of Andrée's misadventure.

The fate of the *Eagle* is also considered in more depth in Richard Montague's *Oceans, Poles and Airmen* (New York: Random House, 1971); Vilhjalmur Stefansson's *Unsolved Mysteries of the Arctic* (New York: MacMillan, 1938); and P.J. Capelotti's *By Airship to the North Pole* (New Brunswick, NJ: Rutgers, 1999). All three of these books also examine several other stories in the strange history of polar ballooning, any one of which could have made it into this volume.

CHAPTER 4
DONALD CROWHURST

"The Reward Was Madness" was the measure of the fate of Crowhurst's ambitions in Peter Nichols's *A Voyage for Madmen*.

The definitive work on Crowhurst's life is Nicholas Tomalin and Ron Hall's *The Strange Last Voyage of Donald Crowhurst* (London: Hodder and Stoughton, 1995), but the difficult saga has been told in many forms over the years. Peter Nichols covered all the players in the race in *A Voyage for Madmen* (New York: Harper Collins, 2001). David Roberts compared Crowhurst's story with those of many other fabricators in *Great Exploration Hoaxes* (San Francisco: Sierra Club, 1982). There have also been plays, feature films (*Horse Latitudes*), and a novelization (Robert Stone's *Outerbridge Reach* [New York: Ticknor and Fields, 1992]).

CHAPTER 5
JOHN FRANKLIN

"The Man Who Shouldn't Have Been There" was author Pierre Berton's assessment of Franklin's place in the Arctic.

The telling of Franklin's life story has included several hagiographies, for example, *Sir John Franklin and the Romance of the North-West Passage* by G. Barnett Smith (London: Partridge, 1928); but more honest appraisals of the man can be found in a number of books. Notable among them as sources used here were Francis Spufford's brilliant *I May Be Some Time: Ice and the English Imagination* (New York: St. Martin's Press, 1997); Beau Riffenburgh's *The Myth of the Explorer* (London: Belhaven Press, 1993); Pierre Berton's *The Arctic Grail* (Toronto: Doubleday, 2001); A.H. Markham's *Life of Sir John Franklin and the North-West Passage* (London: George Phillip & Son, 1891); David Woodman's *Unravelling the Franklin Mystery* (Montreal: McGill-Queen's Press, 1991); and Beattie and Geiger's *Frozen In Time* (New York: Dutton, 1988).

CHAPTER 6
JEAN BATTEN

"A Terrible Beauty" was an assessment of Jean Batten by one of her many lovers.

Jean Batten's own books *My Life* (London: Aviation Book Club, 1938) and its augmented reissue as *Alone in the Sky* in 1979 (Auckland:

Airlife) are a partial view into Batten's mind, but a much fuller account comes from Ian Mackersey's *Jean Batten: The Garbo of the Skies* (London: Warner Books, 1990).

CHAPTER 7
ALEISTER CROWLEY

Crowley invited many critical superlatives, including "The Wickedest Man in the World," first heaped on him by a London judge during a 1934 trial, and then happily used as a headline by the British press for years.

Crowley's autobiographical volume *The Confessions of Aleister Crowley* (London: Penguin, 1989) and other collections of his works are fascinating introductions to his story, but making more realistic sense of his story requires more critical biographies. Two I relied on heavily were Lawrence Sutin's *Do What Thou Wilt* (New York: St. Martin's, 2000); and Richard Kaczynski's *Perdurabo* (Tempe: New Falcon, 2002).

CHAPTER 8
CLAUDIO CORTI

The great French alpinist Lionel Terray described his assessment of Corti's attempt on the Eiger quite simply: "Only a Madman Would Try Such a Thing."

Jack Olsen's *The Climb Up to Hell* (New York: Harper & Row, 1962) is the richest account of Corti's story. Additional details were filled out with the help of Arthur Ross' *Eiger: Wall of Death* (New York: Orion, 1982); and Lionel Terray's *Conquistadors of the Useless* (London: Gollancz, 1963).

CHAPTER 9
MAURICE WILSON

The harshest contemporary judgment of Wilson's aspirations for Everest came from London's *Daily Mail* in May 1934 when it called his scheme "An Elaborate Suicide."

Dennis Roberts' *I'll Climb Mount Everest Alone* (London: Robert Hale, 1957); is the primary source for most tellings of Wilson's story, but Wilson's own unpublished diary, now held in the archives of the Alpine Club in London, was required to fill in many of the areas left blank or overdrawn by Roberts.

Other sources that briefly discussed Wilson included Walt Unsworth's *Everest* (Seattle: The Mountaineers Books, 1999); Ed Douglas's *Tenzing:*

Hero of Everest (New York: Simon and Schuster, 2004); and Mick Confrey and Tim Jordan's *Mountain Men* (London: DaCapo, 2002).

CHAPTER 10
EARL DENMAN

"The Romantic Heart" was the force that Denman's nephew Graham felt plagued much of his uncle's life.

Denman's book *Alone to Everest* (New York: Coward-McCann, 1954); takes the reader to the mountain but not much beyond. Denman's unpublished manuscript of the last years of his life (graciously loaned to me by his nephew Graham Denman) was a far more revealing resource. Ed Douglas's *Hero of Everest* clarifies the relationship between Tenzing and the Canadian.

CHAPTER 11
GUY WATERMAN
JOHNNY WATERMAN
BILL WATERMAN

"Walking into Darkness" was a phrase Johnny Waterman used to describe the fear he felt when setting out for his second attempt on Mount Hunter.

Several printed sources were invaluable in telling the Watermans' story. Jon Krakauer's *Into the Wild* (New York: Villard, 1996); Glenn Randall's *Breaking Point* (Denver: Chockstone, 1984); and Jonathan Waterman's *In the Shadow of Denali* (New York: Dell, 1994) all tell Johnny Waterman's story in rich detail. Chip Brown's *Good Morning Midnight* (New York: Riverhead, 2003) is a superb biography of Guy and his family; and Laura Waterman's *Losing the Garden* (Washington: Shoemaker-Hoard, 2005) is a bravely honest assessment of her marriage to Guy. I'm also deeply indebted to Laura for her willingness to share Guy's unpublished manuscript *Prospero's Options*.

index

relationship with Leonard
and Enid Evans, 176, 180-81,
190
second Everest attempt, 195

suicidal ideation, 194-95
Wyvill, Brian
modern measure of Aleister
Crowley, 139

about the author

Geoff Powter is a clinical psychologist practicing in Canmore, Alberta, and has been the editor of the *Canadian Alpine Journal* since 1993. He has climbed extensively in the Himalaya and other ranges of the world, and has been a frequent contributor to adventure magazines. His mountain writing won him a National Magazine Award in 2002.

THE MOUNTAINEERS, founded in 1906, is a nonprofit outdoor activity and conservation club, whose mission is "to explore, study, preserve, and enjoy the natural beauty of the outdoors." Based in Seattle, Washington, the club is now the third-largest such organization in the United States, with seven branches throughout Washington State.

The Mountaineers sponsors both classes and year-round outdoor activities in the Pacific Northwest, which include hiking, mountain climbing, ski-touring, snowshoeing, bicycling, camping, kayaking and canoeing, nature study, sailing, and adventure travel. The club's conservation division supports environmental causes through educational activities, sponsoring legislation, and presenting informational programs. All club activities are led by skilled, experienced volunteers, who are dedicated to promoting safe and responsible enjoyment and preservation of the outdoors.

If you would like to participate in these organized outdoor activities or the club's programs, consider a membership in The Mountaineers. For information and an application, write or call The Mountaineers, Club Headquarters, 300 Third Avenue West, Seattle, Washington 98119; 206 284-6310.

The Mountaineers Books, an active, nonprofit publishing program of the club, produces guidebooks, instructional texts, historical works, natural history guides, and works on environmental conservation. All books produced by The Mountaineers fulfill the club's mission.

Send or call for our catalog of more than 450 outdoor titles:

The Mountaineers Books
1001 SW Klickitat Way, Suite 201
Seattle, WA 98134
800-553-4453
mbooks@mountaineersbooks.org
www.mountaineersbooks.org

The Mountaineers Books is proud to be a corporate sponsor of Leave No Trace, whose mission is to promote and inspire responsible outdoor recreation through education, research, and partnerships. The Leave No Trace program is focused specifically on human-powered (non-motorized) recreation.

Leave No Trace strives to educate visitors about the nature of their recreational impacts, as well as offer techniques to prevent and minimize such impacts. Leave No Trace is best understood as an educational and ethical program, not as a set of rules and regulations.

For more information, visit *www.lnt.org*, or call 800-332-4100.

MORE ADVENTURE READING THAT YOU MAY ENJOY . . .

H.W. Tilman: The Seven Mountain Travel Books
H.W. Tilman

**A Fine Kind of Madness:
Mountain Adventures Tall & True**
Laura and Guy Waterman

**David Roberts: The Mountain of My Fear;
Deborah: A Wilderness Narrative**
David Roberts

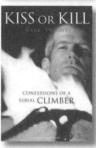

Kiss or Kill: Confessions of a Serial Climber
Mark Twight

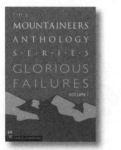

**Minus 148°: First Winter Ascent of
Mt. McKinley**
Art Davidson

THE MOUNTAINEERS ANTHOLOGY SERIES:
Vol. 1, Glorious Failures
Vol. II, Courage & Misfortune
Vol. III, Over the Top: Humorous Mountaineering Tales
Vol. IV, Everest
Peter Potterfield, editor

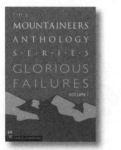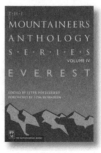